Diplomacy and lobbying during Turkey's Europeanisation

MANCHESTER
1824

Manchester University Press

POLITICAL ETHNOGRAPHY

The Political Ethnography series is an outlet for ethnographic research into politics and administration and builds an interdisciplinary platform for a readership interested in qualitative research in this area. Such work cuts across the traditional scholarly boundaries of political science, public administration, anthropology, social policy, and development studies, and facilitates a conversation across disciplines. It will provoke a re-thinking of how researchers can understand politics and administration.

Previously published titles

The absurdity of bureaucracy: How implementation works
    Nina Holm Vohnsen

Politics of waiting: Workfare, post-Soviet austerity and the ethics of freedom
    Liene Ozoliņa

Diplomacy and lobbying during Turkey's Europeanisation

The private life of politics

Bilge Firat

Manchester University Press

Published by Manchester University Press
Oxford Road, Manchester M13 9PL

www.manchesteruniversitypress.co.uk

British Library Cataloguing-in-Publication Data
A catalogue record for this book is available from the British Library

ISBN 978 1 5261 3362 5   hardback
ISBN 978 1 5261 6368 4   paperback

First published 2019
Paperback published 2022

The publisher has no responsibility for the persistence or accuracy of URLs for any external or third-party internet websites referred to in this book, and does not guarantee that any content on such websites is, or will remain, accurate or appropriate.

Typeset in Minion and Scala Sans
by R. J. Footring Ltd, Derby, UK

*For my dad, the finest connoisseur of human
nature I have ever known*

Contents

Figures

Series editor's preface

Ethnography reaches the parts of politics that other methods cannot reach. It captures the lived experience of politics; the everyday life of political elites and street-level bureaucrats. It identifies what we fail to learn, and what we fail to understand, from other approaches. Specifically:

1. It is a source of data not available elsewhere.
2. It is often the only way to identify key individuals and core processes.
3. It identifies 'voices' all too often ignored.
4. By disaggregating organisations, it leads to an understanding of 'the black box', or the internal processes of groups and organisations.
5. It recovers the beliefs and practices of actors.
6. It gets below and behind the surface of official accounts by providing texture, depth and nuance, so our stories have richness as well as context.
7. It lets interviewees explain the meaning of their actions, providing an authenticity that can only come from the main characters involved in the story.
8. It allows us to frame (and reframe, and reframe) research questions in a way that recognises our understandings about how things work around here evolve during the fieldwork.
9. It admits of surprises – of moments of epiphany, serendipity and happenstance – that can open new research agendas.
10. It helps us to see and analyse the symbolic, performative aspects of political action.

Despite this distinct and distinctive contribution, ethnography's potential is rarely realised in political science and related disciplines. It is considered an endangered species or at best a minority sport. This series seeks to promote the use of ethnography in political science, public administration and public policy.

The series has two key aims:

1. To establish an outlet for ethnographic research into politics, public administration and public policy.
2. To build an interdisciplinary platform for a readership interested in qualitative research into politics and administration. We expect such work to cut

across the traditional scholarly boundaries of political science, public administration, anthropology, organisation studies, social policy, and development
studies.

The triple mantra that Turkey is 'too poor, too large and too Muslim' for the
European Union (EU) dominated political and scholarly debates about Turkey's
accession to the EU for decades. Turkey was the elephant in the room. Between
2005 and 2013, Bilge Firat immersed herself in the political and cultural environment of the negotiations over Turkish accession in Brussels, Istanbul and Ankara.
Her fieldwork encompassed elite interviews, participant and non-participant
observation as an intern, the analysis of policy advice documents, personal
conversations, and informal gatherings of members of her extensive network of
contacts. It is the first book to present ethnographic fieldwork on brokerage by
diplomats and lobbyists in the EU. She seeks to explain Turkey's version of Brexit –
TRexit. Why did the negotiations about Turkey's accession to the EU fail? She
uncovers the everyday understanding and practices of actors in the negotiations
over TRexit. Her point of access was the diplomats and lobbyists who served as the
human bridges between Brussels and Ankara.

This book has three parts. The first lays out her analytical and methodological
approach. The second tells the EU–Turkey enlargement story. The third reports
her fieldwork and is the heart of the book. It describes the cultures of diplomacy
and lobbying, and the arts of its practitioners, inside the EU Council, European
Commission and European Parliament. She provides an account of the everyday
work of diplomats and lobbyists, and the ways in which they managed conflicts
and compromises.

The acute, core argument is that actors impeded accession because their
private, professional, public, personal and institutional interests prevailed over the
policy objective of promoting Turkey's EU membership. Turkish accession was
not the product of negotiations. Rather, accession was a process in which actors
and agents used the negotiations to further their personal, professional and public
ambitions. The negotiations were not about Turkey's EU membership, but about
what the several actors could gain from the process itself. As a result, in her words,
Turkey's accession negotiations with the EU turned into a death spiral.

A key aim of ethnographic fieldwork is get below and behind the surface of
official accounts by providing texture, depth and nuance. It produces rich, thick
descriptions. Bilge Firat does just that and one has to admire the devotion that led
her to take weekend walks in her neighbourhood, reading the names on doorbells
to identify potential interviewees. No one said fieldwork was easy, and it is obvious
why this book was eight years in the making. Working in the library, on documentary sources and in one's room are all part of research but partial and total
immersion in the field poses distinct challenges while offering unique insights.
Bilge Firat's book typifies the difficulties and rewards of such fieldwork.

Professor R. A. W. Rhodes
University of Southampton
Series editor

Preface

Turkey's Europeanisation, which began in 1959 and climaxed in 2005 with the opening of membership negotiations with the European Union (EU), has gradually turned into a death spiral, while those who were mandated with facilitating Turkey's EU membership bid gained more recognition, status and power. Taking this paradox to its centre, *Diplomacy and Lobbying During Turkey's Europeanisation* introduces to its reader the intricate backstage negotiations conducted by formal and informal actors of Turkey's Europeanisation through the corridors of power. Honing in on the role of diplomats and lobbyists during negotiations over Turkey's contentious EU membership bid, now stalled, which drove this candidate country both closer to and farther from the EU, the book presents the everyday actors and agents of Turkish Europeanisation, what their work entailed, which interests they represented, and how they did what they did. Turkey's Europeanisation saga presents a unique opportunity to understand how interstate actors negotiate their interests; what 'common interests' look like from their historically and culturally contingent perspectives; and what happens when actors work for their private, professional, public, personal or institutional interests, even when those interests may go against their mandate. Based on long-term ethnographic fieldwork in Brussels, I argue here that public, private and corporate actors voicing economic, political and bureaucratic interests from all corners of Europe sought access to markets and polities through the Turkish bid instead of their mandate of facilitating Turkey's EU accession. Although limited progress was achieved in Turkey's actual EU integration, diplomats and lobbyists from both sides of the negotiating table contradictorily reaffirmed their expertise as effective negotiators, earning more recognition, status and power.

Organisation of the book

This book is in three parts. Part I lays out the analytical and methodological purviews I adopt in this book. In Chapter 1, I take stock of the Turkish Europeanisation literature and identify its critical drawbacks. Complementing the triple mantra of poor economics, large population and Muslim identity and the associated normative analyses, I suggest an analytical perspective that is grounded in the everyday understanding of actors' and agents' actual roles during negotiations over economy, governance and ideology. Analysis of the worlds and actions of diplomats and lobbyists who served as human conduits during the negotiations offers a better route to understand what ultimately went 'wrong' with the now completely stalled process of Turkish Europeanisation. I lay out my main thesis of how Turkish Europeanisation evolved from an accession framework to an access objective, as its actors began working for their own private, professional, public, personal or institutional interests and against the mandate of making accession happen. I then explain central concepts of the book, such as interest, power and their brokerage. Finally, I walk the reader through the power–interest nexus or the theoretical toolkit I use in this book as I search for the arts of lobbying and diplomacy during Turkey's Europeanisation. Chapter 2 maps out the social topography of Brussels' Europolitics and introduces some of the key actors of Turkey's Europeanisation, mainly from the Turkish side. I identify them as nobles and notables because of their prominent role during Turkish Europeanisation and because, unless otherwise noted, many proved resilient as effective negotiators, even when the EU–Turkey membership negotiations went into a death spiral. The chapter also gives a historical overview of the negotiations since 2005 and explains my research and writing methodology.

Part II reflects on the EU's enlargement ethos. Chapter 3 introduces the reader to the political and technical framework of the EU's enlargement policy and accession negotiations with third countries as soft power. I argue that the enlargement policy has had a 'pedagogical' grounding that emerged from and produced an uneven power relationship between the EU (teacher) and Turkey (student). On the flip side, the accession pedagogy elicited Turkish governmental responses that were often defensive, defiant and counterproductive. These responses make sense when one considers them within the context of Turkey's post-imperial, neo-nationalist ambitions for constructing its own soft power (neo-Ottomanism) to counterbalance power inequality with the EU. Politicians', diplomats' and lobbyists' manipulation of where technical prerequisites for accession end and where political interests begin framed this accession pedagogy and its neo-Ottomanist derivative. Based on comparative readings of Turkish and EU diplomats' and lobbyists' accounts, this chapter discusses how Turkish and EU actors performed policy work and their power–interests within such a pedagogical framework.

Part III hones in on the arts and cultures of diplomacy and lobbying inside the EU Council, European Commission and European Parliament. Chapter 4 maps the complex machinery of how corporate interests influenced the construction and conveyance of 'national interests' of EU member states regarding Turkey's Europeanisation, which were expected to mould 'common European interests' and investments in Turkey's future sovereignty and statecraft. I map out the role of Brussels-based EU member state diplomats as permanent national lobbies during this process. Together with corporate lobbyists, EU diplomats sculpted the terms and conditions of Turkey's EU accession responsibilities during their twice-weekly meetings of the Council Working Group on Enlargement. I show how the everyday (in)formal communicative practices of sovereignty by diplomats and lobbyists, behind closed doors at the Council and faced with pressures from advanced European capitalism, shaped the interests of EU member states and Turkey in each other away from accession. Whereas EU member state diplomats enjoyed greater flexibility in performing their duties of diplomacy and lobbying, Turkish diplomats participated in the construction of Turkish national interests less than they might have done, due in part to how Turkey's EU policy and accession negotiations were organised by the Ankara government. In this tight environment, Turkish diplomats carved a wedge between Turkish and EU interests, instead of integrating them, to make their services useful. Their efforts came at a price, however, as they disengaged from the Eurocracy, facing enduring problems of collocution.

Chapter 5 focuses on encounters between bureaucrats, diplomats and lobbyists from both sides at several significant moments of the deepening of economic (but not necessarily political) integration between the EU and Turkey, beginning with the EU–Turkey customs union and the free trade agreement (FTA) on steel. The customs union has turned towards protectionism to manage the political and economic costs associated with Turkey's EU accession and to satisfy key business interests from both sides to protect their market access in the face of the receding prospect of accession. One means by which Turkish elites tried to compensate for such losses was to resort to dramatic expressions of state power. The chapter reveals how mistrust, wariness and differences in cultures of lobbying and negotiation deeply alienated Turkish and EU actors from one another. Using the customs union and steel contact group and other sectoral meetings as a trope, I analyse bureaucrats' inter-institutional and interpersonal encounters with one another and their symbolic dimension. As my EU and Turkish interlocutors often communicated, the apparent mismanagement and distortions of the customs union and other economic regulatory instruments such as the FTA in steel manifested a disjuncture in common interests regarding the overall objectives of EU–Turkey economic integration – a disjuncture marked by unequal power relations. Even though dramatic expressions of state power entered this process to remedy (or cover up) Turkish actors' perceived power deficit vis-à-vis their EU counterparts, they ended up exacerbating actors' alienation from one another. Appearing as bureaucratic inertia, such alienation had implications for the membership talks, with Turkish officials at individual and collective bureaucratic levels experiencing loss of control during negotiations with EU officials. As traced from the transnational day-to-day encounters of techno-bureaucrats, this process put the future of economic integration at risk.

Chapter 6 maps exchanges of information, interest and influence in the production of the European Parliament's annual reports on Turkey's reform performance. In this chapter, I delve into the Parliament's textual repository on Turkey as a site and medium where EU actors and their Turkish counterparts negotiated interests invested in (or disinvested from) Turkey's bid for EU membership. I analyse successive draft reports and amendment proposals put forth by MEPs which were largely initiated upon the request of those who lobbied them from both within and outside this EU institution. I argue that such political documents contributed to bureaucratic politics in both the EU and Turkey. Those who drafted or circulated them or who influenced their writing increasingly relied on them to sustain communication between otherwise reluctant parties. In return, political documents served as the means through which actors maintained the demand for their expertise. This human contact ultimately reveals complex negotiations over what matters most, to whom and to what end in Europe's encouragement (or discouragement) of Turkish membership.

Considering the increasing authoritarianism of the Turkish government, the changing regional problems and their implications for the EU, and the recent refugee crisis and the bargain that gave Turkey extended rights in Europe in exchange for heightened protection against outsiders, I conclude the book by shedding light on the possible outcomes of that bargain and how the EU and Turkey may initiate future negotiations regarding similar and novel troubles that await the region at large.

Acknowledgements

Since its inception over a decade ago, with the research that went into it, *Diplomacy and Lobbying During Turkey's Europeanisation* has accumulated great debts to many people. Without the assistance and encouragement of accomplished librarians at Bartle Library of Binghamton University, Library of the European Economic and Social Committee, Bibliothèques de Université Libre de Bruxelles and the Central Library of the European Commission this book would have been a poorer one. Colleagues and mentors at Binghamton, Istanbul Technical and Texas A&M Universities and, more recently, the University of Texas at El Paso helped this book see the light in myriad ways. I would like to thank, in particular, Howard Campbell, Carmen A. Ferradas, Josiah M. Heyman, Douglas R. Holmes, the late William F. Kelleher, Robert R. Shandley, Aydan Turanlı, Thomas M. Wilson and Tuncay Zorlu. Thomas M. Wilson, my mentor and friend, has taught me how to produce responsible scholarship and that, if used properly, ethnographic analysis can be a great tool to hold power and the powerful accountable. My fellow Europeanists at Binghamton, in particular William V. Pavlovich and James E. Verinis, made life enjoyable in the Southern Tier. The Cornell–Binghamton Consortium for the Anthropology of Europe (now defunct), which some of the above names made possible and of which I was a founding member, contributed to my academic career in its infancy.

I also thank the staff at the Inter-institutional Relations and Relations with National Economic and Social Committees unit of the European Economic and Social Committee, the 'Committee', which provided a home and an institutional shield at a time when my return to Brussels to do fieldwork remained uncertain. Philippe Bon, Sonia Calvy, Eva Michiels, Vasco Oliveira, Jerome Roche, Véronica Tomei and the interns of autumn 2008 took me under their wings and allowed me time and collegiality during the early phases of fieldwork in Brussels. Thanks are also due to Professor Marianne Mesnil and the Centre de recherche en ethnologie européenne, Université Libre de Bruxelles, for hosting me as a visiting researcher in Brussels. A timely Wenner-Gren Foundation grant made fieldwork in Brussels feasible.

While in Brussels, I received welcomes from the offices of Turkish and EU interest representations and diplomatic circles, in particular the offices of the Turkish Industry and Business Association, the Centre for Turkey in Europe and ABHaber.

During fieldwork in Brussels, Istanbul and Ankara and beyond, Dilek Ateş, Özlem Aydoğan, Nur Beler, Monika Berdys, Meltem Çakır, Manolis Dardoufas, Birsen Demiriz, Gamze Ege, Onur Eryüce, Gökalp Gümüşdere, Sanem Güvenç-Salgırlı, Yeliz Hacıosmanoğlu, Tuğçe Işıkara, Canan Karaosmanoğlu, Maria Ketsetzi, Kıvanç Kılınç, Bilge Köprülü, Ender Mersin, Suna Orçun, Burak Özgen, Arzu Şengün, Maresi Starzmann, Aslıhan Tekin, Didem Vardar, Nicholas Whyte, Sarah Williams and Seda Yalçın offered shelter, friendship and much-needed laughter. Bomani Shakur and Jason Robb, presently at Ohio State Penitentiary, offered decade-long love and friendship.

Binghamton University's inaugural Richard T. Antoun Fellowship made initial writing of this book possible. But Denis A. O'Hearn, my partner in life, is responsible for it appearing in this final version. If it was not for his endless encouragement, the book might not have seen the light of day. Howard Campbell, Jaume Franquesa, Sanem Güvenç-Salgırlı, Josiah M. Heyman, Iver B. Neumann, Denis O'Hearn, Robert R. Shandley, Jaro Stacul and Tom Wilson read the manuscript in parts or in its entirety and helped sharpen my arguments. Robert Sauté and Ralph Footring improved its language and clarity. My editors at Manchester University Press stood by me and saw the book through.

A portion of Chapter 3 was published as 'The Accession Pedagogy: Power and Politics in Turkey's Bid for EU Membership', *Anthropological Journal of European Cultures* 23 (1): 99–120. It is reprinted here by permission of Berghahn Publishers. A much earlier version of a section of Chapter 5 appeared as 'Failed Promises: Economic Integration, Bureaucratic Encounters, and the EU–Turkey Customs Union', *Dialectical Anthropology* 37 (1): 1–26. It is reprinted here by permission of Springer Netherlands. Portions of Chapter 6 were published as 'Political Documents and Bureaucratic Entrepreneurs: Lobbying the European Parliament During Turkey's EU Integration', *Political and Legal Anthropology Review* 39 (2): 190–205. They are reprinted here by permission of John Wiley & Sons.

Finally, this book owes a great debt to my diplomatic and lobbyist interlocutors in Brussels who took their invaluable time to explain painstakingly to an outsider the everyday complexity of doing politics and policy along the EU–Turkey axis. For reasons of anonymity, their names shall remain with me. Last but not least, I thank my family for their patience with my occasional absences from their lives. Here is a partial explanation.

Part I

Inside the private life of politics

Figure 1.1 Aerial photo of Brussels' European neighbourhood, with the Commission's cross-shaped Berlaymont building (lower left-hand side), the Council's Justus Lipsius building, with a helipad on top (slightly above and to the right of the Berlaymont building), and the Parliament complex, with ellipsoid Paul-Henri Spaak building (upper right). Source: Google Earth

The elephant in the room

'Dream of a rosy-pink Europe'

While she escorted me out of her triplex condo, I asked Leyla whether she had ever thought about what might happen to her self-professed vocation as a lobbyist if Turkey were to join the European Union (EU). Previously, I had read her writings and watched her speak with great poise on television or during conferences on Turkey–EU affairs. Leyla mulled over my question for a while and recalled what a friend from a central European state had told her some years before. Reflecting on her own country's EU accession process, Leyla's friend, a fellow lobbyist, commented with dismay: 'After accession, there is less need for lobbying'. Over a decade has passed since Leyla made that remark. In those years, Turkey initially moved closer to joining the EU but then moved far away; over the same period, many of Leyla's diplomat and lobbyist colleagues from both Turkey and the EU achieved professional advance as a consequence of their experience and involvement in the tortuous accession process. This book is an effort to understand these contradictory dynamics that moulded the history of Turkey–EU relations.

Despite its bid for EU membership, Turkey is presently undergoing its own Brexit moment, which some refer to as Turkey's de-Europeanisation (Aydın-Düzgit & Kaliber 2016) or TRexit (Ülgen 2016).[1] TRexit is Turkey's home-grown post-application condition – not in the sense of its securing EU membership to which Leyla's friend referred but perhaps eclipsing the idea thereof. This book is an effort to explain what went 'wrong' between Turkey and the EU, which ultimately led to this TRexit moment. Based on over two years of ethnographic fieldwork conducted in Brussels, Istanbul and Ankara between 2005 and 2013, it sheds light on the conditions that led to TRexit from the everyday perspectives of diplomacy and lobbying.

Diplomacy is the conduct of interstate politics to reach an agreement. Assembling information and knowledge, relaying influence and negotiation over interests are common practices for diplomats (Neumann 2012). If diplomacy is the art of formal negotiations of 'different positions held by different polities' (Neumann 2012: 7–8), lobbying refers to informal negotiations among public and private stakeholders. Like diplomacy, lobbying depends on accumulating and transmitting knowledge and expertise on how host polities work, and brokering information, influence and interests. Both practices depend on actors' capacity to gather high-quality information and intelligence, plan policy briefs based on this information and persuade their addressee to trust their expertise and to act on this information. Though diplomacy remains a formalised practice, both diplomacy and lobbying use formal and informal channels of communication in relaying information, influence and interests. That the information and intelligence diplomats and lobbyists produce or gather gain value only when shared makes both activities relational. Today, a variety of people and institutions perform diplomacy and lobbying, representing states, governments, transnational corporations, non-governmental organisations (NGOs) and international organisations (Neumann 2012, 2013; Ross 2007). While diplomats increasingly lobby and lead informal negotiations, interest representatives and lobbyists heavily inform or perform paradiplomatic work. They are increasingly two sides of the same coin.

When we consider international relations, we often take for granted that states negotiate their interests. States – essentially an abstraction – per se cannot do things; only particular people who conduct particular actions in their name can do so (Abrams 1988; Feldman 2019; Mitchell 1991). Accordingly, in contexts beyond the usual diplomatic negotiations, when we say 'states negotiate' we need to know who negotiates what, when, where and how. However, we take diplomacy for granted and assume that state representatives re-present or relay 'state interests' formulated elsewhere. Our understanding of what constitutes 'state interests' or 'national' interests' thus remains equally unyielding and needs refinement, especially when those state interests reflect an admixture of private, corporate or institutional interests, represented by a variety of state and non-state actors.

Adding Turkey–EU affairs to the mix extends what we do not know about how national, governmental, corporate and state interests are formed and communicated to parties of interstate negotiations between a supranational entity, such as the EU, and a candidate country for EU membership, like Turkey, which is also a nation state. But the EU–Turkey membership negotiations also present a far more significant challenge to our normative understanding of international relations: what happens when actors who are entrusted with facilitating interstate relations through diplomacy and lobbying work for their own private, professional, public, personal or institutional interests, even when those interests may go against their commonly understood mandate? While political anthropologists are oblivious to this question because of their disdain for 'high-level' politics, political scientists and international relations (IR) scholars – the traditional arbiters of such questions – remain silent about the non-normative conduct of politics and policy at the interstate level. A combination of disciplinary forces is needed.

Calling attention to actors' agency in shaping the structures of power in which they operate and which they are shaped by, this book reveals how diplomatic and lobbying actors, such as Leyla and many others I introduce throughout the book, who were entrusted, after 2005, with facilitating Turkey's EU membership bid, conducted the EU–Turkey membership talks, until those talks lost steam. Here I argue that actors and agents of Turkish Europeanisation from both sides in fact impeded accession because their private, professional, public, personal and institutional interests departed from their mandate of facilitating Turkey's EU membership. Instead, there was a widespread but tacit prioritisation of the acquisition of resources and power, implicitly at the expense of genuine progress towards accession, given that such resources and power would be lost if accession actually happened. This shift occurred as the structures of power between the EU and Turkey bred a culture clash of sovereignty and statecraft during what I call the EU's pedagogical treatment of Turkey (see Chapter 3) and Turkey's post-imperial rejection of this treatment. Throughout the long course of negotiations, membership talks and political communication became perturbed. Although some progress was made towards Turkey's EU integration, diplomats and lobbyists from both sides of the negotiating table contradictorily reaffirmed their expertise as effective negotiators and thereby earned more recognition, status and power over the period.

Taking diplomacy and lobbying as its cue and entry points, this book presents the intricate backstage negotiations that surrounded Turkey's EU bid, negotiations which drove this candidate country both closer to and farther from the EU. In this volume, the reader will find the everyday actors and agents of Turkish Europeanisation and learn what their work entailed, which interests they represented and how they did what they did, which I could capture only through long-term ethnographic observation of actors' everyday patterns of action. Assuming that conflict, contestation and compromise are the *sine qua non* of any negotiation, the book walks the reader through the conflicts of interest and compromises that occurred during actors' everyday encounters with one another through the Turkish and EU corridors of power. I present how the power–interest nexus that surrounded negotiations affected the actual, daily policy work that interstate negotiations require, and discuss whether it was culturally specific. Diplomacy and lobbying present a unique vantage point from which to examine a decade of power and interest negotiations between Turkish and EU actors, in which those actors articulated what 'common European interests' looked like from their historically and culturally contingent perspectives – a process otherwise known as Turkish Europeanisation.[2]

'Europe' has long been a charged concept in Turkey. Turkish modernity and state formation were calibrated for it during much of the twentieth century. Schoolchildren in Turkey learned from an early age that their country, post-Atatürk, belonged in the imaginary that the Nobel laureate Orhan Pamuk (2010) called a 'dream of a rosy-pink Europe'. At the dawn of the twenty-first century, roughly since the 1996 EU–Turkey Customs Union Agreement, Turkey has largely framed its relations with the European region within the context of the country's integration into the EU. In December 2004, EU leaders made the historic decision to start accession talks with Turkey on 3 October 2005, which opened a new chapter in these long-running relations, one that began with great hope and expectation

By 2009, that expectant mood had evaporated. That year, the Eurobarometer survey recorded that only 38 per cent of the people in Turkey trusted the EU, and only 43 per cent had a positive image of the Union. The results of the German

Marshall Fund's Transatlantic Trends 2009 survey, the results of which circulated in EU meetings and hallways, showed even more dramatic numbers: 32 per cent had a positive image of the EU and a third (34 per cent) said they felt they shared common values with the West and by implication with the EU. According to the same survey, and most significantly, while 48 per cent of the Turkish people believed Turkey's EU membership would be a good thing, 65 per cent thought it was not likely to happen, compared with 54 per cent in the EU who believed Turkish membership was inevitable.

Turkey's membership negotiations with the EU have coincided with the rule of the Adalet ve Kalkınma Partisi (AKP; Justice and Development Party). The AKP came to office in 2002 after it had fervently campaigned for Turkey's integration into the EU. Soon after accession talks began in 2005, both Turkey and the EU had shifted their interest from membership to access to markets and polities. While successive AKP governments kept failing to deliver the substantive domestic reforms the EU required of it, several EU member states openly expressed opposition to Turkey's EU membership, even though the European Council decision to begin (and end) membership talks requires unanimity. Since then, conservative forces have gained ascendancy in both European and Turkish politics. Today, Turkey's EU membership is little more than a pipedream. And, as I suggest in this book, the arts of diplomacy and lobbying have a lot to do with this outcome.

The human bridge

Leyla did not become a lobbyist overnight. Born into an extended family of politicians, public officials and journalists, she was a vocal feminist, a staunch human rights supporter and an ardent believer in Turkey's European future well before her self-made career in lobbying. After studying journalism in Belgium, Leyla worked for over a decade as the bureau chief of a (now defunct) Turkish private news agency and the Brussels correspondent and head of French broadcasts for Turkey's state television network, the Turkish Radio and Television Corporation (TRT). Long before politicians and civil servants sat down to talk about the nuts and bolts of Turkey's accession to the EU, Leyla reported about Turkey–EU affairs at the heart of Europolitics. Moving back to Turkey in the mid-1980s, her weekly columns in Turkey's popular newspapers – before being terminated twice in her career by political pressure from the very top – often focused on the country's EU integration. Over the same period, she had been actively involved in the women's rights movement that had formed after the 1980 coup d'état, at a time when official censorship was rampant and political activism risky.

When we met, Leyla was living and working from her home-office in Levent – one of Istanbul's most affluent neighbourhoods, populated by many who worked in the media, advertising and finance. She ran (unsuccessfully) for parliament for the Cumhuriyet Halk Partisi (Republican People's Party) during the 3 November 2002 general election. That election resulted in a coalition government being replaced by the AKP. The coalition had undertaken some initial reforms and had paved the road for EU–Turkey accession talks to begin, as they did under the

AKP. A few years later, Leyla would write: 'Europe will enhance its multicultural identity with Turkey'. Her optimism, though, was not without a hint of caution, since she belonged to modern Turkey's founder Ataturk's republican elites, the old, more liberal-leaning elites, which the new self-proclaimed 'conservative democratic' rulers of the country threatened to replace.

Shortly before her failed try at a political career, Leyla had gone into professional lobbying. Shuttling between Brussels and Istanbul every couple of months, she had joined a Turkish consultancy firm with offices in Brussels and Washington, DC, which a Turkish lawyer-lobbyist had founded. Leyla ran the Istanbul office and advised the board, but soon left the company because of intense personal and professional differences with its founder. Leyla then set up a consultancy business operating out of that Levent condo, which allowed her to use her political, cultural, intellectual and social capital pertaining to Turkey–EU politics and markets, but now with a new professional partner, one who had expertise in communication and public affairs. The opening of accession negotiations improved business. In this new line of work, Leyla's personal politics did not prevent her from doing business with AKP elites. She actively sought clients from any sector, from pharmaceuticals to insurance to construction. Meanwhile, she initiated the (now defunct) Turkish-language edition of Euractiv, a prominent web-based EU media outlet. In Brussels she cooperated with a global consultancy firm while joining the ranks of another. She also established the Centre for Turkey in Europe, a non-profit platform that was to serve as a think-tank, in Brussels' *quartier européenne* – a conspicuously Eurocratic neighbourhood.

Unlike many others whose deeds, accomplishments and non-actions I present in this book, Leyla was not exactly part of the 'higher circle' of power that Charles Wright Mills (1956) discussed in his classic monograph *The Power Elite*. She did not occupy a formal political or an administrative position in Turkey's EU membership negotiations. Those negotiations officially took place between Turkish and EU leaders and their diplomats and bureaucrats. Although some of her fellow lobbyists had held public office in the past, Leyla's career as a lobbyist did not rest upon public service. Nor was she a member of the policy elite. While Leyla and her colleagues actively represented a variety of public and private corporate interests inside Turkey and at the heart of Europolitics in Brussels, politicians and businesspeople consulted her and other professionals about matters pertaining to Turkish Europeanisation.

Leyla was thus a human bridge: she tied together different interests and different sources of information and influence, and channelled them through the corridors of power. Such interests and sources vied to steer Turkey's Europeanisation, as power oscillated between the centres and peripheries of a wider Europe. The power–interest nexus surrounding Turkish Europeanisation attracts the attention of students of European integration and Turkish politics because it relates to questions of what matters most, for whom, in what ways and for which end-results in today's Europe and Turkey.

In their responses to these questions, experts, who commonly conducted benchmark analyses and public opinion surveys, have often found Turkey 'too poor, too large and too Muslim' for EU membership. I argue that this triple mantra of poor economics, large population and identity talk, on which experts have long relied as their analytical compass, has, in the main, fallen short in explaining the process under scrutiny. In fact, it may have pointed students and experts on Turkish Europeanisation away from understanding the main dynamics of accession negotiations. In this chapter, I take stock of the Turkish Europeanisation literature and identify its critical drawbacks. Leaving aside the triple mantra and the associated normative analyses, I suggest an analytical perspective that is grounded in an everyday understanding of actors' and agents' actual roles during negotiations over economy, governance and ideology. Analysis of the worlds and actions of diplomats and lobbyists who served as human conduits during the negotiations offers a better route to understanding what reportedly ultimately went 'wrong' with the process of Turkish Europeanisation. I lay out my main thesis on how Turkish Europeanisation evolved from an accession framework to an access objective, as its actors began working for their own private, professional, public, personal or institutional interests and against the mandate of making accession happen. I then explain central concepts of the book such as interest, power and their brokerage. Finally, I walk the reader through the power–interest nexus or the theoretical toolkit I use in this book as I search for the arts of lobbying and diplomacy during Turkey's Europeanisation.

The triple mantra

When Turkey entered a customs union with the EU in 1996, became a candidate for EU membership in 1999 and began negotiating the terms and conditions of its accession in late 2005, it elated many at home and abroad. The large number of young, skilled Turks promised to reinvigorate Europe's economic sectors, while the country's growing and diverse consumer society would create greater market opportunities for European businesses. Its secular stance could have made Turkey a unique model of Muslim democracy in the Middle East while potentially stabilising troubled European multiculturalism. The negotiations were expected to take only five to six years, in line with the precedent set by other EU candidates (the central and eastern European countries), but they are still ongoing, with no end in sight. In addition, the century-long privileged position of 'Europe' among the country's different social classes seems to be waning. Today, most experts agree that Turkey's membership is unlikely, due to Turkey's weakening economy, large population and religious identity. In short, Turkey is 'too poor, too large and too Muslim' for the EU.

This triple mantra has dominated political and scholarly debates on Turkey's EU affairs for decades, making experts of European integration treat Turkey, in the words of one of my European Commission interlocutors, as an 'elephant in the room'. Concentrating on normative aspects of institution-building, scholars mainly in political science, economics, sociology and law have produced numerous benchmark assessments of the economic challenge Turkey's integration could bring to the EU, including its cost to member states, with sectoral policy analyses in agriculture, telecommunications, regional development policy and so on. Future technical projections of the harmonisation with the EU *acquis communautaire* (common law) became rampant. Comparative analyses of the capacity of EU member states and institutions to accommodate the possible scale of Turkish migration were common, as were those on citizenship policies. Public and elite opinions on Turkish membership were regularly surveyed in both Turkey and the EU.[3]

I find the triple mantra of poor economics, large demographics and identity talk dubious for several reasons, pertaining to facts, theoretical outlook and methodology. First, facts. In relation to the first element of the triple mantra, with the EU–Turkey customs union, Turkey's economy has matured, making Turkey less 'poor', especially from the perspective of qualifying for structural funds that are available to EU member states. In relation to the second, and as a European Parliament interlocutor explained, since a member state's population determines its voting power in the EU, critics fear demography will make it difficult for EU institutions and actors to 'get Turks to do things' if Turkey joins the EU before it registers substantial progress in undertaking EU reforms. But in any case, Turkey's population has stabilised over the last couple of decades, at a level on a par with Germany. Regarding the third element of the mantra, religion is as much a contentious issue in Turkey as in the EU. But religion is a nominal category, and people in Turkey will believe in whatever they want to believe in, regardless of EU membership. Thus, factually, the triple mantra is rendered moot.

Many analyses of Turkey's EU accession that rely on the triple mantra remain theoretically ill-suited to explain the accession dynamics. On the one hand, available accounts of Turkey's Europeanisation regard accession as a transfer of norms and as a straightforward top-down project of technical adaptation from the supranational polity to the nation state, steered by elite decision (cf. Richardson & Mazey 2015). They thus depict the negotiation process as if it were body-less, devoid of agency and without contention. On the other hand, according to neo-functionalist theories of European integration, experts anticipated that closer economic cooperation would bring political integration, or at least enhance Turkey's ability to participate in the EU's common decision-making processes and structures (Rosamond 2000: 50–73). Contrary to this expectation, however, EU–Turkey membership talks have stalled, while economic integration proceeds (manifested in trade in manufactured industrial goods, market liberalisation and the circulation of capital) – though with burgeoning troubles that in turn yield a reverse 'spill-over'.

Finally, future technical projections, benchmark analyses and opinion surveys fail at a more important, methodological level. Attitude surveys, whose results could be used to sensationalise EU–Turkey relations, may capture self and other perceptions at one moment in time, as the 2009 Eurobarometer and German Marshall Fund surveys helped to do, but they do not explain why relations have reached the bleak point they have. In fact, none of the experts actually foresaw the opening of the EU–Turkey accession negotiations in 2005, or ultimately the de facto (but not yet de jure) suspension of the EU–Turkey membership talks a decade later, rendering Turkish interests and (dis)investments irrelevant to negotiations over sovereignty, governance and statecraft between the centres and peripheries of Europe. The kinds of account that political actors of earlier rounds of EU enlargement wrote and that provide insiders' perspectives (Grabbe 2006; Vassiliou 2007) are non-existent in the Turkish case. That is, there are no suggestions as to who the agents of this process were, how and where they did what they did, and what motivated them to act or what restrained them from action. Lack of grounded, empirical evidence is a major factor in the failure to make accurate predictions, but so are the particular analytical and methodological frameworks scholars commonly use to explain the Turkish EU bid. When anticipation does not correspond to reality on the ground and when analyses of *actual* negotiations are nil, the triple mantra becomes all the more captivating, leading experts to call upon notions of 'Turkish exceptionalism' or the idea that the Turkish case can be explained only self-referentially (Arvanitopoulos 2009; Grigoriadis 2009).[4] What remains missing, in other words, is an analysis that problematises how Turkey's EU accession process is managed, what it ultimately means for its actors and agents, and what implications all this may have on the EU and on Turkey.

Most importantly, from technocrats to diplomats to lobbyists and other interest brokers from both sides, none of my interlocutors expressed the triple mantra in their work for Turkish Europeanisation, except on a few occasions where they grappled with it at a personal level or tested its viability as a negotiation tactic. I met no insider of Turkish Europeanisation who was concerned about the triple mantra, even though insiders remained acquiescent to it because they ultimately benefited from its masking effects vis-à-vis the situated dynamics of the negotiation process and their complicit role in it.

This does not mean that economy, governance and culture have been irrelevant to Turkey's Europeanisation. While experts and the public were busy mulling over the triple mantra on an everyday basis, the EU–Turkey membership talks primarily concerned technical issues, such as alcohol taxation, chemical regulations, state aid for steel and agriculture among others, that are in the main harmonised into thirty-two distinct policy areas. Setting aside simple policy talk, what politicians, diplomats, bureaucrats, interest representatives and lobbyists *actually negotiated* behind closed doors between Ankara and Brussels were their cultural differences in sovereignty, statecraft and governance.

Against the backdrop of the triple mantra, then, I invite the reader to explore a different perspective and an alternative explanation for Turkey's failed EU membership bid. As I followed my interlocutors while they negotiated their cultural differences in sovereignty, statecraft and governance, listening to the issues they were passionate about, observing the conflicts they handled through Brussels' political labyrinth, I came to wonder whether Turkey's EU accession was anyone's end game. What if Turkish Europeanisation was not so much an end or a *product* of negotiations, but a *process* – a process wherein actors and agents imbued membership talks with their personal, professional and public ambitions, impassioned calculations and competing interests? What if their negotiations were not about Turkey's EU membership but about what they could gain *from the process itself*? And if so, how could we account for this power–interest dynamic? Such an investigation would require first-hand access to what went on behind closed doors, and this volume is the first to offer that very perspective.

Leyla between accession and access

When we first met, in 2007, neither Leyla nor I could have predicted the emergent forces that were to yield TRexit. Yet Turkish Europeanisation was already caught up in its death spiral, which forced Leyla to close up shop in Brussels a couple of years later and go back to Turkey. Nonetheless, while negotiations were still underway, Leyla and I were optimistic about Turkey's EU membership prospects.

Admittedly, I, like many of my fellow Turks, was naive to take for granted that membership negotiations were simply that: discussions aimed at reaching an agreement whose ultimate goal was membership of a group. In his *How Nations Negotiate* the Swiss sociologist Fred Charles Iklé (1964: 3–4) defined negotiation as 'a process in which explicit proposals are put outward ostensibly for the purpose of reaching agreement on an exchange or on the realization of a common interest where conflicting interests are present'. Iklé's definition is still in use today. Accession negotiations between a supranational/intergovernmental entity like the EU and a nation state with the characteristics of Turkey, however, defied common norms of international negotiations and how one state may join a group of states. They also required special coaching.

Precisely because the EU framed accession talks as negotiations, many of my Turkish interlocutors took this definition to heart and behaved as if they *could* negotiate with the EU *en bloc*. Meanwhile, in Turkey, many believed that Turkish diplomats and lobbyists were effective negotiators with Brussels. In line with this popular view, my Turkish interlocutors aimed at nothing less than membership – at least superficially – *if* they could negotiate the terms and conditions of this membership on equal terms with their EU colleagues.

Unlike scholars who commonly find Turkey 'too poor, too large and too Muslim' for the EU, I found that it was not so much that economy, demography and culture/identity barred Turkey from EU membership, although they made membership difficult at times. Rather, Turkish membership would have ultimately opened up the decision-making processes and structures of the country to EU member states and those of the EU to Turkey, and this bore for both sides too big a cost to see it through.

Economy, population and ideology are matters central to how to govern, as Michel Foucault (1991) has taught us. While there might be some truth to the triple mantra, I find it most unhelpful in explaining the actual dynamics of accession talks. During my fieldwork, I often observed that Turkish and EU elites managed the cost of Turkish Europeanisation with a bureaucratic politics of *non*-membership based on tactics of containment. In effect, the actors dragged out the negotiations for over a decade, until they ran out of steam. At the individual bureaucratic level, such tactics led to actors' disengagement from one another, while paradoxically contributing to their standing as 'effective negotiators' within their own policy communities, without actual progress in negotiations. The process was one of dis-integration.

To explain this Turkish 'anti-case' of EU membership as seen through the cultures of diplomacy and lobbying, I contend that the nature of public, private, corporate, personal and professional interests gave *access* to power and resources in both Turkey and the EU and took precedence over *accession* or full membership. In the end, the EU–Turkey negotiations hardly 'went sour' but instead too many parties benefited from the negotiations themselves to bring them to a close. This book lays out how diverse public, private and corporate actors voicing economic, political and bureaucratic interests from all corners of Europe sought access to markets and polities through the Turkish bid for EU accession and how this access dialectically (in)formed the cultures of sovereignty, statecraft and governance between Turkey and the EU. This book ultimately seeks to bring interests and their brokerage back to the centre of social and cultural analyses of power, policy and politics. In the context of Turkish Europeanisation, it is those institutional bureaucratic, personal and professional ambitions, calculations and interests about which actors and agents of the process negotiate on a daily basis.

Interests and their brokerage

'Interest' bears a complex polysemy laden with multiple meanings of legal and financial claims and concerns in modern times. Raymond Williams traced the concept to the Latin word *interesse*, meaning 'to be between, to make a difference, to concern' (Williams 2015 [1976]: 123). Pursuing the concept from its French use to its roots in Latin, Irène Bellier (2000a: 54) defined it as 'to be at a distance' and 'to matter'. Both scholars referred to two later meanings of the term as a borrowing charge and injury or loss. In modern Turkish, 'interest', *çıkar*, means expedient option or indirect gain as in when someone benefits from a situation indirectly, for which one also uses the Arabic word *menfaat*. Whereas *çıkar* may describe collective and more neutral interest (as in 'interest group', *çıkar grubu*), *menfaat* almost always carries a negative connotation and is often used to denote concealed, individual gain.

Economist Albert O. Hirschman (2013 [1977]) argued that 'interest' artificially separates various motives that drive human action, when in fact it is another term for tamed passions. In transforming passions into 'interests', modern rational beings choose between *Zweckrationalität* and *Wertrationalität* (Weber 1978) or between acting rationally and instrumentally and acting according to their value compass. Hirschman (2013: 32–8) reported that interest's reference changed from a general concern (as in the 'national interest' being represented by the ruler of the state) to a set of differentiated concerns held by various groups and individuals who were interested in advancing their power, influence and wealth:

> 'Interests' of persons and groups eventually came to be centred on economic advantage as its core meaning, not only in ordinary language but also in such social-science terms as 'class interests' and 'interest groups'. But the economic meaning became

dominant rather late in the history of the term. When the term 'interest' in the sense of concerns, aspirations, and advantage gained currency in Western Europe during the late sixteenth century, its meaning was by no means limited to the material aspects of a person's welfare; rather, it comprised the totality of human aspirations, but denoted an element of reflection and calculation with respect to the manner in which these aspirations were to be pursued. In fact, serious thought involving the notion of interest first arose in a context entirely removed from individuals and their material welfare. (Hirschman 2013: 32–3)

In this book, I show how 'interest' as the totality of concerns and aspirations invested in Turkish Europeanisation oscillates between the term's collective and individual referents.

Anthropologists have had a long-term engagement with interest as a group category. Dating back to the decolonisation and modernisation of the 1950s and 1960s and transactionalism in the 1970s, many have encountered interest groups as informal actors and interest brokerage as informal political practice, connecting local systems of power to the nation state (Koster & Leynseele 2018; Lewis & Mosse 2006; Lindquist 2015; Mosse & Lewis 2005; Vincent 1990).

Eric Wolf (1956), one of the pioneers of this anthropological engagement with interest brokerage, called attention to the important role interest brokers played as guardians of 'crucial junctures or synapses of relationships which connect the local system to the larger whole'. In a passage that, for me, best explains Leyla's predicament between accession and access, Wolf wrote:

> The position of these 'brokers' is an 'exposed' one, since, Janus-like, they face in two directions at once. They must serve some of the interests of groups operating on both the community and the national level, and they must cope with the conflicts raised by the collision of these interests. They cannot settle them, since by doing so they would abolish their own usefulness to others. Thus they often act as buffers between groups, maintaining the tensions which provide the dynamic of their actions.... [T]hey must also maintain a grip on these tensions, lest conflict get out of hand and better mediators take their place. (Wolf 1956: 1075–6)

Following Wolf, Jeremy Boissevain (1974: 148–9) described brokers as those 'who control strategic contacts with other people, who control resources directly, or who have access to such persons'. He further suggested that 'a broker's capital is [the] actual communication channels he controls', while 'his credit consists of what others think his capital to be. [Brokers] are thus dealing in expectations – future possible services – rather than dead certainties' (Boissevain 1974: 159). Brokers, according to Boissevain (1974: 149), 'manipulate people and information for profit'. The profit that the brokers achieve, however, need not always be monetary, as I show in this book. Trading favours for allegiance and loyalty, brokers benefit from this exchange by accumulating more status, power, influence and prestige. Following these transactions, the broker's services become indispensable

With the death of patron–client studies in anthropology, anthropologists began to downplay interests and the role of brokerage, which they now took as signs of class hegemony, corruption and weak statehood, crying cronyism, nepotism and clientelism in sub-state regions and localities (Mosse & Lewis 2005). Here, brokers were taken to be tangential to, if not anomalous within, the conduct of modern politics. Today, the anthropological attention to interest politics has been partially reinvigorated by ethnographic analyses of the role of affect in governance (Graham 2002; Laszczkowski & Reeves 2017; Masco 2014; Navaro-Yashin 2012; Tate 2015) and the role interests play in actually existing neoliberalisms in a variety of policy contexts, ranging from economic to cultural to human rights and foreign-policy programmes around the world (James 2011; Merry 2006; Tate 2015; Wedel 2009).

Informed by anthropological work on interests and brokerage, I believe that there are significant parallels between local- and national-level brokerage relations and EU lobbying. EU institutions regularly consult specific interest groups, NGOs and other representatives of civil and economic society on the Union's industrial, trade and enlargement policies, among others. Since enlargement is in fact a meta-policy cross-cutting all other policies, all EU institutions require fresh information and expert knowledge about what goes on in candidate countries regarding their preparation for membership, which is why Eurocrats welcome lobbying.

In the reverse direction, for EU actors' consulting with interest groups and others, informal actors lobby EU institutions on behalf of their clientele. Formal actors such as diplomats and informal actors such as interest representatives and lobbyists have access to and sometimes control over basic resources: power and policy elites inside the EU, legitimacy, political support, funds, knowledge, expertise and information, resources that their clients or whomever they are accountable to want (Binderkrantz et al. 2017; Dür 2008). Here access is the primary but not the only requisite for effective representation. As political scientist Pieter Bouwen (2002: 366) remarks, 'ineffective political actors might gain access to an institution without being able to translate this advantage into policy [or the desired] outcome'.

Contemporary forms of political brokerage differ from the clientelisms Wolf and others observed. Even though I suggest taking today's diplomats as having limited autonomy and taking the lobbyists as mobile brokers, protection, favours and loyalty are no longer the goods patrons, brokers and clients exchange but information, influence and interest.[5] However, to appear to be effective in their work, diplomats, interest representatives and other lobbyists have to convince their clientele that their access to EU institutions and actors remains exclusive and critical to the interests of those clients (be they states, governments or businesses), hence the enduring need for their service. Compared with professional lobbying, the efficacy and success of diplomatic work are more enduring, but same conditions apply to both lines of work.

EU politics depends on lobbyists and diplomats channelling information, expert knowledge, advice and influence from one level of policy-making to the other and from the outside to the inside. During my fieldwork, I often observed how diplomats and lobbyists as actors and agents of Turkish Europeanisation experienced and exhibited similar everyday personal and professional dilemmas to those which Wolf wrote about in the passage quoted above. These dilemmas were primarily due to diplomats and lobbyists occupying the category of what Max

Weber called 'professional politicians'. As Weber (1994: 314) eloquently explained in his *Politics as a Vocation*, these are people who do not want to become rulers or politicians but instead commit themselves to serving those rulers' political agendas and policies, all the while being invested in the latter either by making a living from this service or by personally believing in those agendas and policies. Weber classifies MPs as 'part-time politicians', since they are active only during parliamentary sessions. As professional politicians, diplomats and lobbyists blur the boundaries between Weber's two ways of making a career out of politics: living 'for' politics and living 'from' politics.

From street demonstrations to international negotiations behind closed doors, politics has been about governing emotions, concerns, passions and aspirations, in short, interests, which run through social interactions. Following Hirschman, Wolf and others, my use of 'interest' has less to do with material aspects of a person's or organisation's wellbeing – although those may incentivise people's actions. It does not exclude affect, identity or values, or an individual's daily or long-term concerns with job security, family wellbeing or steady income. I use 'interest' to include the concerns, aspirations and passions of a person who, in my case, may act in the name of a state, a government or a corporate entity. These concerns, aspirations and passions may be personal, private (self-serving), public, systemic, structural, or institutional (Neumann 2012). Interests, thus defined, pertain to power, governance and statecraft, or what matters to actors most. From an anthropological perspective, interests are nothing more than what those who have a claim to them say they are, how those who represent them according to a collective or peer-recognised mandate enact them, and how those who act upon them perceive them to be. As I show in this book, while stalling negotiations, interest in Turkish Europeanisation continues to matter to its agents and actors, but for reasons that remain hitherto undisclosed to the public.

A political anthropology for future accountability

The move from political anthropology to an anthropology of politics has required researchers to shift their focus from the conduct of formal politics to its agents and institutions and their expectations of and exceptions to bargaining over the conduct of conduct (Abélès 1997; Vincent 1990). 'Political anthropology has never distinguished itself by researching the corridors of power; the challenge to "study up" was not widely accepted', as Joan Vincent (1990: 400) observed some three decades ago. Today, anthropologists and ethnographers of politics are a bit more at ease with the corridors of power and those who – like the elite, the powerful, the professional or the expert – operate in such spaces. Anthropologists study these actors and agents of power and policy-making up and down, sideways and through.[6]

Taken as an elite project, which sits uneasily among the peoples and politics in the local, regional and national levels, anthropologists commonly studied the EU and European integration from the perspective of 'nascent Europeans' at the top or from the prism of everyday contentions the EU may elicit from below.

Though few in number – but burgeoning – ethnographic analyses of the EU have most commonly concentrated on polity-building and the cultures of policy professionals to see whether a common European identity was emerging among EU elites. Probing essentially neo-functionalist theories of elite socialisation in the EU (March & Olsen 1998; Suvarierol 2009; cf. Shore 2000), ethnographers tested whether EU elites would converge because of 'culture contact' in the EU's multicultural institutions, that provide the necessary socio-physical infrastructure for different governmental, techno-bureaucratic and political/societal concerns to flourish (Abélès 2009: 43).[7] Although they reached no consensus on that, an-thropologists have ultimately shown the European project to be a dynamic site of meaning-making, over which larger questions of sovereignty, statecraft and identity are conveyed.

The EU is indeed an elite, expert-driven project. Yet, I contend that ethno-graphic studies of particular EU actors and agents have been overshadowed by analyses of their widely publicised knowledge and narratives (what they say and what they say they do) at the expense of investigations of their practices, policies, expertise (what they actually do; could do but don't do, or cannot do) and in-terests, or what matters to them most, within and beyond their own institutions of power. In effect, this privileging of elite/expert discourses over practices led scholars to downplay the role of informality in EU politicking and policy-making.

Having studied Brussels' Europolity in spaces that diplomats, lobbyists and other interest representatives also frequent, where brokerage relations commonly take place, anthropologists have long encountered such brokers as constitutive of informal, pluralist politics in the EU. But perhaps because these encounters were not the subject of targeted research, diplomacy and lobbying figured only tangen-tially in anthropological research. Hence, interest brokers were treated as low-key actors in the political field and were given insufficient space within the general description of the political life of EU institutions.[8] Despite persistent calls to the contrary (Bellier 2000a; McDonald-Walker 2000; Muntigl et al. 2000), nowhere in the scholarship did lobbying figure as constitutive of (in)formal politics and policy-making in the EU or a significant politico-cultural practice warranting the ethnographer's critical, systematic attention. In the rush to embrace performativ-ity, identity and fluidity, anthropologists lost sight of aspects of power central to politics, such as competition, conflict and interests.[9]

Even though no systematic ethnographic research on brokerage by diplomats and lobbyists has been hitherto available, representation, mediation and negotia-tion of interests remain key to understanding contemporary politics, especially in Europe, where non-governmental actors are not only encouraged to get involved in policy-making but their involvement is institutionalised through enforced rules and observed norms of the EU's changing political culture. Their exchanges with governmental actors are regular and non-codified but in ways that are not publicly sanctioned or transparent.

Critics have indicated the difficulty in doing anthropological work on politics and 'the political' today. Two problems stand out. One criticism concerns the post-Foucault tendency to see 'power' (Sahlins 2002) and 'political' (Candea 2011;

Curtis & Spencer 2012) everywhere. This book is explicitly about actors performing power and politics and prefiguring 'the political'. Following political theorists Andrew Barry (2001) and Chantal Mouffe (2005), I use 'political' in referring to those things whose meaning and boundaries remain contested. Even though the highly technical accession process was supposed to tame it, Turkey's Europeanisation remains contested to this day. Relations have long suffered from a democratic deficit, which ultimately yielded a breakdown of communications. This book ultimately aims to contribute to the democratisation of EU–Turkey relations by holding the powerful accountable through cultural analysis.

Second, Jonathan Spencer (2007) critiqued classical political anthropological work for its narrow focus on finding social order in places that were otherwise torn by contradiction and conflict. Focusing on interests, factions and individuals, classical political anthropology, according to Spencer, actually downplays structure and system by neglecting social relations and cultural processes. Ethnographic enquiries pivot around data collected through long-term cultural immersion within and participant observation of the lives of those who participate in (and bar others from participating in) cultural production and meaning-making on a daily basis (Greenhouse et al. 2002; Joseph et al. 2007; Schatz 2009). As an ethnography of politics in the EU, this book attends to 'the pace of political action, the texture of political life, and the plight of political actors' (Auyero & Joseph 2007: 2). It seeks to uncover the *human dynamics* of failed integration between the EU and Turkey. It privileges actors and agents over structures, honing in on their practices and relationships of power, but, following Spencer (2007), without neglecting those structures and institutions of power to which they are accountable and that are infrastructural to the everyday work of Turkish Europeanisation. A state-centric, structural-institutionalist approach would have foreclosed the possibility and potential for a scholarly analysis of the power–interest entanglements embedded in Turkish Europeanisation. For even if it might have allowed a partial study of diplomacy as the representation of state interests, state-centric approaches ultimately fail to account for lobbying, which is an informal, elusive, unexpectedly transparent yet equally opaque communicative practice. The significance and centrality of diplomacy and lobbying in EU decision- and policy-making and Turkish Europeanisation are accessible only to their practitioners (see Atan 2004; Ülgen 2005) and to an ethnographic eye, but only when one looks beyond formal, state-centric framings of power and interests. In doing so, this book maintains that power operates flexibly at the top (Wedel 2009, 2014).

Political and policy processes have their own myths, symbols and rituals that help embed power relations in policy structures and in actors' relationships with one another. Unlike political scientists' concern for normativity in EU policy-making, anthropologists have most commonly interested themselves in unearthing 'the human dimensions' of policy processes, which otherwise tend to be neglected (Greenhalgh 2008: xiii). They have found policy to be a particular relationship of power, a way actors have of relating to each other that arises from their cultural differences, including their (political or otherwise) class positions and roles in the policy field. Through political communicative practices such as diplomacy and lobbying, actors – who may or may not know each other or even share a common moral universe but who act within the negotiated boundaries of the policy universe, with its own norms and forms – operate in the EU's political and policy 'fields' on an everyday basis (Bourdieu 1998; Georgakakis 2015; Georgakakis & Rowell 2013).[10] As a field where cultural production occurs, policy is a space whereby actors and agents negotiate these norms and forms within the given and emerging power and boundary relations. Shifting relations of inequality operate inside this space, in which actors struggle, at the same time, for the transformation or preservation of the field. Examining their struggles calls attention to how actors make and remake field and group boundaries.

In the EU's enlargement policy field, national officials who represent EU member states in Brussels with diplomatic capacity liaise between their respective governments, other EU members and the EU institutions. European Commission technocrats at different directorate-generals (DGs), along with members and administrators of the European Economic and Social Committee (EESC) and the Committee of the Regions (CoR) and EU agencies, propose policy recommendations to the European Parliament and the EU Council. Members of the European Parliament (MEPs), along with their assistants and advisers, and the administrators of political groups and parliamentary committees and their advisers deliberate over changes proposed by the Commission. An item of the EU's enlargement policy, Turkish Europeanisation is, in the classic definition of the term, the 'policy problem' that these institutions and their agents need to solve in the negotiation process. Pan-European industry, trade and labour associations and unions, including those that have Turkish members or that do business in or with Turkey, strive to influence their work. Through formal and informal networks, all exchange influence and interests within and outside of governmental purview. People like Leyla are important go-betweens within and among these networks and constitute a third group; and they do this professionally. Successful EU diplomacy and lobbying require the capacity to integrate or at least to appear to have integrated into the EU's enlargement networks. Per Boissevain (1974), what constitutes diplomats' and lobbyists' professional capital/power is their long-cultivated access or appearance of access to these policy networks. But this appearance of having capital/power needs constant reinvention (Nordstrom 2000; Wedel 2017). Often, as Janine Wedel (2014: 26) has so eloquently put it, 'the very power of the power brokers stems from their ability to be unaccountable'. During research for this book, I found the power of diplomats and lobbyists as interest brokers to be, post-Foucault, much more relative and relational than they portray. Originating from public as much as a scholarly concern, this book ultimately calls for accountability for Turkish Europeanisation, a heretofore overlooked dimension of Turkey–EU relations.

The power–interest nexus and symbolic politics

Diplomacy and lobbying are forms of political communication whose examination provides a lens onto cultural interactions between actors while they politick.

Throughout this book, I use these two aspects of diplomacy and lobbying (cultural interaction and politicking) in a mutually enabling framework. Here I follow Francis Snyder's (1989: 192) productive maxim that 'thinking about "interests" is another way of thinking about power'. I maintain that an ethnographic explanation of Turkish Europeanisation could benefit from a multi-dimensional and multi-level conceptualization of power, such as the one suggested by political and social theorist Steven Lukes (2004 [1974]; also see Heyman 2003).

According to Lukes (2004 [1974]: 25), power is first about exerting control over decisions that are already on the political agenda or that are in the making. This is what most politicians, public officials and community leaders do and how political scientists theorise power. Here, power operates by framing the policy process and the practices and behaviour of policy actors (Colebatch 2002). But not every issue makes its way on to the political agenda. If one focuses on the non-decisions and silences in the policy-making processes, one encounters a different dimension of power. In this second dimension, some framing is done to forestall certain types of policy behaviour. Here, power is still about controlling the political agenda, not by pushing some issues onto it but rather by controlling 'the ways in which potential issues are kept out of the political processes' (Lukes 2004: 25). The making of non-decisions here may also refer to 'the practice of limiting [the] scope of actual decision making to "safe" issues by manipulating the dominant community values, myths, and political institutions and procedures' (Bachrach & Baratz 1963: 632). With its (sometimes forced) silences and non-decisions in policy-making processes, power in its second dimension is difficult to study, yet carries immense potential for policy research. To silences and non-decisions, non-verbal ways of communication, such as body language and gestures, need to be added as rich ethnographic moments of policy analysis (Shore & Wright 1997; Yanow 1996). However, argues Lukes (2005: 486), real power lies in the capacity to 'shape, influence or determine others' beliefs and desires, thereby securing their compliance'.[11]

Coupled with Foucault's governmentality and micro-physics of power, Gramscian hegemony and Bourdieu's field theory, political scientist, policy and IR scholars and political anthropologists have long focused on power's third dimension, which, centring on practice, requires an interpretative analysis to understand how and why policy actors do what they do. Anthropologist Richard Jenkins (2007: 34) suggested taking policies as 'processes of representation and of the production and the reproduction of meaning'. Based on practice theory, IR scholar Rebecca Adler-Nissen (2016) distinguished between ordering and disordering practices that (de)stabilise the worlds of policy and politics. Finding politics itself an interpretive engagement, political scientist Claudio Radaelli (1999: 41) argued that '[a]ctors offering interpretation are in a pivotal position because policy is an attempt to understand and decode a complex reality'. In that sense, policy-making is a political act whereby 'making policy (and changing it) can be a vehicle for opening up issues, and allowing a wider range of players to enter the game' (Colebatch 2002: 3; see also Colebatch et al. 2010). In this book, I take the EU's enlargement policy and its application through accession negotiations as a politico-cultural field of meaning-making and social interaction. Here, diplomats, who are humbly bureaucrats when at home (Neumann 2012), and lobbyists often do the interpretive work that policy formulation requires. I leave my analysis of how multi-dimensional power works in Turkey's Europeanisation to later chapters, but suffice it to say here that the absence of (mainly Turkish) interest mediation in certain policy fields and networks has been equally instructive as much as their presence. So has the symbolic politics EU and Turkish actors often engaged in.

Much has been said about diplomacy being a political and a cultural institution (Constantinou et al. 2016) reflecting the political cultures of nation states. Unlike diplomacy, the relationship between culture and lobbying remains unsettled. Political scientists have examined organised interests' access to individual EU institutions (Bouwen 2002, 2004; Chalmers 2013; Mulcahy 2015; Pleines 2005), their strategies with respect to whom to lobby and when (Broscheid & Coen 2003; Mahoney 2008; Marshall 2010; van Schendelen 2010), the success or impact of lobbying in the EU (Dür 2008; Eckhardt 2015; McGrath 2005; Rasmussen 2015) and the framing of the arguments and contexts of lobbying (Voltolini 2017). While they normatively debate whether culture plays any role in EU lobbying (Carroll & Rasmussen 2017; Dür & Mateo 2010; Christine Mahoney quoted in Panichi 2015; Woll 2012), empirical research on the cultures of EU lobbying, grounded in systematically collected field data, remains unavailable.

My response to this debate is that both lobbying and diplomacy are deeply cultural matters. Actors are over time acculturated in the diplomatic and lobbying knowhow and common practices (or successfully pretend to have done so, since culture is also performative), which they share interpersonally. In her study of the cultures of expertise among central bankers, anthropologist Annelise Riles (2018: 34) described the cultural institutions of elite experts as 'collections of human beings, with all of the tensions and biases, disagreements, uncertainties, common aspirations, career trajectories, and ideological orientations that define any other group of human beings'. Whereas diplomatic theory can be taught at school, gaining command over the subtleties of diplomatic practice requires young diplomats to apprentice before they become masters of their trade. While good knowledge of different political systems and policy-making traditions is desired and can be taught at school, lobbying is ultimately a 'watch and learn' profession. At a more important level, success in both lines of work depend on how culturally competent diplomats and lobbyists are, and how well they understand their own polity *and* the polity of those to whom they direct their energies. These aspects of the job circumscribe lobbying and diplomacy as cultural work.

For those who take diplomacy and lobbying as cultural work, an understanding of the work of diplomats and lobbyists requires the analyst to study the social and cultural relationships among them, between them and their clients, and the 'more inclusive social fields within which contacts and relationships are played out', as anthropologist Don Handelman (1978: 9) put it in his programmatic take on the anthropology of bureaucracy. This book argues that the social and cultural relationships of diplomats and lobbyists are both constituted by and constitute their capacity as actors to bring outside and in-group influences into their encounters

with counterparts from all levels of political life. As in every political act of instituting, their ways of doing so have manifest and latent symbolic qualities, not
least the rites and rituals of institutions (Bourdieu 1996, 1999; Douglas 1986) (for
an application of this argument to the EU–Turkey accession negotiations, see
MacMillan 2016).

Studying the role of bureaucrats and consultants in development policy and
other policy areas, anthropologists have suggested that researchers focus on
the 'ritual[s] and [the] production of meaning ... rather than [the] production
of effective policies per se' (Hansen & Stepputat 2001: 17) or the measurement
of policy efficacy and effective implementation schemes, much favoured by
political scientists.[12] Others have argued that bureaucrats and consultants are
meaning-producing cultural performers 'whose product should not be judged in
terms of its supposed practical ends' (Stirrat 2000: 43; see also Herzfeld 1992; Riles
2000) because, as the argument goes, their working conditions, the outcome of
their work and the way their work is perceived have little to do with whether they
produce effective policy implementation.

I concur with this line of anthropological interpretation that cautions against
exaggerating the importance of policy product over process and practice, but only
if the researcher does not *normatively* separate the work of diplomats and lobbyists, the outcome of their work and the social contexts within which they come to
work – or policy from practice or product. To do so would wrongly suggest that
the domain of policy-making is isolated from other realms of culture and a place
where legitimacy emanates from within.

For these reasons, to study the work of public (read: national, state, governmental) and private interest brokers and the practical policy results of their work
at the same time is imperative. If diplomats and lobbyists act as cultural actors,
then they act in a cultural environment that ultimately shapes and is shaped by
their actions. If one takes consultative practices independent of their environment
(i.e. their immediate and wider bureaucratic and political culture) – or the policy,
its process, practice *and* product – it becomes impossible to establish democratic
legitimacy and accountability, especially troubled in the current EU (Shore 2006)
and Turkish contexts. So does relating the 'policy worlds' of professionals and
experts (Shore et al. 2011) to the worlds of others with no or limited access and
standing in expert worlds.

At another level, attention to process, practice *and* product improves our
enquiry. Policy worlds and processes are circular rather than linear, and contestation and renegotiation occur at multiple times during the 'social life' of a policy
(Appadurai 1986). To capture this circularity in anthropological studies of policy,
Wedel (2009, 2014, 2017) has consistently recommended network analysis. But
what if a major product of diplomats' and lobbyists' work concerns a different kind
of politics, one which is predominantly symbolic?

Surely, all forms of power are symbolic so long they are communicative. 'Power
relations are objectified, developed, maintained, expressed, or camouflaged by
means of symbolic forms and patterns of symbolic action', as anthropologist Abner
Cohen (1979: 89) observed long ago. 'Ordinary symbolic performances such as a

dancing ball, a university graduation ceremony, a funeral service or a wedding festivity [or meetings between EU and Turkish actors] repetitively reproduce or modify power relations' (Cohen 1980: 66; see also Kertzer 1988, 1996).

In Europe, the symbolic dimension of the EU's normative power often accommodates a measure of efficacy when 'the production of an appearance of coherence and order', 'being seen to have a policy – as opposed to actually effecting the outcomes specified by policy' takes precedence (Jenkins 2007: 25). Here, the 'art of symbolic politics' or the 'art of being seen to do something' is as much a constitutive part of the art of governance as things that are actually done (Jenkins 2007: 28; see also Abélès & Rossade 1993; Cohen 1979, 1980; Kertzer 1988, 1996; Mosse 2005). This is both due to the high costs involved in administering a policy (Colebatch 2002) and because policies (from an emic perspective on organisations) mainly function to foster political support, as well as to 'account upwards, legitimis[e] expertise, signify alliances, or conceal differences' (Mosse 2006: 939; see also Garsten & Jacobsson 2007; Müller 2011).

During my fieldwork, I found that diplomats and lobbyists from both sides of the aisle engaged in symbolic politics quite extensively. 'The *image of the effective broker* who knows the way through the political-economic labyrinth is central to a[ny] … regime of power', as anthropologist Monique Nuijten (2003: 3, original emphasis) observed in another context. Due to the competition among and the diversity of interests represented in Brussels, if lobbying is defined solely as the exertion of influence to meet targeted results of legislative change or favouritism, not all lobbying is successful. But if one takes diplomacy and lobbying as communicative practices of (in/formal) power vital to modern politics, one observes that actors' efficacy depends on how well they perform symbolic politics. With symbolic politics I do not mean 'optical effects' (Goffman 1986: 7), such as fakery, fraud or deceit, but a particular strategy for self-endurance and a technique of negotiation, which the actors and agents of Turkish Europeanisation commonly employ, even though they may use some of those optical effects to obscure their symbolic politics.

The communicative arts of diplomacy and lobbying

Since the 1987 Single European Act (SEA), Brussels has hosted increasing numbers of lobbyists and interest representatives – some 40,000 according to recent estimates, although full-timers make up only one-seventh of that number (European Public Affairs Directory 2018). A couple of months before the SEA went into force, Turkey had applied for membership of the European Economic Community (EEC), the predecessor of the EU – even though its application would not generate any response until the end of 1989. Following the application, national-level big business associations with the widest domestic networks, sectoral associations like textile exporters, and business-supported NGOs from Turkey opened offices in Brussels to represent client interests in shaping the emerging prospects for economic and political integration between Turkey and the EEC. Their efforts were coordinated with associations from EU member states, which also intensified their representational activities in Brussels in response to the SEA (Mazey & Richardson 2003). Thereafter, the involvement of private interests in EU policy-making dramatically increased both in Turkey and in Europe.

As European integration unfolded, increased lobbying activities curbed government and state monopolies over national representation within 'a multi-cultural platform with rules in which national officials [may] not necessarily [be] well trained' (Bellier 2000a: 56) or act flexibly. Traditional diplomatic actors had to give way to new ones who, despite lacking official credentials, increasingly replaced diplomats in performing diplomacy (Hamilton & Langhorne 2010; Neumann 2013). Today, non-state actors, be they consulting firms or individuals acting as special envoys, increasingly perform paradiplomacy on behalf of third states (Marsden et al. 2016; McConell et al. 2012). Many former diplomats themselves go into lobbying and consultancy work mid-career or after they retire. In Europe, through their access and ability to broker interest, information and influence between different levels of public and private sector hierarchies, lobbyists appeal as much to politicians as to bureaucrats. In Turkey's case, however, non-governmental actors' relations with the EU still depend on whether their relation to the Turkish state and government is contentious or amicable. At the same time, diplomats have had to perform diplomatic work not only on military and political fronts but also on other sectors of life, such as climate change, economic and financial crises and refugee flows. Today, lobbying counts as a natural part of a diplomat's job in the EU (Geuijen et al. 2008; Spence 1993, 2002; van Schendelen 2010), making the boundary between diplomacy and lobbying ever more slippery.

To counter this ambiguity, some twenty years after the SEA, the then EU commissioner for administrative affairs, audit and anti-fraud, Siim Kallas, called for an end to the lack of transparency, integrity and accountability in EU decision-making by recommending that 'organisations, groups or persons in the ambit of European institutions which offer advice, represent clients, provide data or defend public causes' reveal 'who they are, what they do and what they stand for' (Kallas 2005). The Estonian politician put forth an initiative to 'ensure a proper functioning of the decision-making process, to gain the trust of the public, and to protect policy-makers against themselves' (Kallas 2005). His Green Paper, 'European Transparency Initiative' set out the most extensive definition of lobbying available today: 'All activities carried out with the objective of influencing the policy formulation and decision-making processes of the European institutions'. Lobbyists, then, are 'persons carrying out such activities, working in a variety of organisations such as public affairs consultancies, law firms, NGOs, think-tanks, corporate lobby units ("in-house representatives") or trade associations' (European Commission 2006a). Efforts to distinguish diplomacy from lobbying, like that of Kallas, remain important for reasons of accountability but may not always yield greater insight into these practices.

Normative understandings of lobbying from political science and political anthropology imply that it is an outsider's practice (Drutman 2015; Mahoney 2008), even though in international (and national) negotiations actors often exchange interests, information and influence and they do so both formally and informally

(Black 2001; Christiansen & Piattoni 2004; Kleine 2014). Treating influence as an external technique along with 'intrigue, diplomacy, bluff, bribery, activation of commitments, threats of resort to force and promises of rewards for support', one popular political anthropology textbook identifies lobbying as an outside exertion of influence along with 'patronage, conspiracy, subversion, the acquisition of wealth, peaceful infiltration of the antagonists' ranks, espionage' (Swartz et al. 2009: 32). Yet, EU lobbying in Brussels is hardly an outside activity. In fact, EU lobbyists are very much a part of Eurocracy (Broscheid & Coen 2003; Coen & Richardson 2009). The Commission's emic definition of lobbying above points at a similar flexibility when one considers who lobbies whom and the porous boundaries of inside/outside.

Turkey's EU accession process opened a field of interest to many. People and institutions that were not technically diplomats or lobbyists were lobbying on different aspects of the EU's enlargement policy towards Turkey. It was not only Turkish nationals who sought to represent Turkish interests, and nor were Turkish nationals the most effective (cf. Polo & Visier, 2007; Visier 2009; Visier & Polo 2005). Representatives of diverse interests from EU institutions and member and non-member states actively lobbied the EU and each other during Turkish Europeanisation. Their lobbying was often much more intense than that of Turkish agents. The kind of 'lobbyists' I expected to observe lobbying for Turkey's EU membership were Turkish actors, but they were nowhere to be seen in Brussels or were lobbying for clients who had objectives other than Turkish accession. Some of those objectives were antithetical to the reforms Turkey had to undertake as part of its preparation for EU accession.

In the main, Turkish public and private interest representatives were a small but significant part of Eurocracy. Many Turkish diplomats and lobbyists would insist that they were not newcomers to Europolitics. Yet I found their EU lobbying not to be on a par with their presumed experience. For one, they were deeply entrenched in internationalism and had less patience for and appreciation of supranationalism (relinquishing state sovereignty to a collective) and intergovernmentalism (cooperative decision-making) as practised in the EU. Evidently, they lobbied the European Parliament (instead of the Commission, which proposes policy) and 'older', 'bigger' and 'Turcophile' EU member states, such as Germany (until the 2000s) and the UK (from the 2000s), which they considered to have more sway in the EU than 'newer' or neutral members. Second, Turkish national political culture, much like that of France, Italy and some eastern European countries, is unreceptive or antagonistic towards lobbying, which it equates with unsolicited advice-giving at best and political meddling at worst.

The main difference between the lobbying done by EU and Turkish actors in Brussels, I would argue, is that lobbying is now relatively institutionalised in the EU and not at all in Turkey. Lack of institutionalisation does not mean that lobbying is absent in domestic Turkish politics. In fact, consultancy firms typically surround the Turkish parliament and government ministries, whereas individual bureaucrats lobby from within, attesting that lobbying political and policy actors and institutions in Ankara remains an important politico-cultural communicative practice in its own right, but without a public presence or established rules. Some practitioners surely enjoy this non-transparency.

Lobbying during the process of Turkish Europeanisation was not restricted to those who practised it professionally, for a fee, or to those who lobbied the EU from outside. First, lobbyists need not always lobby in exchange for monetary compensation. Nor need compensation constitute an end for them. Second, those who lobby need not do this in a professional capacity. From diplomats to techno-bureaucrats to politicians from both inside and outside the EU – all players in the EU's enlargement policy field frequently lobbied each other regarding the nuts and bolts of Turkish Europeanisation. During my fieldwork, I encountered many diplomats from both the EU and Turkey who lobbied and who did so sometimes even more effectively than professional lobbyists.

Unlike conventional understandings of lobbying as an outsider's activity, then, this book shows that actors from both outside and inside EU institutions lobbied during Turkish Europeanisation. Both EU and Turkish diplomats lobbied decision- and policy-makers as much as professional lobbyists and interest representatives did. And they did so as insiders and outsiders to the system. At the level of international negotiations and bargaining, as Turkey's EU bid exemplifies, many Turkish bureaucrats, diplomats and other public and private interest representatives lobbied the EU and Turkish governments, despite their outsider position due to Turkey's non-member status. Their colleagues who represented Turkish private interests also lobbied EU decision- and policy-makers and structures through their embeddedness in Eurofederations. Their numbers were limited, which might partially explain their (in)efficacy. But other factors played a greater role in this outcome than their sheer size.

One major conundrum was that few Turkish representatives operating in Brussels defined their work as lobbying, which they typically associated with nation or country branding, public diplomacy or organising cultural events (cultural lobbying). Most EU lobbyists, diplomats and policy-makers, however, operate based on a shared understanding of lobbying akin to its meaning in Anglo-Saxon political culture, which refers simply to influencing the EU's decision- and policy-making processes. As per their Turkish colleagues, ambiguity and aversion towards defining lobbying as part of their job contributed to their estrangement from Brussels' enlargement circles. In many respects, they took representatives of EU member states, institutions and organisations as their 'constitutive outsiders' (Laclau & Mouffe 1985). As representatives of 'Turkish' interests, they believed that their job was beyond lobbying. They equally need not lobby due to Turkey's presumed importance for the EU. While lobbyists from the EU quickly moved on to substance, Turkish diplomats and lobbyists sank into permanent self-defence as agents of 'Turkish' interests, operating from a latent assumption that those interests were either too important or alien to Europe. Self-denying Turkish actors contributed much to the 'anti-case' of Turkey's Europeanisation. Their perceived outsider-ness was due in part to their inability to follow or influence the shaping of the EU agenda proactively, even when it directly pertained to Turkish Europeanisation. This incapacitation perpetuated their self-marginalisation.

Although many Turkish diplomats and lobbyists felt estranged from their task (Turkish Europeanisation), they continued to occupy a central position in the EU's enlargement policy field as human contacts conveying information, influence and interests between Brussels and Ankara.

In return, the Turkish government, state and business circles did not necessarily appreciate their agents' roles in Brussels. The marginalisation of the Turkish public and private interest brokers was also due to the centralisation of negotiations with the EU by the Turkish state, government and their business acolytes. Instead of allowing their representatives to do their job as experts in both political systems, by asking them to take greater initiative and say, Ankara and Istanbul (read: political and economic elites) dictated the terms of the process to their agents in Brussels, undermining their capacity to mediate properly. In the Turkish anti-case, the centralisation of EU-level negotiations away from Brussels constitutes a counter-pattern to the dominant style of EU negotiations. To overcome this incapacitation, Turkish public and private interest representatives *cum* lobbyists resorted to symbolic politics and bureaucratic entrepreneurship in myriad ways, which helped them keep their otherwise tenuous positions during the negotiations.

Working in Brussels with or without diplomatic capacity, each actor and agent of Turkey's Europeanisation was entrusted with (in)directly channelling Turkish priorities through public and private interests from the EU, its member states, Turkey and other interested third parties to the negotiation table. How their differences in cultures of negotiation and compromise helped shape the outcome of these negotiations make up the crux of the Turkish anti-case, as well as the blueprint of this book. Diplomacy and lobbying as (in)formal frontstage/backstage negotiations (Goffman 1959) engage the ethnographic lens, refracting the power–interest nexus through the EU's enlargement policy and associated policy-making processes engendered along the EU–Turkey axis, breeding their own 'private life of politics'.

Notes

1 Aydın-Düzgit and Kaliber (2016: 5) define de-Europeanisation broadly as 'the loss or weakening of the EU/Europe as a normative/political context and as a reference point in domestic settings and national public debates'. The UK's referendum on its departure from the EU ('Brexit') was held in June 2016.

2 Harmsen and Wilson (2000: 14–18) documented eight different uses of Europeanisation:(1) emergence of new forms of European governance, (2) national adaptation, (3) policy isomorphism, (4) problem and opportunity for domestic political management, (5) modernisation, (6) 'joining Europe', (7) reconstruction of identities and (8) transnationalism and cultural integration. Also see Diez et al. (2005) and Featherstone & Radaelli (2003). My definition calls specific attention to the power–interest dynamics that are embedded in membership negotiations.

3 See Akipek & Akçay (2013); Avci & Çarkoğlu (2013); Aydin-Düzgit (2012); Burrell & Oskam (2005); Çarkoğlu & Rubin (2003); LaGro & Jørgensen (2007); Müftüler-Bac (1997); Müftüler-Bac & Stivachtis (2008); Piran (2013); Tocci (2011) and Uğur &

Canefe (2004). For Turkish elites' scepticism towards EU membership on the grounds of economic problems, population size and religion, see McLaren (2002). For a recent reiteration of the triple mantra, see Müftüler-Bac (2016).

4 Current accession countries are Albania, North Macedonia, Montenegro, Serbia and Turkey. Croatia began accession negotiations at the same time as Turkey did and acceded to the EU in 2013.

5 Pieter Bouwen (2002, 2004) argues that EU lobbying is marked by an exchange logic whereby information, which he calls an 'access good', is the most sought-after item in EU institutions.

6 For ethnographic studies of experts, professionals, elites and the powerful, see Abbink & Salverda (2012); Ardener & Moore (2007); Crewe (2005); Crewe & Müller (2006); Hertz (1998); Hertz & Imber (1993); Ho (2009); Holmes (2000, 2013); Marcus (1983); Mosse (2011); Niezen & Sapignoli (2017); Nuijten (2003); Pina-Cabral & de Lima (2000); Schumann (2009) and Shore & Nugent (2002). For studying power up, down, sideways and through, see Rhodes et al. (2007) and Stryker & González (2014).

7 Although the cultures of policy professionals still captivate the anthropological imagination, others have investigated the technical blueprints of policy. For a review, see Firat (2014).

8 For pioneering anthropological studies of Europolity, see Abélès (1992); Abélès et al. (1993); Bellier (2000b); Geuijen et al. (2008); Holmes (2000); McDonald (1996, 2000); Shore (2000); Thedvall (2006); Zabusky (1995). For ethnographic encounters with lobbyists, see in particular Abélès (1992) and Bellier (2000a, 2004).

9 I thank Emma Crewe for this insight.

10 In *On Television and Journalism*, Pierre Bourdieu (1998: 40–1) defined the field as 'a structured social space, a field of forces, a force field. It contains people who dominate and people who are dominated. Constant, permanent relationships of inequality operate inside this space, which at the same time becomes a space in which the various actors struggle for the transformation or preservation of the field. All the individuals in this universe bring to the competition all the (relative) power at their disposal. It is this power that defines their position in the field and, as a result, their strategies.'

11 Lukes' concept of real power approximates that of Goffman (1959), Mills (1956) and Weber (1978). In its simplest form, this is how ideology or common sense works. Others have given it a different name: 'symbolic power' (Bourdieu 1979, 2009 [1991]), 'governmentality' or 'the conduct of conduct' (Foucault 2003) and 'structural power' (Wolf 1990).

12 Political scientists, whose work the cultural interpretive turn influenced, share this social constructivist inclination (Christiansen et al. 2001; Colebatch 2002; Radaelli 1999; Yanow 1996).

Fieldwork among the no(ta)bles

Pilot: Bruxelles/Brussel/Brüssel/Brussels

The trains from Brussels' Zaventem Airport to the city centre carry thousands every day. When I took the trip late one evening in July 2005, a Dutch development consultant returning from Africa sat next to me. I had found an apartment in Brussels online. For the next four weeks, I was going to be an intern at the EU representation office of one of the most powerful interest groups from Turkey. I had never been to this post-industrial, northern European, polyglot city Turkish people call *Brüksel*. Belgium has never been much of a tourist destination for Turks like me.

With a total population of close to 1.2 million, one-third of whom are foreign nationals, Brussels harbours manifold political, social, economic and cultural topographies, which I needed to canvass.[1] Brussels has hosted institutions of the EU and its forerunners since the late 1960s, but the EU presence grew notably in the early 1990s. That the Belgian government gives tax breaks to thousands of officials who populate the EU institutions, organisations and agencies must have helped to boost the influx (Hein 2000; Lagrou 2000; Papadopoulos 1996).

With every effort to advance European integration, Brussels has attracted ever more diverse political and economic interests from all over Europe and beyond. Some scholars took the 1987 Single European Act, which bore provisions for a common market to be operational beginning in 1992, as the main reason for interest representatives to flood into Brussels; others stressed that the rise in interest representation contributed to the EU becoming a self-sustaining – that is, independent of its member states – mature, political system (Andersen & Eliassen 1996a; Mazey & Richardson 1993). Today, such interests range from steel producers to consumer organisations to environmental groups and others. Politicians and bureaucrats from EU institutions, government officials and diplomats from EU member states and lobbyists make up Brussels' urban cultural mix and social dynamism. They move to the city for short-term (one to four years) or long-term (over five years) jobs. Like Leyla, some also commute from across Europe.

Belgium became a de facto federal state in 1970 and an official one in 1993. With federalism and regionalism, Belgian political society multiplied. Regionalism for

Figure 2.1 Upper image: Expired Commission visitor badges. Lower image: Local bus stop in the European quarter with discarded badges

Belgium meant that, next to the federal parliament and government offices, each region formed its own parliament and administrative offices. Belgium is now home to a tri-partite system of linguistic (Walloon, Flemish and German-speaking) communities and administrative (Wallonia, Flanders and Brussels Capital) regions. Historically, the Flemish communities engaged in farming. Except for mines in the northern part of the country, Flanders was predominantly an agricultural land, while Wallonia in the south was industrial. Deindustrialisation and mine closures reversed the power and wealth dynamics in Belgium. Today, more people move out of Wallonia and Brussels Capital regions to Flanders.[2] Political parties that propagate Flemish nationalism use this socio-economic gain to their advantage (Pinxten 2006).

When they first came to Belgium in the 1960s, labour migrants from Turkey settled in the Belgian industrial valley (in northern Wallonia) or joined mining communities in Brussels and northern Flanders. A decade later, when the coal-mines started to close, more families moved to Brussels and its suburbs. There they built Turkish-Belgian civic lives. Today, third-generation 'EuroTurks' (Kaya

Figure 2.2 Car plate with the Turkey and EU symbols either side

& Kentel 2007) are equally distributed across the Brussels Capital, the Flemish and the Walloon regions (Jacobs et al. 2006; Aksöyek 2000). Some earn college degrees and own homes and businesses, becoming employers themselves. Some hold public office at various governmental levels and serve as members of regional parliaments. During the heyday of Turkish Europeanisation, their cars could commonly be seen circulating through Brussels' urban traffic displaying allegiance to both their own place of birth and that of their grandparents.

They furnished their licence plates with stickers of EU, Belgian and Turkish flags – much like many people in Turkey did at the time (except the Belgian flag, of course). Brussels' long-term Turkish quarter, Schaerbeek, underwent a profound transformation, with newcomers moving in and notable departures of upwardly mobile Turkish-Belgians leaving the neighbourhood in search of better-integrated futures for their children in other parts of the city or the country.

Turkish AKP governments as well as earlier ones have serviced the lives of Euro-Turks by sponsoring mosques, schools, religious foundations and social centres. Initially, migrant remittances were critical to offset Turkey's shortage of foreign currency. Some also went into financing conservative political parties like the AKP and its predecessors (Turam 2007). When the second- and third-generation EuroTurks became business owners and employers, and gained citizenship and voting power in Europe, they also became a pressure group in the diaspora. Past and present Erdoğan governments considered EuroTurks as much a source of electoral and economic power in Europe and in Turkey as citizen-diplomats, and encouraged them to perform active, vocal advocacy on behalf of their homeland (and its government) in Europe through civil society and lobby groups.

Some of these groups were initiated or backed by Erdoğan himself, such as the Union of Turkish Associations, the Confederation of Businessmen and Industrialists of Turkey – which the Turkish courts outlawed after the 15 July 2016 coup attempt due to its ties to the Gülenist movement – and the Union of European Turkish Democrats (now Union of International Democrats). Founded in 2004 in Cologne, Germany, the latter has branches in fifteen European countries, twelve

of which are EU member states, including Belgium; Erdoğan's party representative to the EU serves among its executives. Represented by a law student and
second-generation EuroTurk during my fieldwork, the group recruited young,
college-educated EuroTurks for its lobbying and country-branding activities.
From Islamophobia to the headscarf issue (favourite topics for Erdoğan himself),
its members built issue-based alliances with other Turkish organisations and with
non-Turkish conservative European associations inside the countries in which
they were established. The group also organised international congresses of Euro-
Turks and Erdoğan's election rallies in Europe.

For instance, in early 2009, on his first stop after Germany, in Hasselt in Belgium,
then prime minister Erdoğan addressed his fellow citizens and electorate before he
visited his EU counterparts in Brussels the next day, signifying his preference for
'the nation' over EU business. Thousands poured into Hasselt, a small town about
eighty kilometres east of Brussels, close to the German border town of Düsseldorf,
home to many German Turks. Belgian police placed signs along the road from the
train station to the hangar-like structure where Erdoğan's 'Grand Reunion' was to
take place. A German-Turkish scholar once labelled many of Erdoğan's supporters
in European countries the 'new Jews of Europe' (Yurdakul 2013). Others might
identify them as 'black Turks' due to their working-class background and religious
piety. Erdoğan, too, identified as a 'black Turk' (Sontag 2003).

With flashing lights, a high-end sound system, a bombastic presentation by
his favourite tout and his cabinet members parading on the stage, that afternoon
Erdoğan called on his Turkish-Belgian audience, much as he had done with his
Turkish-German audience a few days before: 'Yes to integration, no to assimila-
tion'. The next day everyone in Brussels was mulling over his words.

Considering the Flemish–Walloon conflict and the transnational Turkish
nationalism, Belgian-Turks had adapted well to their new regional cultures and
identities. One day, I was out shopping in Antwerp, the biggest and most prosper-
ous city in Flanders. Being aware of the Flemish people's aversion to the French
language and not being able to speak Flemish myself, I mostly used English, a
little French but also Turkish with Turkish-looking Belgian shopkeepers. Hearing
me speak Turkish, one of them asked her colleague from the back of the shop to
help me. As I was paying, the Turkish-Belgian salesperson caught me off guard
when she said: 'Il faut parler la langue [One needs to speak the language]!' The
shopkeepers thought of me as a newcomer to Flanders, perhaps a new Turkish
migrant, and suggested that I learn *the* language, namely Flemish. As I left the
shop, I made a mental note to myself about this Flemish–French duel. Years later,
when my participant observation led me to work for Leyla in Brussels, we always
wrote to Belgian MEPs from Flanders in English.

Besides the Belgian federal government and EU institutions, Brussels is home
to international organisations such as the North Atlantic Treaty Organization
(NATO) and the World Customs Organization. When these organisations moved
to Brussels they brought their own administrative staff and families and a broad
range of professionals, such as journalists, lawyers and lobbyists, who followed
their policies and actions. Transparency International estimated the number of

Figure 2.3 Erdoğan's *Büyük Buluşma* (Grand Reunion) inside Athias Arena, Hasselt, Belgium, 2009

full-time lobbyists accredited to EU institutions to be more than 6,000 in 2016, though the wider circle involves close to 40,000 individuals, with a doubling of the number of lobbyists and the number of full-timers increasing by a quarter from a decade previously (European Public Affairs Directory 2018).

I became interested in lobbying and diplomacy and their role in Turkey–EU relations as a concerned citizen. I was not born yet when Turkey signed an association agreement with the European Coal and Steel Community (the 1963 Ankara Agreement) and the Additional Protocol with European Economic Community (EEC) in 1970 – both predecessors of the EU – and was too young to remember when it applied for EEC membership (1987) the same year when the SEA took effect. Those born around the time of the 1980 military coup in Turkey spent their early adolescent years in a climate where politicians and officials had been picking petals off a daisy: 'Loves me, loves me not? Will Turkey become an EU member, will it not?' Anyone from my generation would remember the day when the EU–Turkey customs union came into force. We were teenagers then. One morning at school, the voice of the principal poured out of the classroom speakers: 'As of today [1 January 1996] our country has entered a customs union with the EU. Congratulations to our nation. May it bring prosperity to all of us!'[3] Opinions on the customs union among the public differed between the elites and the laity, between businesspeople and workers, between the political right and the left. The centre-right coalition government argued that deeper economic integration with the EU would boost Turkish manufacturing, mature industry and increase wages. Punning on the EU's 'common market', the opposition chanted: 'Onlar ortak, biz pazar! [They are the commoners, we are the market!]'.

A year later, in 1997, the commoners in Turkey heard their politicians lamenting that EU leaders did not include, in their Luxembourg meeting, Turkey within the long list of EU candidates, but did include ten former Soviet countries and Cyprus, damaging Turkey's relations with Luxembourg in particular forever. Two years later, in Helsinki, EU leaders named Turkey as a candidate, marking the kick-off of a long-term reform process in the country. The Helsinki announcement took a great amount of powerful backdoor politicking and last-minute deal-brokering among EU member states, Turkey and the United States (Öniş 2000; Tocci 2011).

The early 2000s began with a frenzy of initial democratisation reforms, which were necessary for accession negotiations to begin. The Turkish parliament banned capital punishment and granted Kurds, the largest ethnic minority in Turkey, the right to speak their mother tongue in public. The air was full of enthusiasm for Turkey's prospective EU membership. My personal curiosity turned into an intellectual interest around this time. I wanted to look deeper into the background of this rapprochement. But where was I to begin?

Consider the following depiction of the events on 3/4 October 2005, when the European Council formally started accession negotiations with Turkey:

In western Europe, a forested area between the Rhine basin and the Atlantic Ocean. In the Grand Duchy of Luxembourg, somewhere outside the city limits, in a series of buildings reconstructed from a hangar. At one end, the Council of EU

Ministers meets. At the other are hundreds of journalists, commentators, observers and cameras at the international media centre. News arrives and everybody steps outside. It is a dark night. In the light from the door stands British foreign minister Jack Straw. As the president of the EU Council, he takes the stand to welcome expected guests. Next to him are the EU's high representative for foreign affairs, Javier Solana, and the EU commissioner for enlargement, Olli Rehn. There is red carpet on the floor. A crowd from the media press around. In front of them an empty, wide, dim parking lot. Soon, the lights of vehicles appear in the distance. They arrive at the parking lot slowly, one by one. The foreign minister of the Republic of Turkey, Abdullah Gül, and minister of state, Ali Babacan, emerge from their cars. Victorious after two days of meetings, diplomats follow them. Accession negotiations between Turkey and the EU begin. It is the third and a half of October. Details of the story are hidden in this virtual time slot between 3 and 4 October.[4]

The main actors in this snapshot were the usual suspects of high state politics: the national ministers from EU member states and Turkey, their diplomats, two of the EU's top politicians and members of the media. But there was another actor, whose seeming invisibility as the narrator of the events contributed much to the credibility of its telling. I call him Deniz.[5]

No(ta)bles of Turkish Europeanisation

Deniz was the archetypical inhabitant of a liminal space-time constructed by the accession-versus-access dialectic of Turkish Europeanisation. A crucial figure in Turkey–EU relations operating in Brussels, his mission was to lobby the EU for Turkish accession but his particular vocation was to represent the specific interests of the 4,500 top Turkish companies in the capital of the EU. His mission was thus secondary to his vocation. True to his vocation, his organisation's alliance with the pan-European business lobby, the Confederation of European Business (Business-Europe), an alliance which began with Turkey's application for EU membership in 1987, framed his representational activities.

After pursuing doctoral studies in Istanbul and Brussels, Deniz, a Francophone, settled in the latter. Following the customs union agreement, he represented the Turkish Confederation of Employer Associations and the Turkish Industry and Business Association in Brussels. Under his tenure, the latter grew and now maintains offices in Washington, DC, Berlin, London, Paris and Beijing. The architect of several of today's EU edifices in Brussels helped Deniz find an office building by Tervuren Park, a ten-minute walk from the European Parliament. The two were 'old time friends', the architect told me years later.

Deniz's office was neither the first nor the second Turkish representation in town. Before the military takeover of 12 September 1980, Talat was working at the legal unit of Turkey's Confederation of Progressive Unions. In the aftermath of the coup, courts tried and convicted many leading trade unionists. As part of its international awareness campaign against trials of its leaders, the Confederation asked the European Trade Union Confederation (ETUC) for its support. Meanwhile, Talat left Turkey for a meeting with ETUC in Brussels. This was his first trip abroad, he told me when we met in Brussels a couple decades later. Once he had left, he returned to Turkey only for holidays and family visits. In Brussels, he set up an office and intensified campaigning internationally for the release of his colleagues. Talat helped turn the Confederation, a member of the Soviet Confederation of Labour Unions, towards Europe by making it a part of ETUC in 1985 and a full ETUC member in 1992.

With the 1992 Maastricht Treaty, ETUC's representation of European workers within the European Social Dialogue framework, next to BusinessEurope, took on a binding nature. Via the Confederation's ETUC membership, Talat represented Turkish workers' interests on a par with Deniz's representation for their bosses. Believing in 'Social Europe' and the merit in joining the European working class, the Confederation's leadership and Talat lobbied the Party of European Socialists (PES) of the European Parliament to vote 'yes' for the EU–Turkey customs union. Meanwhile, in 1995, the European Economic and Social Committee (EESC) upgraded relations with Turkey from a working group to a joint consultative committee (JCC).[6] The Confederation joined the EU–Turkey JCC – even though some of its members perceived sitting next to the representatives of the bourgeoisie as 'class submission' – and actively participated in it until 2006, when it left the JCC to protest against the Turkish government's slow pace in legislating labour reforms, including the right to organised action.

The Economic Development Foundation followed the Confederation in opening a representation office in Brussels. The Foundation, whose members are well respected business and industry associations, is an Istanbul-based, business-supported NGO formed in 1965 to nurture Turkish–European relations. Anticipating Turkey's EU membership application before it transpired, in 1984 the Foundation bought a three-storey building in a neighbourhood that once hosted Brussels' foreign corps community. After his public sector work as an economist and financial expert at various government offices, most notably the undersecretariat of treasury and foreign trade in Ankara and the permanent delegation of Turkey to the EU in Brussels, Orhan became its representative in 1995. He and Deniz assumed their new positions around the same time. Whereas Deniz's organisation represented individual companies, Orhan's was an umbrella organisation of business associations, in which Deniz's stakeholders were also active. Cross-listed memberships, limited resources and wavering interest in Turkey's EU membership bid caused enduring competition, rivalry and questions of redundancy between the two organisations and their interest representatives.

Part of Orhan's job was to represent the Union of Chambers and Commodity Exchanges of Turkey, a founding associate member of Eurochambres in 1966. Several years later, Orhan delegated his responsibility to Biray, his partner in life. Like Orhan, Biray had had a career in the public sector before taking over at the Union. For many years, in Brussels, she worked in an office next to her husband, which they also used as their main residence. Orhan and Biray often compared Belgian and Turkish 'ways of life', from education to urban planning. They mulled, not very enthusiastically, over what kind of a future their children might have had had they grown up in Turkey.

Later, Biray's organisation appointed a Turkish expat businessman as its main representative, rendering her position auxiliary. The Union and the Foundation also moved to an address closer to the EU institutions. Erdoğan, at the time Turkey's prime minister, inaugurated this office in its new location directly across from Deniz's office by Tervuren Park.

Back in the mid-1990s, textile exporters opened their own representation office, with Altan as their Brussels representative. Like Orhan, Altan worked at the undersecretariat in Ankara. Before he moved into the private sector, he served in the Turkish delegation in Brussels. While working at the undersecretariat, Altan specialised in textile exports and foreign trade. With the customs union, Turkish textile exports to the EU grew dramatically, increasing Turkish manufacturers' market share vis-à-vis their European competitors. At the delegation in Brussels, Altan looked into the problems of textile exporters such as export quotas when they traded with European countries. A decade earlier and as a rookie reporter, Leyla followed Turkish textile exports to Europe. By 1981, textiles represented 15 per cent of Turkey's total exports to Europe, leading the Community to apply quota restrictions to Turkish cotton yarn. When the Istanbul Textile and Apparel Exporter Association, a regional branch of the Turkish Exporters Assembly, approached Altan to become its Brussels representative, Altan accepted the job and quit public service. He set up the Brussels representation office of textile exporters at a location close to the top two pan-European sectoral associations in textiles, the European Apparel and Textile Confederation (EURATEX) and the European Federation of the Cotton and Allied Textiles Industries (EUROCOTON), both of which operated from the same address. His new office was also within walking distance of the Turkish delegation.

EURATEX posed a problem for Altan. Like many other associations in Europe representing the collective voice of producers or consumers, it only took members from EU member states. 'We made them change their bylaws', Altan told me, and he explained further: 'We reminded them that EURATEX is not a political organisation but a platform for business and trade, yet their membership criteria were political!' Today, several of the EURATEX board members are from Turkey and they occupy important decision-making positions. They are not alone in this trend.

For many years, Altan followed customs union and foreign trade negotiations as a government observer. With his new identity as a private sector representative and lobbyist, and the EURATEX and EUROCOTON memberships as allies, he moved on to negotiate the EU's textiles and trade policies as an insider with counterparts he knew well. When they first met, Altan and his Commission counterparts were junior officers. A decade later, they had all become seasoned officials (e.g. directors or heads of units). Their relationships were based on mutual trust. For Altan, 'mutual trust' also meant access to privileged information and exclusive access to insider documents.

Several years after Deniz, Orhan and Altan had established themselves in Europe, Zehra founded an Istanbul- and Brussels-based private consultancy firm, where Leyla worked before starting her own company in Istanbul and think-tank in Brussels.[7] Following the Helsinki announcement, Zehra targeted Turkish companies and assumed their EU advocacy in Brussels, to which she was no stranger. She had previously worked for several leading US law firms based in Brussels and had done an internship at the European Commission. Boasting her role in Turkey–EU affairs, she once claimed in an interview to the media that she was the only Turkish lawyer to have helped draft the EU–Turkey customs union. Successful lobbying in her world involved having privileged access to internal EU documents and information such as the draft Turkish progress reports, which the Commission and the European Parliament regularly prepared, before they were made public.

Elif, a Turkish-Belgian woman and Zehra's closest aide and confidante, went through a career trajectory similar to Zehra's, except Elif did an internship at the Parliament and had an assistantship to a British MEP. Together, they brought the Istanbul Metropolitan Municipality to Brussels, setting up an office and a cultural centre for Istanbul in the middle of Brussels' busiest business district. Zehra chaired its board and won the Chairwoman of the Regional Representation Award in 2008. Later, the centre was taken from the Municipality and turned into a culture office of the Turkish state.

Whether Zehra's assertions about being at the centre of Turkish Europeanis-ation were true or not, she was clearly well connected to politics, business and bureaucracy in Brussels, Istanbul and Ankara. After her untimely death in 2015, higher echelons of the Turkish government, including Erdoğan himself, attended her funeral. Yet, she was notoriously disliked, even feared, by other Turkish expats in Brussels. Her employees found her work ethic extremely objectionable and her labour practices questionable. People who worked for her pointed to her ruthless competitiveness. But she was also a go-getter.

As a political move, Zehra set up her office a block from the Turkish delegation to the EU. Since the 1963 Ankara Agreement, Turkey has maintained a permanent delegation to what is now the EU. Turkish diplomats took great pride in constituting a 'delegation', denoting equality with EU member states, instead of a 'mission' like other candidate country representations. After the Turkish embassy to Belgium, the consulate-general in Brussels, the permanent representation to NATO and the North Atlantic Council (NATO's political body), which stand outside Brussels, the delegation is the fourth diplomatic mission representing Turkey in Brussels. With its 1987 application for membership of the EEC, all Turkish diplomatic missions operating in Brussels gathered at one address. At the corner of Rue Montoyer and Arts-Loi and at a short walk from the European Parliament, the Turkish flag flew next to Romanian, Armenian and Greek flags. Since then, the diplomatic corps of many other countries have left this urban spot for the Schuman Roundabout, where the Commission stands. The Turkish delegation, too, has moved, but for different reasons and in the opposite direction, away from EU institutions and Europeanisation.

The strategy of housing the delegation, embassy and the consulate-general in the same location instigated more conflict than cooperation between Turkey's diplomatic representations. Personal differences between the three Turkish ambassadors (to Belgium, the EU and the NATO) led to diplomatic power struggles between them.[8] Per Pierre Bourdieu (1996), their differences emanated largely from whether they attended Francophone or Anglophone schools, where they leaned politically and how they viewed Turkey's EU membership. Zehra helped to find a new place for the delegation. Around the corner from the old building, still far away from the European Parliament and the Commission, today the delegation stands a block away from the Turkish culture centre and the AKP's EU representation (which came later) – and two blocks from Zehra's office. The move partially improved the spatial conflict but not the personal-political clashes in which the Turkish diplomatic corps was continuously embroiled.

Finally, Deniz, Orhan, Altan, Biray, Zehra and Leyla had all been members of the Turkish Business Association – Brussels. Twice a year, all met for a concert or dinner at which high-level Belgian or Turkish-Belgian political figures spoke.[9] Founded, towards the end of the 1990s, as a friendship group by a network of Turkish and Belgian businesspeople living in Belgium, this was overwhelmingly an association for the urban, upwardly mobile, middle-class, secular, college-educated, professional expatriates who identified with Turkey *and* Europe, as opposed to those who associated with rural, working-class, pious, migrant Turks. The association promoted 'white Turks' as opposed to 'black Turks' (Arat-Koç 2007; White 2014; Yavuz 2000). While Brussels' 'black Turks' may amount to a 'community' in the anthropological sense, its 'white Turks' did not even like to be associated with that concept and its referent. They did not have much in common or to do with Brussels' 'Turkish community', even though they yearned for familiar foods and occasionally shopped in Schaerbeek.

Due to their proximity to Brussels, I imagined, my protagonists had first-hand experience and closer involvement in Turkey–EU affairs and the rapprochement that paved the way for accession negotiations to begin. After all, the common impression in Turkey regarding its lobby in Brussels was and (still is) that it is effective. But if there was a success, I pondered, who would reap the benefits?

When, in December 2004, the European Council signalled that accession negotiations between Turkey and the EU could start the following October, expectations ran high. But to make it happen, Turkey had to sign a protocol extending its customs union agreement to the EU's ten new member states, including Cyprus, and lift its embargo on Cypriot flag-flying vessels and aircraft or whose last port of call was Cyprus. On the eve of the opening of the membership talks, I landed in Brussels.

Canvasing Brussels – *alla Turca*

My formal business was to do an internship at Deniz's office, where a few strong Turkish professional women, two of whom were economists, managed the representation office. While Deniz was busy with meeting EU politicians, technocrats and businesspeople during breakfast, lunch or dinner hours to discuss issues specific to Turkish–EU trade or was speaking at public events about the benefits of Turkish Europeanisation for the EU, the staff, who rarely accompanied him to such meetings, connected member companies with their EU counterparts or prepared specific policy briefs about the potential effects of a particular change in EU regulation for Turkish–EU trade from the perspective of sector players.

A few also attended BusinessEurope meetings or conferences, seminars or social events organised by Brussels-based think-tanks, such as the Centre for European Policy Studies, the European Policy Centre, the German Marshall Fund, the European Stability Initiative, Friedrich Naumann Stiftung, the International Crisis Group, the Council for International Relations and others. My hosts and other Turkish representatives had contracts with these think-tanks to help organise events about different aspects of the Turkish bid in Brussels. EU politicians and administrators attended these events because of the think-tank's credibility. When commenting on his institution's contracting of studies and events to outside experts in this way, one Commission interlocutor revealed: 'Sometimes it's better when some things are said by others'. When initiated by think-tanks, this practice is called 'deep lobbying' in the United States (Clemons 2003; Garsten 2013; Garsten & Sörbom 2018). Think-tanks' deep EU lobbying was only good to keep Turkey's Europeanisation on the EU's agenda.

During my internship at Deniz's office, I followed leads to potential interlocutors. One day, I came across a phonebook-like directory of Brussels' lobbying community. Aside from the Commission's later efforts to make EU lobbying transparent, the European Parliament set up a voluntary registry for lobbyists back in 1995. A decade later, this registry was accessible online, with the contact details, areas of operation, aim and budget information of thousands of associations, firms and individuals working in Brussels' EU labyrinth – a modest goldmine for a researcher. Later, when I frequented the European Parliament, I observed how lobbyists' brown badges marked them apart from the MEPs and their staff, who carried blue badges, and journalists with their yellow badges.

The registry helped me in both intended and unintended ways. The first time I used it I went through all the names and noted down those that sounded Turkish. To assume that Turkish-sounding names would lead me to Turkish interests was a 'culturally intimate' moment (Herzfeld 1997).[10] And throughout the fieldwork for this book, I had many such moments. I met Orhan, Biray and Altan through this registry. I also met others who, despite their Turkish-sounding names, had nothing to do with representing 'Turkish' interests in the EU: with their Turkish-Belgian, Kurdish-French, Turkish-German or Kurdish-German dual identifications, these individuals put the social fact of Turkey in Europe in a new perspective.

Using the office phone to schedule interviews with these contacts, I stumbled upon deep divides within the Brussels-based Turkish-interest community. Before I could pursue a potential contact, my prospective interlocutor, who might have initially cherished the idea, needed to be convinced that it was not 'the office' calling them but a junior academic researcher, albeit based in that office. On one occasion, after telling me that there is no reason to meet face to face, the representative of a low-key Turkish interest group blurted out that his single 'successful' lobbying accomplishment of the year was to help block the proposal at the European Parliament for the Armenian genocide to be officially recognised.

The office also helped me socially. Back then, it was the only Turkish office to welcome trainees. I made long-term friends there. Some were on their way to various Commission internships, thanks to Deniz's backing. Though many applied, few were successful, due to the intense competition. In hopes of later having a professional career in Turkey–EU affairs in Brussels or elsewhere, working in Turkish interest representation offices was a stepping-stone in the careers of many of my friends. Those who came to Brussels to learn how the EU worked, upon returning to Turkey carried their knowledge and experience into the public sector, while others became advisers and communicators in the corporate world. Several generations had prepared for Turkish Europeanisation in the hope that, one day, their expertise might come in handy. Some worked full time, with pay, but on student visas, at Turkish consultancy firms based in Brussels. No matter how little their bosses paid them, aspiring Turkish 'Eurostars' (Favell 2008) took any opportunity that came their way.[11] The younger generation communicated EU priorities better than their bosses, who often only wanted to showcase their interns or staff instead of using their skills for politico-cultural translation. The bosses publicly argued that Turkey was now 'modern' and 'European', but they privately entertained all forms of self-orientalising, based on constant comparisons in many sectors of life, ranging from urban planning ('European cities were planned while Turkish cities lacked basic planning') to state bureaucracy ('Our bureaucrats are cheeky') to women's clothing. Once, during the early years of Turkey–EU negotiations, a friend told me that her boss had asked her and her female colleagues to attend public seminars and raise a hand to speak, to show 'how modern [read: secular, urban, educated] young Turkish women *actually* dressed'. Needless to say, my friend did not wear a head-scarf, spoke official languages of the EU and had liberal views – an ideal candidate for 'white Turk' imagery.

Towards the end of my term at Deniz's office, Turkey declared its intention to extend the customs union to the new EU members. I witnessed the sighs of relief from interest representatives and their congratulations to themselves and to each other. With the vote at the European Parliament, Deniz had not only successfully lobbied that EU institution for the opening of accession talks with Turkey (see Chapter 5) but also had given AKP politicians a new political identity, who there-after branded themselves 'conservative democrats'.

Next, the representatives wondered whether the Turkish government's man-oeuvring would convince EU publics that the 1970 Additional Protocol sufficiently covered the divided island of Cyprus and whether it would be able to convince the Turkish public that this did not mean that Turkey recognised the Republic of Cyprus.[12] After four weeks, I left Brussels with various versions of how complicated it was for the Turkish interest representatives to work in the EU environment, where Turkey was a mere outsider and where representatives were doing their best for a glorious partnership soon to be crowned with EU membership! My later meetings with their bosses in Istanbul and Ankara largely affirmed these narra-tives. Little did I know, at the time, of these difficulties in representing Turkey, but I knew this: the interest representatives fed these sentiments to enthusiastic researchers who parachuted in and out of Brussels for short-term engagements.[13] The ethnographer in me sensed that much.

Brussels proper

In early 2008, the chief public prosecutor of Turkey's Constitutional Court pressed charges relating to anti-secular activities against Erdoğan's AKP. Before its deliberation, the Court referred the indictment to a group of constitutional rapporteurs. The case became known as the AKP closure trial. News of the closure trial and I arrived in Brussels around the same time. Before the court case exited the Turkish political scene, it took the full-time attention of Turkish diplomats and their EU colleagues, many of whom I was only just getting to know.

During the short-lived AKP closure trial, I worked as a *stagiaire* at the EESC (the 'Committee'), one of the two EU bodies that represented the collective voice of European business and civil society. Later, I conducted fieldwork in other capacities, such as a 'network officer' at Leyla's think-tank, a reporter-trainee for an online-based EU–Turkey news network, and a student of Turkey–EU relations from a white, urban, middle-class background, who spoke English with a US (meaning not British or Turkish) accent. I also went back to consuming tobacco. While waiting to meet my interlocutors, smoking helped initiate many conversations with people who populated Turkish or EU offices.

During my term at the Committee and rite of passage through Brussels' Euro-politics, I carried a badge that opened doors of EU institutions (literally) and allowed me to sit in on official meetings between the EU and Turkish officials as an insider – much to the confusion of the Turkish participants, who would later express appreciation of my presence. Political and social relations among people maintained administrative rules and norms, which in return solidified those relations. This was as much the case at the top as at the bottom.

At the start of my internship at the Committee, I had a rough time with fellow trainees, who suspected me of harbouring ulterior motives, like joining Brussels' Eurocratic labour force and competing with them for future EU jobs. Later, however, my cohort helped me advance my research in significant ways. As a group, we visited many international, national and European organisations, like the Organisation for Economic Co-operation and Development (OECD), the United Nations Education, Scientific and Cultural Organization, the French Foreign Affairs Ministry and the Secretariat General for European Affairs in Paris, as well as the International Criminal Tribunal and European Police Office in The Hague. During these visits, if I had not already found an opportunity to do so, my fellow interns would pop 'the Turkish question' to stir a debate around Turkey–EU relations among members of the international policy communities, who saw the issue from their organisations' vantage point.

While I was away, newly minted offices increased the number of Turkish interests represented in Brussels. Between 2005 and 2008, this number went from twelve to twenty-one, and to twenty-eight after 2008: political movements and party representations, from two to four to five; civil society, labour and trade unions, and business organisations, from nine to twelve; city municipalities, from zero to two; and professional lobbying and consultancy firms, from one to three to four. The number of news agencies also increased, along with the numbers of journalists and Brussels correspondents. Some old friends and soon-to-be friends worked in these offices.

Transnational encounters of the Eurocratic kind

Defne was one such friend. After getting her undergraduate degree in law and her MA degree in European studies, in Turkey, she came to Belgium to do her doctoral studies in EU law. To pay for her living, though, she needed to work. Her international student visa made her employment situation precarious. Potential Belgian employers did not want to hire her and Turkish employers did not want to pay for her social security. When word reached her that Leyla was looking for someone to set up an office for a think-tank in Brussels, Defne got happily involved with the project. She found an office space for the think-tank inside the busy International Press Centre, along with Bloomberg, Associated Press, Euractiv, TRT and others. Her office was now conveniently located across from the Commission's Berlaymont building. A non-profit organisation under Belgian law, this think-tank was a corporate social responsibility project of Leyla's Istanbul-based consulting firm. To promote Turkey's European integration in areas outside of high politics, diplomacy and international relations, Defne and Leyla organised artistic shows, cultural exhibitions, seminars and conferences. After some months, Defne moved to a Commission internship. Five months later, word reached her that the Women Entrepreneurs Association of Turkey, which promoted entrepreneurialism among businesswomen in Turkey, was looking for a Brussels representative.

One month into my internship at the Committee, Defne invited me to her office inauguration party. Office openings took place quite ceremoniously in Brussels. They provided an opportunity to make a good name for one's organisation within Eurocratic circles. Being an offshoot of Deniz's association, Defne's workplace occupied the top floor of Deniz's office building. On the evening of the opening party, all four floors were booming with people and music. A well-known college folk band played popular songs in multiple languages native to Turkey. VIP guests were chatting in every corner of every room. From Turkey, they included the government minister responsible for women and family affairs, members of the diplomatic corps, the first woman rector of Turkey's top public university, well-known EU experts, artists, novelists, journalists and others.

I remember standing with my back to a grand portrait of modern Turkey's founder, hanging at the top of the stairs, and watching people socialise into the late hours of the evening. Those who were well known for their institutional, or other-wise self-interested, role in Turkish Europeanisation attended this party. At the time, I knew so few faces. Apart from the Turkish faces, I recognised the European Parliament's Turkey rapporteur and her colleague, the Dutch socialist chairman of the EU–Turkey Joint Parliamentary Committee and his Turkish wife, who had worked in the past as a war reporter and later as the Brussels correspondent for a Turkish media network.

For the next year, I shadowed, interviewed, observed and worked with many of these individuals (181 of them in total, to be exact). The 'Turkey file' on the EU table and the 'EU file' on the Turkish table consumed their everyday professional (and, to large extent, personal and private) lives. I interviewed Commission technocrats who drafted EU regulations with region-wide effects; diplomats who translated these regulatory changes back to their countries and channelled national responses to the Council. I observed MEPs, their advisers and staff, and the parliamentary committee and political group administrators and country advisers as they deliberated on those changes. I asked representatives of organised interests from all corners of Europe to tell me about their work on Turkey's Europeanisation. I talked to Turkish-EU citizens and members of resident and non-resident Turkish-European communities and their representatives; listened to journalists, students and artists about their hopes and concerns regarding Turkey's European saga. Some became key interlocutors; others provided bits and pieces of the everyday picture.

After the evening of Defne's office party, I attended nearly 100 events, ranging from political meetings, cultural activities, public lectures and press conferences to reception and dinners. I made it my business to find my way into the rooms where the EU–Turkey encounters took place. Some days I had two to three interviews scheduled back to back, as well as VIP gatherings to attend during the rest of the day. Lunch and dinner meetings organised on behalf of the higher echelons of the Turkish state were more like political spectacles. All provided the necessary social platform for various members of the EU's enlargement policy community, especially for those who otherwise might not have known each other face to face but nevertheless regularly communicated by other means. In such spaces, participants of the enlargement policy community socialised and learned about where their claims originated or might lead. For political ethnographers, these meetings are full of rich moments for participant and non-participant observation. I used them to observe the transnational encounters of my interlocutors as they negotiated Turkish Europeanisation on a daily basis. Their day-to-day negotiations took place both formally, that is, during official meetings, and informally, during their encounters with one another outside official meeting rooms, much like Defne's office opening party.

Formal meetings among political actors have become popular as productive sites for ethnographic research (Brown et al. 2017; Høyer Leivestad & Nyqvist 2017; Sandler & Thedvall 2017; Schwartzman 1989). While my accounts of formal meetings at the Committee, CoR and European Parliament are from first-hand experience, my accounts of lower-level access-restricted technical meetings between the EU and Turkish bureaucrats, diplomats and lobbyists in the Council, the Commission and elsewhere come from my triangulated information from interviews with participants who had been at those meeting. These meetings may appear as mundane sites compared with more high-level political negotiations attended by EU and Turkish heads. But their mundanity does not mean they are unimportant.

In fact, lower-level technical meetings carry more import in the social life of European politics than high-level meetings of 'talking EU heads', not least because they are where actors encounter one another face to face to negotiate their differences, interests and investments.

Negotiations of interests at the international level are often thought to be matters of high politics, with restricted access. Yet, I found Brussels' Eurocracy to be more accessible than national administrations – at least to an unattached researcher. Many of my interlocutors represented public, private, institutional and corporate interests from all over the continent and beyond. From their privileged position at the heart of the EU and due to the unique nature of their vocation, most strove to influence the political decisions and policy actions that set the parameters for the EU's enlargement policy and Turkey's Europeanisation. All stood to lose their privileges if Turkey's EU membership were to materialise. While politicians, bureaucrats and private interest representatives lacked a post-accession vision and complained about the proliferation of pseudo-experts in Turkish–EU matters, the common sentiment among EuroTurks was an ambivalence over Turkey's EU membership. Some supported their homeland in this endeavour, while others feared losing their privileged way of life if more Turks migrated to the EU (Kaya & Kentel, 2005, 2007). Bringing such different people into a conversation, this book discusses how situated actors managed this contradiction to the best of their ability, knowledge and competence – albeit not always effectively, as I show in the following pages.

The T. files

Each year, EU institutions and consultative bodies prepare reports and policy briefings assessing Turkey's progress in instituting the domestic reform stipulated as necessary for its EU membership. In addition, during political, technical and sectoral meetings at the Council, Commission, Parliament and other venues, participants take notes and minutes for internal use. Transnational encounters by actors and agents of Turkish Europeanisation, thus, produce a vast repository of both discursive and material artefacts, some of which is publicly available, whereas one can access others only by establishing good rapport with insiders. Some 'T.' (Turkey) files like the Commission's annual Turkey reports are more techno-bureaucratic in nature. As instruments of policy-making, they aim to inform decision-makers how to fashion better policies and compel the involved governments to take further action. One could classify others as political documents, such as the Parliament's Turkey reports and the Turkish counter-reports they elicit. These documents do not create politicians and bureaucrats but contribute to their professional careers in myriad ways.

Actors exchange documents and, through them, information, influence and interests. During the report-writing season, member-state officials update their Turkish colleagues on the proceedings of internal EU meetings about Turkey's progress in reform. Sometimes one's ability to influence the documentary content is *the* measure of success – however elusive that effort might be. But in most cases successful lobbying amounts to finding a copy of the documents through one's contacts before they enter the public domain.

Formal and informal modes and channels of policy-making sustain such exchanges. This exchange takes on material, non-material and verbal forms. In the EU's complex policy field, where actors do not regularly meet face to face, material products such as official documents, policy papers, research reports, non-papers (*aide-mémoir*), information notes and their draft versions gain a special communicative value. Even though the EU's system for archiving documents is highly sophisticated, more developed and more flexible than its national counterparts, the EU runs a bureau system, wherein all policy documents and communications are digitally filed (and some also as hard copies). Policy actors' transnational encounters take place in this bureaucratised environment through text. Whether they concern public or private bureaucracies, competing policy intentions, acts and actions are heavily documented in the EU.

In this book I treat these documents as objects with manifold meanings. They are codifications of human intent, products of human interactions and, as I argue, also the objective of such interactions. Archaeologists and palaeographers know this best. According to Bruno Latour (1988: 26), anthropology, however, has long mistreated files and records as 'the most despised of all ethnographic objects'. Several reasons may account for that. According to critics, documents are 'unconscious maps of the mundane' (Comaroff & Comaroff 1992: 36) that reflect routinised actions. Meeting reports, for example, 'born in the work of staff and the recommendations of committees, circulate among and are given specific substance by individual[s], and go on to figure centrally in the decisions made at other meetings' (Brenneis 2006: 42). Critics also question whether the textual meaning of documents is available, accessible or even relevant to outsiders to the group which initially produces, uses and circulates them. The mere existence of a particular policy document, critics argue, may further mislead in presupposing the need for action in a policy area (Ferguson 1990). Finally, critics observe that a great deal of social life does not appear in textual documents, as they, unlike human interlocutors, do not readily communicate with the ethnographer (Riles 2006) – although, whether they live under liberal or illiberal systems, what people may say often differs from what they do (Spencer 2007; Yurchak 2006).

Despite the long-term privileging of people-to-people interactions over the artefacts of human interaction, anthropologists have, since Latour's critique, examined the form and aesthetics of documents such as internal bureaucratic communiqués and international agreements, their affective meaning (as in travel documents) and their associative qualities through which political authorities relate to their subjects (as in land titles, identification cards or transparency documents) (Gupta 2012; Hetherington 2011; Hull 2012a; Navaro-Yashin 2012; Riles 2000; for a review, see Hull 2012b).

Some documents, like the drafts of parliamentary reports I analyse in Chapter 6, are specifically designed to become mundane, especially if seen from inside the institutional settings in which they come into existence (Brenneis 2006). Once their 'careers' (Harper 1998), 'life histories' (Appadurai 1986) or 'social lives' (Appadurai

1986) are over, their relevance retreats to archives (Harper 1998). They become inactive (Hodder 1994). But mundanity, I would argue, does not mean that documents are mute, inaccessible or misleading. In his seminal work on the social life of things, Arjun Appadurai argued that following the things (documents in my case) in motion is methodologically necessary:

> Even if our own approach to things is conditioned necessarily by the view that things have no meanings apart from those that human transactions, attributions and motivations endow them with, the anthropological problem is that this formal truth does not illuminate the concrete, historical circulation of things. For that we have to follow the things themselves, for their meanings are inscribed in their forms, their uses and their trajectories. It is through the analysis of these trajectories that we can interpret the human transactions that enliven things. Thus, even though from a *theoretical* point of view human actors encode things with significance, from a *methodological* point of view it is the things-in-motion that illuminate their human and social context. (Appadurai 1986: 5, original emphasis)

When looked at from an emic perspective, political documents constitute institutional communication between the EU and Turkey. Here, I pursue them as artefacts-under-production-while-in-exchange because they provide a lens on the power–interest relations between Turkish and EU actors.

Lobbying and diplomacy are contemporary forms of political communication of diverse interests. They also foster bureaucratic encounters of a political nature with enduring after-effects. Political communication in advanced bureaucracies such as the EU commonly takes place on discursively. As mundane objects of politicking and policy-making, these documents provide privileged access to what matters most today to those who manage Turkey–EU affairs. Following Appadurai, I take these documents as material evidence of and complementary to ethnographers' observations of the larger socio-cultural context throughout which their transactors operate and encounter one another transnationally.

During my fieldwork, getting access to textual information from EU interlocutors was relatively easy. Eurocrats shared copies of their documents without quibble. Some offered a copy of a particular document; others let me look at it. Once, I took a more militant approach and briefly intercepted the exchange of minutes from an internal EU meeting between a member state official and a Turkish lobbyist.

Schuman Roundabout, European quarter – back to Leyla

Some months after my term at the Committee, Defne arranged a meeting between Leyla and myself in an upmarket patisserie on the European side of Istanbul, where Leyla asked me to manage her NGO/think-tank in Brussels. After Defne, she had hired a Turkish-Belgian woman to run the office but now she, too, was leaving. I accepted her offer. What better way was there to do ethnographic fieldwork on lobbying than working as a lobbyist? I worked in that office for several months.

My first inclination, as for many who did this line of work, was to prepare our organisation's distribution list. Whether it was about announcements of our upcoming events or the monthly bulletin Leyla and other board members put together, we used this contact list of about 3,000 names as our primary audience, which I regularly updated. At some point, a younger lobbyist friend cautioned me against sharing my list with anyone. He pointed out how invaluable these network lists were for practising lobbyists.

Between large lobbying firms and one-person offices, it was quite common for a representation office, consultancy firm or an NGO in Brussels to have a staff of a few people. The annual European Public Affairs Directory, the quintessential address book on EU lobbying, shows this to be so. Turkish offices fit the norm, except those Deniz and Zehra ran: theirs were relatively well staffed and well funded. The biggest budgetary constraint an office faced was full-time employment of staff based in Brussels, which was very costly in Turkish currency. But one did not need a lavish office space or an army of people to do the job effectively. Often, a phone line and an e-mail address sufficed. To cut costs, some offices procured stationery from Turkey. The pay of a Turkish intern was usually a third of that of an EU intern.

Every day I would leave my apartment, which I shared with a Bulgarian journalist and an Italian trainee, and walk to the office a few blocks away, passing by many who worked in EU institutions, NGOs, law firms and consultancies scattered throughout the European quarter. In this neighbourhood the roads were always in need of repair, security was subtle but tight and the physical edifices of the EU's political infrastructure were always impeccably sanitised. True to Europe's social fact, many people who attended to the EU's material maintenance as janitorial staff, receptionists and security guards spoke my native language. The concrete, glass and wire mesh around me were also strangely familiar. The world-renowned Turkish architect who helped Deniz find his office designed them. His most recent works include Erdoğan's presidential palace (Aksaray [White Castle]) and his decade-long dream for Istanbul, the Taksim Mosque.

I never wore a lobbyist's badge, but I represented Leyla's interests by helping organise outreach activities or attending those others organised. During my brief time with Leyla, we organised several 'high-level' (read: exclusive, access-restricted) meetings where practitioners would exchange views on political economic matters related to the future of Turkey–EU relations, or cultural events that were to contribute to Turkey's portrayal as a peace-building member of the European community. Carefully packaged before and after for Leyla's different constituencies, each event was well attended. They contributed, in the main, to debates on various politico-economic aspects of Turkish Europeanisation and to keeping the T. file on the EU's agenda. Leyla's expertise in journalism helped spread the word at various media outlets.

A few months later, I left my post at Leyla's organisation (which was then taken by a younger, energetic friend). Nonetheless, I continued to update my network list, interview members of Brussels's enlargement policy community and attend formal meetings and informal gatherings where Turkish and EU politicians, bureaucrats, lobbyists and others encountered one another. On weekends, when the workday occupiers of the European quarter commuted back home to neighbouring countries and cities, I would take long strolls through our neighbourhood. During my walks I made it a habit to read names on the doorbells. Thousands of lobbyists, consultants and interest representatives surrounded the EU institutions. If I suspected a person worked on Turkish Europeanisation, I would contact them. After learning about my research, some contacted me for updates on the T. file.

Towards the end of my fieldwork, my interlocutors also saw me sitting at the journalists' row as a *stagiaire* correspondent of a Turkey–EU news network. A long-term follower of Turkey–EU relations, Adem introduced me to his community of reporters at the European Parliament. I followed sessions and wrote news reports about what went on during parliamentary meetings for his online news network. Adem's was more of a one-man's-show. His website had been reporting on Turkey's Europeanisation for over a decade and a half. He received internship requests from budding young Turkish journalists and taught many the nuances of news-reporting in Brussels. His task was to get word out before competing news outlets. My reports did not look anything like my field notes, nor like the online news reports Adem wrote. He found mine more 'balanced'.

Liminal analytics for reflexive accountability

This book uses liminal analytics that neither privilege nor stand for any particular group of actors. Its critical reflexive lens inverts how political life unfolds at the heart of Europe from the perspective of those who managed membership talks on an everyday basis, all the while remaining observant of the thrills and perils of everyday policy and political work.

Policy workers and influencers are known to be too busy to talk to outsiders. Various anthropologists (Liebow 1995; Marshall 1984) and political scientists (Morris 2009; Voltolini 2017) have pointed out the problems of interviewing elites and experts, who may be reticent about sharing their views and sought-after documents with an outsider, or who may manipulate the interview, using power differences between them and the researcher. In that regard, my time with Turkish and EU diplomats and lobbyists radically differed. 'Too busy' is shorthand for someone who does not see why he or she should spend valuable time and energy explaining what they do to outsiders, from whom they hardly receive anything in return. This is what I encountered with my Turkish interlocutors, who were often puzzled by my presence in places where they did their job. While some talked with me freely, others simply ignored me. To others I was at best simply citizen to whom they did not feel accountable or at worst a planted agent!

Perhaps because of the criticism of democratic deficit, because they developed close encounters with lobbyists and third-party representatives in general or because their work was well compensated, I found many EU bureaucrats to be open to outside contact, including contact by academics. As for professional lobbyists, contacts with members of the media and scholars were habitual. Both bureaucrats and lobbyists perceived talking to a researcher as part of their job description. For them, I was one more person to talk to. Equipped with political science, law and economics degrees, some were even enthusiastic to talk to an anthropologist, an exotic species in Brussels, from their point of view!

Considering sensitive information interlocutors might feel pressured to reveal during interviews, 'too busy' was a valid concern regarding the professional and personal implications meetings with outsiders might have. The case of a gun lobbyist posing as an anthropologist in Washington, DC, continues to serve as a warning (Ridgeway et al. 2008). However minor, my 'anthropologist' identity was a matter of concern to a few potential EU interlocutors who felt compelled to verify my academic affiliation before being interviewed by me.[14]

Diplomacy and lobbying have historically been classed and gendered professions (Bilgic 2016; Kuus 2014; Neumann 2012). Most of my Turkish inter-locutors were members of the elite (or aspiring to be so). In these terms, my research could be seen as an attempt to 'study up' in both literal and ethnographic senses. If defined as access to economic, social, governmental, juridical or political capital, per Pierre Bourdieu (1987, 1996, 1999), most of my interlocutors were from the upper or upper-middle classes (few would have identified themselves as middle or working class) and the majority were men. By their sheer size, EU interlocutors were more diverse.

My passport, my class and gender and my communication skills have both facilitated and impeded research. After I had waited several months for a Belgian travel visa, the authorities rejected my application. For my Committee internship, Brussels contacts suggested that I get a tourist visa. I applied for a Schengen visa from France, instead, and, once there, bought a one-way train ticket from Paris to Brussels. In Brussels, my middle-class background did not create a significant problem. I might have been better off than some of my interlocutors regarding intellectual capital but it was no use in Brussels. Occasionally, my anthropological knowledge of other cultures and polities in Europe helped turn a formal interview into a more dialogical conversation with my EU interlocutors, who otherwise talked to me as if I was a metonym of Turkey, addressing me with 'you' when they meant the Turkish government, state, people and so on.

Dressing up every day for work highlighted my gender identity. It also revealed associated gender stereotypes that are not unique to Turkey's patriarchal society. In Istanbul, one male lower-level AKP bureaucrat from a city municipality abstained from shaking hands with me as a woman when our interview was over – though he changed this behaviour during our later encounters, in Brussels, in public; perhaps because I was one of the few faces he recognised in the crowd. On another occasion, during a seminar break in Brussels, Orhan asked me to pour coffee for Pascal, the French head of the Turkey desk at the Commission's DG Enlargement. Orhan's request caught me off-guard. Once the culturally intimate moment wore off, I flatly refused. Though Pascal was French, he was well versed in Turkish culture. He also knew of patriarchy, ageism and other forms of inequality from his own cultural origins. Pascal, thankfully, had not registered Orhan's request.

Interlocutors on both the EU and Turkish sides exhibited such essentialisms to a limited degree. Unlike a colleague who was told by a German official that Turkey was a mediaeval country, none of my interlocutors uttered an explicitly orientalist statement during our conversations. Nor did any direct their orientalism towards me as a Turkish national – except one time when, comparing the US and the EU educational systems regarding their degree of openness towards young academics like myself, a Commission interlocutor suggested that the US welcomes Turkish students because it 'doesn't have the problem of integrating you [Turkish students, Turkish people] into its society'. Even so, many of my interlocutors 'act[ed] from an unacknowledged position of power': EU interlocutors due to their Eurocentrism (Neumann 2012: 31) and Turkish interlocutors due to their state-centrism, a governing bias in their exercise of power. To manage these complexities, I had to experiment with ad hoc measures and thus I carved a liminal vantage point for myself.

With my unisex name and research topic, most interlocutors assumed that I must be a political scientist and a man. The former Bulgarian EU chief negotiator expected to meet with a male researcher, but I showed up instead. My uncovered hair (or the lack of a headscarf, depending on your politics) prompted statements like 'Like you, not all Turkish women are covered' or 'There are more women with head-scarves in Brussels than in Istanbul'. In both cases my outfit indexed my gender and national identities. Once again, my presence in the field as a researcher served as a metaphor for contestations of culture and power during Turkey's Europeanisation. When we sat down to talk about the actual nuts and bolts of Turkish Europeanisation, however, barriers and markers quickly dissolved.

Two things that helped me most as a 'native' anthropologist who studied cultures of expertise were my command of several EU languages and my humble background in dramaturgy.[15] Besides English, I speak German – a legacy of my teen years spent at an Istanbul high school built and funded by the German federal government for the children of Turkish return migrants from that country which was soon incorporated into Turkish public education – and some French, both of which I used to get a sense of the people around me and to review EU documents drafted in those languages. My background in dramaturgy helped me to traverse gender and class boundaries not by pretending to be someone else but by adjusting to the cultural milieu.

Native anthropologists and ethnographers are said to speak and write with an accent. What helped me most while in the field was that I spoke English with an American(ised) accent, which was still rare in Brussels but was much admired for reasons that are not entirely clear to me. (Perhaps it is a legacy of US hegemony since the Cold War?) My Americanised accent carved a third space (neither Turkish, nor European, nor EuroTurkish), from where I could communicate with many who came from and assumed different walks of life.

During my fieldwork I met many policy workers and influencers. Hardly any failed to answer my e-mail requests to meet. Most people whose experience and expertise I consulted during fieldwork for this book welcomed my approach. We often met in their offices or at public spots in or outside the EU offices. Some exhibited a mix of disbelief and relief that after several years of the opening of accession talks someone wanted to 'talk Turkey' again. In our talks about how, where and why they did what they did, and what they observed others doing or not doing, it would be naive to assume that they shared with me all the intricate details their jobs revealed to them. In this book, I report on those conversations and interviews, as well as the observations of those who had been in office long enough to feel confident of sharing their experience and expertise.[16]

Unlike the common parlance of reflexivity in social sciences, which privileges the role of the researcher, the reflexivity in my account comes from practising liminal analytics, where reflexivity is applied to the socially constructed relationships between the insiders and outsiders of fields laden with power. Here, I use reflexivity less to render problematic my own positionality in the field and more as a research tool to triangulate my interlocutors' field positions, with an aim of establishing accountability. This means that I often asked my interlocutors to tell me both what they do and what they know about others' doings. I thus reached a significant conclusion that, in this field of politics and cultural production, power is never absolute but is always relative, so much so that actors labour to maintain their fragile power and field positions. I certainly encountered many 'para-ethnographic' moments during the fieldwork (Holmes & Marcus 2005). But instead of taking my interlocutors' telling about their political and cultural work from the field as the outcome of my analysis, I used them as measures of their own reflexivity towards establishing accountability. All the while, I kept my ethnographic sensibilities critically aligned with holding the powerful accountable by means of cultural analysis.

Conclusion

In the end, the art of lobbying and diplomacy turned out to be as much an anthropological exercise as ethnographic analysis. Those who excelled in this line of work did so by using their human skills to analyse the negotiating field and by strategising how best they could communicate the interests they were to relay to those whose decisions they worked hard to influence.

Through politico-cultural immersion, elite interviews, participant and non-participant observations among experts, and analysis of the production and circulation of textual policy advice, I reached the natural boundaries of this policy universe. By the end of my fieldwork, some interlocutors came to me for information. My shifting field positions helped me gain social acceptance, while keeping my critical approach towards the ongoing power–interest dynamics sharp. My research thus enjoyed an unusual scholarly privilege: while attending to the dynamics of a troublesome institutional process at a historical moment, I was fortunate to observe why and how membership negotiations plunged into a seemingly terminal decline, or what I heard described as a death spiral. My later visits to Brussels confirmed that the new members of this policy field were well attuned to the norms and forms of cultural interaction that took place during Turkish Europeanisation in Brussels.

After a decade of negotiation over Turkish accession, none of my initial interlocutors remained in office, or held the same job, except the no(ta)bles of Turkish

Europeanisation I introduced at the start of this chapter and others I will present later. The paid advocates navigated the tumultuous political waters surrounding Turkish Europeanisation while performing impeccably as professionals. Some moved from peripheral to central positions in their organisations, by increasing their powers and perfecting their ability to channel interests, influence and information through the corridors of power. Newcomers with no job security filled the peripheral positions vacated by them. Others gained their additional status, power and prestige even while there was no hint of progress in the accession negotiations. Although the steady demand for their expertise never waned, many risked being cut off from Turkish Europeanisation, since it was extremely hard to move to the inner circles of the policy community in a turbulent political landscape – albeit not impossible. In the following, I tell of the myriad ways in which all this happened. Before doing so, a few words about the EU's enlargement policy and the Turkish counter-discourse are in order.

Notes

1 'Belgium in Figures' from https://statbel.fgov.be/nl (accessed 9 May 2019).
2 'Belgium in Figures' from https://statbel.fgov.be/nl (accessed 9 May 2019).
3 I thank G. N. Bedirhanoğlu for sharing this experience with me.
4 Real names. Unless otherwise noted, all translations from Turkish are mine; all names are pseudonyms.
5 To protect the identities of those I encountered within my participant observations, pseudonyms are used throughout this account except where noted otherwise.
6 The EESC shares facilities with the Committee of Regions (CoR), a pan-European meeting platform for local and regional actors. In 2006, CoR members established a working group with Turkey. Despite repeated requests by CoR from the government to upgrade this working group to JCC level, the Turkish government is reluctant to grant representation at supranational level to Turkey's eastern regions with openly Kurdish mayors. Every year, the EESC and CoR prepare their own opinion on the Commission's annual Turkey progress report.
7 I tried to interview Zehra or work for her for research purposes but neither option worked out. Nevertheless, I had many opportunities to observe her and her work. I interviewed her long-time aide and second in charge at her firm and talked to others who worked with her or competed with her.
8 At the time of my fieldwork in Brussels, Turkey's representatives to the NATO, the EU and Belgium all began their Brussels terms around the same time, in 2006, 2005 and 2005, respectively. By the end of 2009, new representatives had replaced them. The then Turkish ambassador to NATO went on to serve as the international security director-general at the foreign ministry, was then appointed as Turkey's permanent representative to the Organization for Security and Co-operation in Europe and later as NATO's assistant secretary-general for public diplomacy. Upon his retirement from public service, the then Turkish ambassador to the EU became an AKP member of the Turkish parliament. The former Turkish ambassador to Belgium became a foreign policy adviser to the prime minister, before he retired from public life. The North Atlantic Council is the political authority of NATO, of which Turkey has been a full member since 1952. It is housed at NATO headquarters, five miles from Brussels city

centre. Due to the complexity of the issue, I have left out Turkey–NATO relations and the role of the defence industry and its lobbying activities. Suffice it to say here that these are extremely important issues that have direct effects on Turkey–EU relations but on which further research is due.

9 Its website states that this association 'conducts … activities to support constructive efforts that reinforce Turkey's membership in the European Union; contributes to the establishment of a "positive" Turkish image starting with its immediate neighbourhood, in Belgium (and to the extent possible in larger environs); increases the extent of relations with Turkey; deepens knowledge of Turkey and keeps alive members' interest in Turkey; and creates opportunities to support the Turkish community in Belgium.'

10 Anthropologist Michael Herzfeld (1997: 3) defines cultural intimacy as 'the recognition of those aspects of a cultural identity that are considered a source of external embarrassment but that nevertheless provide insiders with their assurance of common sociality'.

11 Adrian Favell (2008) describes Eurostars as members of an emergent class of educated, middle-class young professionals who benefited most from physical and socio-economic mobility European integration provided. Eurostars live and work in cities with favourable policies on housing, schooling and health care.

12 Before Cyprus joined the EU, United Nations Secretary-General Kofi Annan proposed a referendum on the reunification of the island in 2004. Turkey, Greece and the UK, as guarantor countries, along with the Turkish-Cypriot and Greek-Cypriot majority leaders, supported the referendum. The EU's concern about indexing the fate of the Cypriot accession to the UN referendum was about a possible Greek veto of the fifth wave of enlargement altogether, should the Cypriots failed to unite. It was a big blow to the Turkish government when the Greek-Cypriots in the south rejected unification in the UN referendum, whereas the Turkish-Cypriots in the north voted for it under the terms set by the Annan Plan. Despite the results of the vote, Cyprus joined the EU as its twenty-third member state. On all occasions since then, Turkish politicians and bureaucrats have reminded their EU counterparts about the UN referendum results. The Turkish government blocks Cyprus's access to important NATO documents concerning defence and security policy within the framework of the NATO–EU cooperation agreement known as Berlin Plus, which was signed a year before Cyprus joined the EU and to which both Turkey as a member of NATO and Cyprus as a member of the EU are now party.

13 In cataloguing the Brussels-based NGOs involved in Turkey's Europeanisation, existing scholarship on the Turkish lobby in Brussels mainly provides descriptive accounts, devoid of explanatory or interpretive power (e.g. Polo & Visier 2007; Visier 2009; Visier & Polo 2005). Compared with those accounts, mine includes voices and transnational encounters with public and private practitioners of lobbying from all sides.

14 Only towards the end of my fieldwork did I learn of a rumour about me that nevertheless did not damage my integrity as a researcher. The person spreading the rumour suggested that I was working as an agent for Zehra, reporting to her who did what in Brussels. This incident and those on two occasions when my interview requests were denied (one by a Commission official and the other by a member state diplomat) on the basis of my nationality were the only such setbacks during the fieldwork. I also received lots of career advice and life coaching from several Turkish interlocutors. Some asked me to work for them, while others suggested I had ulterior motives for doing research in Brussels and advised me to become a journalist or to marry a local for EU residency. As an anthropologist, I knew of the risks of the job and felt nevertheless fortunate because of the low number of obstructions I had to cope with while in the field.

15 For elaboration of dramaturgy as a research method to understand social interactions, see Goffman (1959).

16 Most of those who had already left office for a different role and of those who only recently had started their job did not want to be interviewed, as they felt that their expertise was out of date or not yet formed.

Part II

Framing EU membership

You expect us to say 'Yes, Sir, Europe, Sir!'
I'd like to remind you that this is not the way we do politics in Turkey.

Onur Öymen (real name), former diplomat and opposition MP
(Republican People's Party), during the third session of the sixty-first
meeting of the EU–Turkey Joint Parliamentary Committee, Brussels

3

The accession pedagogy

Enlargement from soft power to pedagogy

When the Turkish foreign minister revealed his government's desire to apply for membership of the European Economic Community on 14 April 1987 with letters hand-delivered to the Belgian foreign minister and president of the Community and to the president of European Commission, no one in his cabinet anticipated the post-1989 reterritorialisation in Europe (Keskin 2001). A little over a year earlier, in 1986, the Community had enlarged for the third time with the accessions of Spain and Portugal.[1] A month after the fall of the Berlin Wall in 1989, the Commission responded to Turkey's application negatively, citing the EU's recent enlargement and Turkey's relations with Greece in view of the ongoing Turkish–Greek conflict over the island of Cyprus as major impediments for Turkey's EU membership. It took a whole decade for the Commission's negative recommendation to the European Council to turn affirmative.

Meanwhile, the break-up of the Soviet Union and debates about what shape the EU's political future might take challenged EU leaders. The enlargement policy was pronounced in 1991 to tackle these problems.[2] Dubbed the EU's 'soft power' (Nye 2004), 'enlargement' became the key policy to bring political stability and capitalist dynamism to the EU's margins in post-Cold War Europe.[3] During the 1990s and early 2000s, this policy appeared to work. The Community (i.e. the EU in Eurospeak) deepened from an economic organisation to a fully fledged political union. Two waves of enlargement were seen in 1995, with the accessions of Austria, Sweden and Finland, and in 2004, with the 'Big Bang' enlargement when eight former socialist states from central and eastern Europe as well as Malta and Cyprus joined. Thereafter, however, proponents of the enlargement policy had to grapple to maintain support for it as public disenchantment steadily grew. In response, EU policy-makers engaged with European peripheries in a much tighter framework, which those on the receiving end of EU policies perceived to be as much pedagogical as serving political ends. Turkish negotiations for EU membership were initiated, in October 2005, within this political context.

The AKP's 'silent revolution' or neo-Ottomanism
as soft power *alla Turca*?

When the first AKP government officially broached the opening of accession negotiations with the EU, the party's ideologues were developing their own ideas of becoming a regional power, softly. Prime minister Erdoğan's much-admired long-term foreign-policy adviser Ahmet Davutoğlu (2001) reframed Turkey's geo-politics according to his 'strategic depth' theory. He argued that Turkey held politico-cultural influence over the peoples and countries in its wider region – stretching from the Middle East, to North Africa, the Caucasus and the Balkans – due to its Ottoman imperial past. A professor of political science and a political strategist, Davutoğlu advised Erdoğan for many years before becoming his first technocratic minister for foreign affairs as an unelected member of the third AKP government. When Erdoğan moved to the presidency, Davutoğlu replaced him as prime minister – only to be sacked by him twenty-one months later.

Many equated Davutoğlu's strategic depth theory – which gave Erdoğan's post-imperial vision intellectual clout – with 'neo-Ottomanism', a political and foreign policy programme of revival of the Ottoman imperial legacy. In circulation since the 1940s but attributed to a former *Financial Times* correspondent to Turkey, David Barchard, who suggested it as a foreign policy option in response to the post-1980 deteriorating Turkish–EU relations (Yanık 2016), neo-Ottomanism had become a viable policy direction under Davutoğlu. I heard first-hand accounts of the AKP's neo-Ottomanist vision from two party politicians. Both would fit Yavuz's (2016: 459) profile of 'Ottoman nostalgics':

> [They] share positive memories of the Ottoman period and use this imagined past to criticise the current secular nation-building project of the Republic. Without showcasing actual knowledge of Ottoman history, they are nevertheless united by an ethereal sense of lost dignity and respect, and a yearning for past grandeur. Their sentiment is backed by fictional constructions of culture rather than by the annals of professional, dispassionate historical research and inquiry.

More than mere nostalgia, however, my interlocutors' evocative renderings of history, culture and politics enmeshed ideology with state policy in the AKP's then new foreign policy outlook.

Once a former MP and a founding-member of Erdoğan's AKP, Zekeriya was no ordinary rank-and-file party affiliate but a sophisticated man and a firm believer in AKP's neo-Ottomanism. At the time of our interview he had been a member of Deniz's organisation and been re-elected to the Turkish parliament. As the Turkish member of the Parliamentary Assembly of the Organization for Security and Co-operation in Europe, he served in leading positions, which made me take him at his word. We met by chance on a sticky summer afternoon in 2007 at the Business World Foundation in Istanbul, a conservative platform for like-minded figures from Turkish business and politics. I was there to talk to Salim, the former Turkish minister of industry and trade, to whom I gained access through our shared regional ties. While Salim gave me an account of the AKP's 'party line' on Turkey's Europeanisation, his colleague, Zekeriya, revealed the discourse of party insiders. Whereas Salim's account was to justify his party's rule, Zekeriya's well rehearsed narrative disclosed the inner voice of the party, as would a ventriloquist.

During our talk, Salim explained that Turkey's domestic successes in politics and the economy and its successes in international politics were due to his government's neoliberal geo-economics and geo-politics. For him, Turkey's role as 'an investment hub, a centre of stability' compelled the EU to start accession negotiations. Salim mused:

> The world has come to see Turkey as a laboratory when we consider our good relations with Arabic countries and the new Turkic republics, and the changing perception of Islamic movements post-9/11 – a laboratory to observe the fusion of democracy and Islam sustainably.... The EU did not want to remain outside of these developments, and, as you know, negotiations were opened. An EU commissioner [his counterpart] told me: 'While we [the EU] didn't follow [your progress] due to our stereotypes, you [the AKP, Turkey] made a silent revolution'.

Pundits and party ideologues now refer to the AKP-era reforms in law, society and governance as Turkey's 'silent revolution' (Democratisation Policies Working Group 2013).

While Salim rehearsed his government's official policy on the EU of 'full membership', disclosing that the 'process' was more important than the product or membership ('If Turkey prepared for membership by fulfilling all EU criteria, EU membership would come naturally!'), his colleague and friend Zekeriya joined us. A fellow MP, Zekeriya was a key player in the AKP's stance on the EU.

We talked about whether Turkey and the EU had policies towards one another. According to EU member states' treatment (*tutum*) of Turkey, Zekeriya asserted, the government would slow down or speed up '[accession] relations with the EU'. He explained that AKP governments had come to the awareness of how significant it was to lobby the Commission's expert committees in their work of preparing technical positions for negotiations with Turkey and to place Turkish experts in them. Deniz's organisation had been the first to alert the Turkish government (before the AKP came to power) to this fact.

Zekeriya addressed Turkey's image problem as an obstacle to its EU membership. Between the lines he elucidated the background to the AKP's neo-Ottomanism and 'silent revolution':

> Fifteen out of twenty-five EU member states of today were once territories [*vilayet*] of the Ottoman Empire and [after independence] they had a psychological bruise [*eziklik*] vis-à-vis Turkey. We encounter problems related to this historical fact [while working with EU counterparts]: as soon as the roles are reversed, the relationship between the ruler and the ruled turns into one of hatred and vengeance. We encounter these problems as a nation with an imperial past, a nation that, as an empire, once mastered a large geographical area. Much like the Russians and others ... we cannot refuse our imperial past. Turkey if not a new state; this year [2007] is our 936th anniversary in these lands [referring to the Turkish occupation of Anatolia in 1071]. From the Seljuks [a Turkic empire] to the Ottomans, the state has endured without interruption. With the republican transition, we have said that

those we elect will now rule us. There are things we are to be proud of in our history and things we are to feel sorry about, like any other nation. But the fact remains: we oppressed no one! We can't change the Turkish image [in the European mind] by ourselves but our people right now need to relax and get over their own bruises due to self-critiquing. At the root of the problem of our self-critiquing lies the fact that we came from a culture of empire. Rural folks who may not have seen or lived in a city before would talk about world affairs with great ease; for the culture of governing big [as an empire] has been infused in their genes, such that their worldview enables this kind of worldly perspective. But we still haven't got over the fact that eighty-four years ago [before the founding of modern Turkey in 1923] our land mass was twelve million square kilometres, and now it's seven hundred and eighty thousand, not even one-twelfth of what it was before! We say, 'I should not have [fallen] like this'. For the last 200 years, Turks have continuously lost [land]. This feeling of loss led our people to severe self-criticism and the build-up of a contusion. We go through this fear of losing in our relations with the West as well. We approach the West with scepticism and always worry about whether the West will fool us again or whether we will lose [land, power, etc.] again. To constantly lose and lose so big led us to this complicated psyche which we need to overcome.

In this long tirade, Zekeriya blended self-Orientalism with biological essentialism and warped, partisan historicism. AKP politicians' neo-Ottomanism was in many ways a conservative attempt to heal bruised egos, which the wounded politician interpreted as damage to the nation, both at home and abroad.

Even though the 'silent revolution' at home and the neo-Ottomanist 'strategic depth' abroad arguably did not turn Turkey into a new regional power in the medium or long term, its architects imagined it would serve as a therapeutic device for many at home, like AKP politicians who harboured a deep-rooted trauma concerning 'the lost Empire'. In the short run, however, the 'silent revolution' boosted Erdoğan's presidential ambitions, which eventually led to his programme of technocratic presidential authoritarianism, dubbed the 'new Turkey'.

Nye's soft power theory, one may argue, failed, too when, post-9/11, world leaders returned to the use of hard force to solve disagreements. The EU adopted enlargement as a soft power tool; yet, after the Big Bang enlargement, some argued, EU citizens and states grew tired of it. They developed enlargement *fatigue* as they eventually became tired of the EU itself, attested by their low participation in EU elections and lack of trust in Brussels. After the UK voted to leave the EU in the referendum of 2016, support for the EU grew again across Europe, but not enough to counter the EU's democratic deficit (Kroet 2017). Turkey, on the other hand, moved further away from its twentieth-century foreign policy target of Westernisation *cum* Europeanisation. That is, public support for Turkey's EU integration has plummeted both in Turkey and in EU member states since the election of the AKP government in 2002. Meanwhile president Erdoğan has grown increasingly authoritarian. Equipped with a political ideology that serves him well, Erdoğan uses neo-Ottomanism as soft power to reorganise state bureaucracy at home and Turkey's foreign relations abroad. During his more than two decades of public service with a populist agenda (beginning in 1994 as mayor of Istanbul), the 'government' has gradually replaced the 'state', to the point where his party and presidency have become a synecdoche for the government. Today, Turkey is a sharply divided society run by a president and his party-state.

But how were these high-political developments manifested on the ground? How did they affect the day-to-day power–interest negotiations among bureaucrats, diplomats, lobbyists and other actors while accession negotiations dissipated? Did diplomats and lobbyists develop enlargement *fatigue* or turn neo-Ottomanist or authoritarian themselves? While actors negotiated the terms and conditions of Turkey's EU membership, what dynamics framed their negotiations and set the parameters of their bargaining and brokerage of interests? How, in three decades, could EU–Turkey negotiations move from relative enthusiasm to outright resistance among Turkish citizens and lawmakers, as the epigraph to Part II suggests? Scrutinising the EU's enlargement policy as a means of governance, this chapter responds to these questions with a microanalysis of the mutually constitutive relationship between technical prerequisites and political negotiations over Turkey's EU membership. I identify them as part of the technopolitics of the meta-policy (a policy that informs other policies) of EU enlargement and its pedagogical implementation during Turkey's EU accession negotiations. I go on to analyse the Turkish and other candidate countries' reactions to the EU's accession pedagogy. I argue that, in the AKP's 'new Turkey', Turkish diplomats' and lobbyists' post-imperial defiance of the EU's accession pedagogy was tactical. In the end, however, their actions and discourses contributed to their disengagement from Eurocracy.

Technopolitics of a meta-policy

The EU is often said to suffer from a democratic deficit and is criticised for imposing technocratic politics from above. The concept of 'democratic deficit' became popular during the run-up to the first elections to the European Parliament, in 1979. It refers to a situation where democratic institutions purportedly fall short in representing their constituents, often because of complicated, hidden or technocratic decision-making processes (Marquand 1979). Supplementing democratic deficit, the charge of technocratic politics refers to the rule of experts over democratic institutions and processes of consensus and compromise. In a world where the elected politicians and unelected experts (say, of bureaucracy) vie for power and authority over what constitutes 'the common good', technocratic politics refers to the rule of the unelected. Technocrats receive their authority to rule over the 'mess' of 'chaotic pluralist democracy, where pressure groups, mass movements and self-interested politicians divert the political system from the common good' (Radaelli 1999: 6–7), from their capacity to identify problems and actions to fix them through reason, rather than popular will.

A critical perspective on technocratic politics calls attention to the double movement through which technology shapes and is shaped by politics. In her study of the technopolitics culture of nuclear power in France, Gabrielle Hecht (2000 [1998]: 15) described the rule of experts as the 'strategic practice of designing or using technology to constitute, embody, or enact political goals … a practice of using … [technology] in political processes and/or toward political aims'. In

Hecht's analytics, technology and the 'technical' refer broadly to 'artifacts as well as non-physical, systematic methods of making or doing things' (Hecht 2009: 15; see also Mitchell 2002: 42–3). Through the double movement of technology's shaping and being shaped by politics, however, technocratic politics breeds a paradox: its efficacy depends on the larger political framework in which it forms (Hecht 2009: 90). Technocrats gain their power and authority from expert knowledge, but expertise is not in and of itself a defining condition for technocratic politics: we recognise technocratic politics in operation only when people put their technical expertise to work for political ends, that is, when they design technologies with particular political goals in mind, which are then embedded in these artefacts and practices (see Winner 1980). In its engagement with Turkey, I argue, the EU's resort to technocratic politics was as much to instil desired policy behaviour on Turkey's part as to remedy the EU's presumed democratic deficit.

The EU is not (yet) a technocracy in the absolute sense of the term but technocratic forces and tendencies there have long sought to resolve political contention through decisions and policy-making practices that rely on technology. The Commission, the EU's executive organ with an exclusive mandate to formulate policy and the main arbiter of the EU's enlargement policy, is the most technocratic institution of the EU. In a technocratic regime where technical experts formulate policies and inform decisions taken at the top, lobbying, if defined broadly as influencing policy processes from outside of the mandated group, appears to be counterintuitive. But when considering representation of specific interests among technocrats, lobbying in the form of channelling technical expertise makes great sense. To that end, the Commission is thus the most lobbied EU institution. My focus in this chapter is on the technical artefacts and technocratic/technopolitical practices the Commission engineered to tame public contention over EU enlargement, as well as their implications for the work of other experts in the Council, and on Turkish (and other candidates') responses to their implementation.

Policy ethnographers have scrutinised a range of EU policies which they have viewed as political technologies or technologies of governance (for a review, see Firat 2014). The EU's enlargement policy, in contrast, has not attracted much ethnographic attention. In what follows, I analyse this meta-policy from a techno-political perspective. Technopolitics offers the critical vocabulary and grammar I encountered in the field while working with my Turkish interlocutors, who often expressed their discontent with how their EU counterparts tried to manage Turkey. But my Turkish interlocutors' contention was not with technopolitics as a technology of governance, for, as agents of state technopolitics (Scott 1998), they already excelled in this form of rule. Their discontent was due to being subjected to this pedagogical treatment, when elsewhere they were its implementers.[4] By pedagogy, I mean an uneven power relationship, as in teacher–student relations, where those on the receiving end of EU norms, guidelines and laws feel like these are being imposed on them as if they were being taught in school. As in school, however, some students are unrulier than others.

Of course, the EU does not officially pronounce its relationship with third countries as a teacher–pupil relationship. But evidence from the Commission,

Council and member state diplomats' accounts, and accounts of government representatives from former candidate countries and their Turkish contemporaries, attest otherwise. A pedagogical approach towards candidate countries reportedly began post-1989 (Christoffersen 2007). The Commission systematised this pedagogical approach when Croatia and Turkey began membership talks in 2005 as much to overcome the disenchantment among EU members towards further enlargement as to actually modify either country's behaviour.

Towards those ends, many EU officials preferred the use of familial metaphors in referring to candidate countries, while they characterised EU integration as 'initiation into the European family' and a 'rite of passage' (Bellier 2004; Borneman & Fowler 1997). Such familialism and other forms of collegiality, in the main, mask a deeper problem running through the relations between the Commission and candidate countries. This problem stems from the unequal power relations between so-called partners in the accession process. The enlargement policy promised EU leaders a soft power tool for influencing a candidate country's progress towards Europeanisation, but it also instituted a pedagogical relationship between EU member states and candidates. The Turkish case presented a challenge to this EU-purported dogma of familialism and collegiality at another level. Familial metaphors are largely absent in the Turkish case, except the marriage metaphor, which suggests a voluntary act of association between equal partners, which the Turkish actors took as leverage to negotiate on a par with the EU.

The accession pedagogy manifests itself most blatantly in the anti-case of Turkey's bid for EU membership, since Turkish representatives, unlike those of other accession candidates, put up considerable resistance to playing the role of pupil and often defied the Commission's demands for policy changes to align Turkey with EU law and practice. My analysis of the EU's enlargement policy manifested in the technopolitics of EU accession negotiations and the Turkish reactions to them suggests that despite the marriage metaphor, pedagogy better explains EU–Turkey relations, pulsing with world political macro-developments and emphases on power dynamics.

Accession negotiations are in the main a two-part process. Candidate countries first go through a techno-bureaucratic procedure in which they undergo the EU's scrutiny and receive the 'know-how' of governing in EU ways, which usually takes five to six years, if the precedent of previous EU candidates is an indicator. Subsequently, the European Parliament, the parliaments of EU member states and the candidate country sign an international agreement and ratify it, which may require referenda.

The candidate country's room for manoeuvre is limited during accession negotiations. It must agree to the timeframe in which it will make its national laws compatible with EU law. This is called 'harmonisation' in Eurospeak, as in tuning two musical instruments so that they play the same note at the same time. 'Accession negotiations' are thus a misnomer because candidates have no power to change the *acquis*. They can only negotiate how much time they get to keep the EU *acquis* at bay before it modifies, or in cases of disagreement overwrites, national laws ('transposition' in Eurospeak). Moreover, candidates cannot 'cherry-pick' the *acquis* by accepting some parts and leaving out others (Sajdik & Schwarzinger 2008; Ülgen 2005). As such, accession negotiations are not conversations among equals, aiming at a new joint formation, but more like a development programme whereby the candidates must 'improve' their ways of governance and statecraft to earn membership of the EU.

Accession negotiations are 'technically' conducted between EU member states; during their meetings the Commission brokers on behalf of candidate countries (Christoffersen 2007; Gottfried & Györkös 2007). In the process of negotiating the terms and conditions of third-country relations with the EU, the Commission is the primary actor and agent acting on behalf of EU member states during meetings with candidates and on behalf of candidates during internal EU meetings. Even though the non-EU countries technically must consent to its decisions, the Commission outlines and supervises the steps they are to take, a process to which the Council (i.e. all EU member states) must ultimately agree. In these negotiations, the Commission has to act doubly, as the representative of common member state positions and as the representative of the candidate country.

Throughout its history of institutionalisation, this double role helped the Commission reinforce its representative functions and power. In 1998, the Commission established the Task Force for the Accession Negotiations to negotiate with Hungary, Poland, Estonia, the Czech Republic, Slovenia and Cyprus. In early 1999, a newly established directorate general (DG; a ministry-like organisation within the Commission) for enlargement with more human resources and financial capabilities replaced this task force (Sajdik & Schwarzinger 2008). Turkey moved on to this unit's agenda in December 1999, after the conferral of candidacy. A little over a decade later, the Commission had reduced the priority it had once given to EU enlargement, due perhaps to the said enlargement fatigue. Merging the enlargement and neighbourhood policy portfolios, then Commission president Jean-Claude Juncker revamped DG Enlargement in 2014 as DG Neighbourhood and Enlargement Negotiations. The term 'policy cannibalism', referring to a situation where a set of policy actions eats up resources and enthusiasm vital for another, may better characterise this situation. It seems that the EU's interests in countries beyond its political borders had led it to revise its external relations and policy instruments, as the European neighbourhood policy has 'cannibalised' the accession prospects of some EU candidates while opening room for others to join the neighbourhood, albeit without a ready prospect of political integration with the EU.[5]

'Politically', on the other hand, EU enlargement and the accession of new members are negotiated because of their ramifications for domestic audiences in EU member states and candidate countries. Accession negotiations follow a technical procedure but they are ultimately a political process that depends on 'political will', as all of my interlocutors from both sides indicated, though blaming the lack thereof on each other. Politicians' statements express this political will, but so do negotiations behind closed doors among their diplomats, bureaucrats and lobbyists. It is due to this political meaning of application for EU membership that the EU and candidate countries keep using the term 'negotiation' in their relations with one another.

The boundaries between the technical and the political understandings of accession negotiations are much blurrier than any neat identification as private (between state representatives, behind closed doors) and public (openly discussed by many and not just by heads of states, in public spaces) would allow. In their study of historical changes in health-care policy in western Europe and the United States, sociologists Paul Starr and Ellen Immergut (1987) found that public policies are heavily influenced by competing forces of politicisation and technification, between which, in different historical moments corresponding to major crises in society, competing interests generate push and pull. 'Technical' here refers to issues or practices that have recognised boundaries and that have moved 'out of political discussion or control', while 'political' refers to issues and practices that remain contested and open for negotiation (Starr & Immergut 1987: 221–2; see also Barry 2001).

The technical–political dynamic has been interrogated by scholars of critical development and dispute settlement, who see experts' deliberations over how to render issues technical as anti-political or as having depoliticising effects. Anthropologists James Ferguson (1990) and Tania Li (2007) have both argued that the depoliticisation of development aims at muting public discussion, as if only harmony and consensus exist between those whom development projects target and those who design, authorise and execute them (Garsten & Jacobsson 2013). Laura Nader (1996) called this form of power 'coercive harmony' and discussed how colonisers, missionaries, and wealthy and stronger states used it to coerce the colonised, indigenous, poor, powerless or weaker states into seeking justice through bilateral dispute settlement platforms with compromise as the goal, often to the disadvantage of the latter. But those on the recipient end of development and dispute settlement programmes are equally capable of manipulating the boundaries between the technical and the political, as Nader also remarked (see Müller 2011). In cases with subtler power inequalities, such as EU–Turkey affairs, one cannot easily identify the technifiers and politicisers as in developmentalist and compromise-reaching processes. As any issue at any point is open to the push and pull by both forces, actors from both sides engage in technification and politicisation whenever they believe it fits their interests. If we agree on my take of Turkish Europeanisation as a development and compromise project, the Turkish anti-case for EU membership is an example of how the push and pull between technifiers and politicisers operate on the ground.

Since the latest round of EU enlargement, further enlargement, and the Turkish bid for EU membership especially, have generated greater public contention and have become politicised in both EU member states and Turkey. To counter this, the Commission has developed new methods and instruments. When examined collectively, these policy artefacts make up the ethos of the EU's pedagogical engagement with candidates. As I discuss below, the technical devices and mechanisms invented for Turkish Europeanisation (and applied to Croatia until it acceded to the EU) often became the means for politicisation, which, in the case of the Commission and its enlargement policy, generated further need for technical intervention by experts and for a tightening of the grip of the enlargement policy.

Below I demonstrate how the technopolitics of EU enlargement helped disengage Turkish diplomats and lobbyists from their EU counterparts and how the former used it in return for their tactical purposes, as diplomats and lobbyists moved back and forth between technification and politicisation of the terms and conditions of Turkey's prospective EU membership.

The policy in action

A policy can be narrowly defined as a discursive universe in which its actors and agents target selected issues for (governmental) intervention with an apparent concern for the common good, and devise a toolkit to that end. From a critical perspective, however, a policy 'is first and foremost an attempt to understand and decode a complex reality' (Radaelli 1999: 41). Policy-making therefore requires a critical capacity to abstract and simplify what policy actors deem to be the 'reality out there', to shape it into instruments like laws, regulations, advisory reports and information notes. These instruments are material representations of what a policy is and embody how a policy works (or ought to work) in real life, since policy workers turn to them for proper interpretation of public policies. These tools are often meticulously documented and communicated to those who are targeted by the policy (Apthorpe & Gasper 1996). The act of documenting is in and of itself a bureaucratic act. The curious fact behind this bureaucratic act of putting into the written word how a policy should function is that it also makes any policy 'look real', regardless of any concerns about its implementation or efficacy. I consider the EU's enlargement policy within this framework and will walk the reader through different steps of this policy in action vis-à-vis the Turkish candidacy.

Pre-negotiation screening and chapter negotiations

Commission experts first examine the laws and the administrative system of the candidate country vis-à-vis the EU *acquis* and compile a set of questions for the candidate government to respond to. Upon the latter's response, Commission experts identify necessary changes the candidate country's government has to undertake and catalogue them under thirty-five 'negotiating chapters'. They prioritise issues that require immediate and long-term action by the candidate government – respectively known as 'opening benchmarks', the preliminary conditions for substantial negotiations over a chapter to begin, and 'closing benchmarks', the final conditions for negotiations to be closed. This process is called screening in Eurospeak. After screening, the Commission delivers its evaluation in a report to the Council, which communicates benchmarks to the candidate country. Screening reports function much like scorecards or school reports.

Because of the ever-growing corpus of the EU *acquis* with which candidates have to comply, the Commission concentrates on substantial norms. The Commission advises transparency in the event of problems of transposition, control or application. The Commission transmits in advance lists of all legal instruments in each chapter to the candidates. As it prepares its national position, the candidate government reacts to the Commission's list of demands with a compilation of problematic or doubtful aspects that its experts identify. On these aspects, the negotiators of the candidate government request time with which to comply, or 'derogations' in Eurospeak (Sajdik & Schwarzinger 2008). Technically, only after the candidate government 'satisfactorily' meets these benchmarks can accession negotiations begin (and end) on a given chapter.

In Turkey's case, screening served two purposes. Public servants from the Commission and their Turkish counterparts met in Brussels twice for each negotiating chapter, to engage in a comparative legislative assessment. Between October 2005 and the end of 2006, around 2,000 Turkish officials met their Commission counterparts for sixty-six screening meetings and a meeting on the Lisbon Strategy (TEPAV 2006). The Commission evaluated Turkey's progress according to EU criteria based on accounts of EU and Turkish policy experts and attached Turkey's progress to the overall success of enlargement policy. Limited to the public sector, screening meetings were to provide a suitable platform on which a common scheme of interpretation of the EU *acquis* could emerge between Commission officials and Turkish administrators over the contention of *acquis* adoption. Meanwhile, these screening meetings were to help EU and Turkish officials develop cultural understandings of one another.

Screening officially began for Turkey and Croatia in October 2005. By the end of 2006, Commission experts had screened all negotiating chapters and delivered its screening reports to the Council. After screening, negotiations on particular chapters begin, if both parties agree. During the heyday of the negotiations (2007–8), nine chapters were opened for negotiation. As of 30 June 2016, the number of open chapters was sixteen, with one provisionally closed. Out of a total thirty-three actually negotiated chapters, twenty-five were through the Council. The remaining eight were waiting to be benchmarked. Three of these chapters are among the eight that have remained blocked since the European Council decision of 11 December 2006 in response to Turkey's refusal to recognise Cyprus as an EU member state and open its ports to maritime trade and traffic from Cyprus. In Brussels, many communicate with one another through the use of EU vernacular, such as chapter numbers, as if speaking in code. Knowing and talking in chapter numbers contributes to the symbolic, discursive authority of accession experts.

When discussing progress during negotiations EU politicians, bureaucrats and policy experts often referred to the ethos of the membership process as being larger than simple chapter openings and closings. For their Turkish counterparts, the process of negotiating accession quickly turned into an algebra test and a countdown of the number of chapters that had been opened to negotiation and how many others they could open in the near future before getting into more troublesome negotiations, for example on the free movement of people, which would require heavy politicking.

Even in the case of the opened chapters, no real progress has been registered in terms of the preparation of Turkish national positions and their consideration by EU member states. Because the EU *acquis* is a dynamic body of law and is changing faster in some policy areas than in others, when accession negotiations are stretched out in time, EU policy workers demand that negotiations be revisited if EU law has since evolved. In the Turkish case, this adds further complications for Turkish policy workers who already have difficulty meeting the Commission's initial reform demands.[6] The Commission continues to monitor the legislative assessment and technical preparations for harmonisation and transposition of the EU *acquis* into Turkish law by way of a complex matrix of non-binding soft law tools that are commonly known as benchmarks and progress reports.

Benchmarking and progress reports

In the early 2000s, the Commission introduced a novel technique called 'open method of coordination' to 'calibrat[e] performance' among EU member states to create a policy convergence in the Union and to encourage member states to learn from each other's best practices 'purely by force of example' (European Commission 2001a: 7).[7] Paragraph 37 of the Presidency Conclusions of the Lisbon European Council, 23 and 24 March 2000, explained that performance evaluations were 'the means of spreading best practice and achieving greater convergence towards the main EU goals' (Council of the European Union 2000). The European Council asked the Commission to implement this method which it intended it to bring about:

> A mutual learning process designed to help Member States to progressively develop their own policies, [which] involves fixing guidelines for the Union combined with specific timetables for achieving the goals which they set in the short, medium and long terms; establishing, where appropriate, quantitative and qualitative indicators and benchmarks against the best in the world and tailored to the needs of different Member States and sectors as a means of comparing best practice; translating these European guidelines into national and regional policies by setting specific targets and adopting measures, taking into account national and regional differences; periodic monitoring, evaluation and peer review organised as mutual learning processes. (Council of the European Union 2000; see also European Commission 2001a)

The Lisbon Conclusions indicated that third countries could take part in the open method of coordination if they wished. But with EU enlargement, participation in the open method of coordination was not as voluntary for accession candidates as suggested. Designed primarily for EU member states, the Commission applied benchmarking to Turkey and Croatia to calibrate their accession performance (Tulmets 2010). Today, the Commission and the Council evaluate Turkey's accession performance by means of benchmarks, which are there to indicate where negotiations on each chapter could begin and end. Benchmark assessments take up a large part of the Commission's annual progress reports on Turkey and negotiations between the Commission and EU member states in the Council.

The Commission began to prepare progress reports on Turkey long before the EU opened accession negotiations. EU member states asked the Commission to draft a regular assessment report on Turkey for the first time during the 1998

Cardiff European Council, at which they initially agreed to take Turkey as an EU candidate. The Commission subsequently prepared its first Turkey report in October 1998 (Sajdik & Schwarzinger 2008). Since then, it has prepared progress reports on Turkey and has made them public annually.[8]

Most countries that enter into a partnership or collaboration with the EU accede (sometimes reluctantly) to the EU's authority in definitional matters of what may constitute best practice. Even when the EU is not a direct party to candidate countries' relations with other sovereign entities, it remains a pedagogical (and hegemonic) power that strives (and mostly succeeds) in determining the terms and conditions of relations between third countries, especially in their economic cooperation and trade relations.[9]

Although the Union's pedagogical engagement with countries in the wider region has been an evolving process, the EU insists on dealing with 'each candidate on its own merits', while the 'same criteria apply to all' (Council of the European Union 1993: 11). This approach is part and parcel of what could be called the Commission's dogma, which stipulates that EU accession is a technical, procedural process whereby candidate countries are in no position to negotiate the terms and conditions of their accession. Such a technical view, however, masks the political nature of these negotiations. Between differentiation and standardisation, the Commission often applies descriptive sanitation when outlining technical steps and instruments of accession negotiations that are tailored to common procedure and individual performance at the same time. This fact led one Commission official to characterise progress reports, wherein the Commission's descriptive sanitation is most evident, essentially as 'political documents' (de Lobkowicz 2001).

Drafting progress reports is in and of itself a process. Line DGs prepare draft reports on progress related to negotiating chapters that fall under their responsibility. In June of each year, Daniela, my contact at the DG Internal Market, which was responsible for six and a half chapters, supervised the drafting of chapter assessments. She coordinated between her boss at DG Internal Market and the DG Enlargement's Turkey unit. She also liaised between her DG and the Commission's delegation in Ankara, on the one hand, and between her DG and diplomats stationed at EU representations of member states and Turkey in Brussels. Between June and September, revision suggestions came to her inbox. She streamlined them by September. By mid-autumn, her colleagues at DG Enlargement pieced together the Commission's progress report from input from the DGs.

Major interest holders from Turkey and Europe lobby the Commission during this timeframe to get their input into these reports, DG Enlargement being their main target. The Commission pre-negotiates progress reports with Turkey in an informal manner. DGs contribute to the making of the final report by drafting their sections, a draft of which they may show to Turkish diplomats and lobbyists in Brussels. Turkish politicians pay lip service to these reports, referring to them as 'mirror images' of Turkey.

Murat, a diplomat from Turkey's delegation in Brussels, interpreted his government's access to draft reports as an indication of the special nature and historical maturity of EU–Turkey relations, given that such reports (unlike the final ones) are generally not circulated. That Turkey had 'privileged' access to the EU's textual repository was proof of its power and priority for the EU over other candidates. A reference to maturity carried the assumption that other candidate countries had no such access. Having access to draft copies of progress reports prior to their publication marked those who had this type of access as resourceful. Rumours of illicit access were rampant. Lobbyists and journalists fought to get their hands on the draft reports. Zehra was exceptionally good at that.

Communicated through screening and progress reports, benchmarking is intended to guide third-country governance performance. Studies of the application of EU benchmarking reveal various pedagogical qualities. In the case of the Euro-Mediterranean Partnership, Schmid (2004: 403) observed that the Commission distinguishes between '"good" and "bad" partners' by 'persuasion ... [and] not coercion' (Schmid 2004: 416).[10] The rhetoric of good/bad partners is familiar to critical ethnographers of global development practice (Abélès 2011; Gould & Marcussen 2004; Harper 2000; Mosse 2005; Mosse & Lewis 2005; Stirrat 2000; Wedel 1998). But pedagogical engagements are not limited to socio-economic development. Coles (2007) found that the EU's interventions to promote electoral democracy in European peripheries, such as Bosnia-Herzegovina, exhibited this character. Similarly, Teivainen (2009) critiqued EU practices of promoting democracy via election observation missions in Latin America for establishing power relations between the 'North' and the 'South' that advantaged the former.

During my fieldwork, I encountered additional factors influencing the EU's pedagogical conduct, factors which speak more to the internal dynamics of the Union. First, EU politicians and bureaucrats viewed benchmarking as a necessary tool to generate domestic public support for further enlargement, especially after the accessions of Bulgaria and Romania attracted much criticism, due to the EU institutions' overly optimistic assessments of how well these candidates had prepared for membership. As EU enlargement became contentious, benchmarking was exercised as a panacea. Doris Pack, a German Conservative MEP, speaking at an event promoting Croatian business and EU membership, for example, explained to the audience that some European politicians (including her) felt that they 'cannot sell further enlargements to [their] constituency without the benchmarking system', and that they had to assure voters that 'we are not going to do it the way we did it with Bulgaria.'[11]

Second, benchmarks were a means for making EU candidates 'look like they take real leadership in charge of a policy', as the Luxembourgian diplomat Benoit explained to me. When introducing (and marketing) his DG's progress report on candidates, the then enlargement commissioner, Olli Rehn, told a mixed audience of member state and candidate country representatives during a meeting in the European Economic and Social Committee that benchmarks were tools to test not only the candidate's preparations for accession but also its sincerity: 'If you are serious about accession, you have to prove that you can achieve it.'[12] It was not exactly clear from Pack, Benoit and Rehn how the candidates could 'prove' they were worthy of EU membership. But Benoit's tacit reference to symbolic politics (the art of being seen doing something), or a carefully curated dramatic performance that fits to the EU's 'economy of appearance' (Tsing 2000), well indicates what the measure for candidate states may be.

Relatedly, benchmarking introduced a layer of discipline where candidates like Turkey had to prove to the Commission that the government's reform activities were not fabricated but were real and tangible efforts to meet EU demands or at least to display a willingness to do so. Usually, harmonisation was considered sufficient. In cases of contested candidacies, such as that of Turkey, however, the Commission demanded both changes on paper *and* 'implementation' or proof of reformed policy application.

Reform efforts appeared especially unconvincing if they were stretched over time. Benchmarking reinforced suspicion and mistrust when candidates failed to assure the Commission that they were serious about the reforms required by the EU. This was especially so in the Turkish case, where failure to satisfy the Commission raised suspicions that the government's EU priorities differed from the EU's priorities for Turkey – regardless of whether they were well founded (and sometimes they were). In cases of mistrust and suspicion between the Commission and Turkey, 'certain portions of the *acquis* [became] economically and socially sensitive and politically impossible', as Kerim, a fellow diplomat and Murat's senior, commented to a group of Turkish women entrepreneurs during their visit to the delegation. From the Turkish perspective, some benchmarks appeared trivial, facile matters, or 'unreasonable' (read: political). Kerim exclaimed in dismay to his audience: 'Eighty-seven benchmarks for six chapters!'

Insider accounts demonstrate how benchmarking politicised accession negotiations. The first chapter Turkey and Croatia managed to open to negotiation was on science and research. This chapter was supposed to be an easy one, for it did not require opening benchmarks. While still being discussed at the Council Working Group on Enlargement (see next chapter), the Commission proposed to open and provisionally close this chapter. The French representative argued for a closing benchmark. The Commission disagreed, stating that such a closing benchmark could not simply be invented (Sajdik & Schwarzinger 2008: 364). Discussions continued, with this representative arguing against a provisional closing by referring to the evolving nature of the *acquis* in view of common expectations that accession negotiations with Turkey would take longer. Meanwhile, others reiterated their governments' usual objections to Turkey. Representatives of the other member states found the solution by changing the common end clause from 'the EU may return to this chapter at an appropriate moment' to 'the EU *will*, if necessary, return to this chapter at an appropriate moment' (Sajdik & Schwarzinger 2008: 365, original emphasis). The only chapter Turkey has been able to close, to this day, is Chapter 25, Science and Research, which was closed to negotiation in June 2006, when a technical fix tamed political interests.

Harmonisation and transposition of the EU *acquis communautaire*

The EU's common body of law (the *acquis* in Eurospeak) is composed of non-binding communications, recommendations and guidelines (i.e. 'soft *acquis*') and directives, decisions and regulations (i.e. 'hard *acquis*'), which are binding on member states. The Commission disseminates its work on EU enlargement and candidate countries to the public in a 'communication' format. A communication is 'a formal document in which the Commission outlines to the Council a general problem or the basic considerations for a later proposal of the Commission' (Sajdik & Schwarzinger 2008: 36n5). Unlike directives, which are addressed to member states, and decisions, which are for specified recipients, regulations are addressed to both member states and candidate states. The Commission has the authority to enforce hard *acquis* on member states but has no such authority on soft *acquis* issues (Snyder 1993). Neither can it impose the *acquis* on third countries. EU member states may renegotiate the *acquis*, albeit to a limited extent and after much hardship, and can appeal to the European Court of Justice in cases of dispute, which is not an option for candidates. Candidate countries have to comply with the EU law – and comply with it 'as is' – if they want to become EU member states. Harmonisation and transposition are thus the last steps before membership.

During the round of enlargement with central and eastern European countries, the *acquis* contained about 80,000 to 90,000 pages of legal text. Today, it contains over 120,000 pages. The *acquis* evolves (as does any dynamic body of law) as European integration matures. From the perspective of enlargement, one of the interesting effects on candidate countries was the increase in elements of the *acquis* with which they were expected to comply. The large corpus of the *acquis*, a great source of mystification for various observers, has been a great cause of grievance for Turkish policy workers. With its large volume of law from the *acquis*, the EU appeared to critics even more bureaucratic than Turkey, whose heavy bureaucracy had 'only 70,000 pages of legislation' (Akdoğan 2008: 5)! 'Integrating the *acquis* has become a tool in the hands of the Commission in its attempt to re-affirm the symbolic dimension of the Union' (Bellier 2004: 144). In the absence of external enforcement, displaying a willingness to comply with the EU *acquis* through discursive gestures is the first step towards membership.

Harmonisation and transposition require attention to 'the EU perspective', code for satisfying all member states. As a first step to legal approximation and alignment, translating the EU *acquis* into Turkish required resources. As I learned from Daniela and from Turkish *stagiaires* who interned at various DGs, Turkish bureaucrats in Ankara sometimes sent the revised law in their native language with apologetic notes attached to it, referring to the absence of technical assistance in translation services. A World Bank report in 2014 identified a 'notification deficit' between Ankara and Brussels. The Bank stated 'Turkey notifies just one-quarter the number of technical measures [it adopts] compared to Norway' (World Bank 2014: 27).

This deficit was a further challenge to negotiations. As one Commission official pointed out, translating the EU *acquis* and aligning national regulations to it is one thing, providing correct interpretations of it and making it comprehensible by Turkish bureaucrats is quite another. In the Commission's legal agenda, laws are to be simultaneously known, understood and practised. In its 2001 Turkey progress report, the Commission explained:

As is the case in previous Reports, 'progress' has been measured on the basis of decisions actually taken, legislation actually adopted, international conventions actually
ratified (with due attention being given to implementation), and measures actually
implemented. As a matter of principle, legislation or measures, which are in various
stages of either preparation or parliamentary approval, have not been taken into
account. This approach ensures equal treatment for all the candidate countries and
permits an objective assessment of each country in terms of its concrete progress in
preparing for accession. (European Commission 2001b: 7)

Here, the emphasis on the actuality of progress common to all candidate country
reports of the time was due to the fluctuations in the market of hope in which
candidate countries, including Turkey, bid. Yet, the meaning of actual progress
remained at best ambiguous, if not contested. Every year during report preparation season, Turkish diplomats showered their Commission counterparts with
prospective progress indicators, however anticipatory or unconvincing they
might be.

In reality, candidates do not have to comply fully with the *acquis* or they risk
'overtransposition' by doing it too much by the book, as my Commission interlocutors explained to me. In fact, overtransposition, or the application of EU laws
too literally and with no local adaptation, can be quite unsettling and begets more
problems for candidate governments. It is this nuance between sufficient transposition and overtransposition that seemed to trouble Turkish officials most. This
nuance was particularly important for them to tackle, since Turkish politicians
and legislators also faced contention that arose because the *acquis* appeared to
threaten their statecraft and governance culture and, through the process of pedagogy, turned them into de facto 'special partners'.

While Turkish legislators were busy with complying with the *acquis*, the EU's
communal body of law grew ever larger. Commission officials informed their
Turkish colleagues about major changes in EU legislation during subcommittee
meetings within the framework of what was called updated screening. Turkish
administrators also had access to certain community programmes and policy
expert groups, which allowed them greater exchange of information with EU
counterparts. Sometimes Turkey sought the Commission's approval of changes in
national laws more directly: some Commission officials were asked to supervise
the actual wording of the national legislation and check its compatibility with the
EU *acquis*. If they 'missed' or went overboard on these occasions, Turkish bureaucrats discovered legislative changes in the EU 'through reality', as one Commission
interlocutor summed it up. The World Bank 2014 report gave the following
example regarding the above scenario and the resulting constraints, in this case
regarding trade relations between the EU and Turkey:

Legislation pertaining to motor vehicles accounts for one-third of the *acquis* that
Turkey has yet to align via a via customs formalities. However, Turkey has adopted a
large body of vehicle regulation that has yet to be endorsed by the Commission since
DG Enterprise requires the full body of law to be translated into English and submitted jointly. Since the motor vehicle *acquis* has a large number of technical annexes,

> Turkey has been submitting pieces of the law but the European Commission cannot assess them until they receive the full set. Consequently, Turkey accepts EU-type approvals but cannot issue them itself. So Turkish manufacturers must rely on EU approvals to export their motor vehicles and parts to the EU, which is more costly than if these approvals could be issued in Turkey. (World Bank 2014: 37)

On the other hand, if it took longer for Turkish legislators to enact harmonis-ation and transposition, the Turkish version of the *acquis* ran the risk of differing from the actual EU *acquis*. This was especially the case for legislation that con-cerned greater sectoral interests and stakeholders, who intensely lobbied the legislators to pass a revision that would benefit their industry, even though it might substantially diverge from the *acquis* (see Chapter 5). One could encounter a similar discrepancy between the transposition and implementation of EU *acquis* in Turkey.

Rather than reading the above scenarios as symptomatic of actual discrepan-cies, I look at this apparent disagreement between law on paper and in practice through a productive lens.[13] Any such discrepancy, I would argue, indicates the opening of the space for politicking, while the *acquis* becomes a 'field of law' or 'juridical field' in EU–Turkey relations. In Pierre Bourdieu's terms, this 'juridical field' is as much 'the order of objective relations between actors and institutions in competition with each other for control of the right to determine the Law' as 'the site of [such] competition for the monopoly of the right to determine the law' (Bourdieu 1987: 816, 817). Within the juridical field of the EU *acquis* and its transposition into Turkish law, this rift is a 'confrontation among actors possessing a technical competence which is inevitably social and which consists essentially in the socially recognised capacity to interpret a corpus of texts sanctifying a correct or legitimised vision of the social world' (Bourdieu 1987: 817). Any so-called rift between the codification and interpretation/implementation of the law refers to different forces that envision technical/political interpretations of what the law and the policy ought to be.

But how exactly did the Commission measure the difference between har-monisation and transposition or between transposition and implementation of the EU *acquis*? According to one interlocutor, the Commission gives candidates 'clues' about its interpretation, sense, position and direction of practice on the transposition and implementation of the EU *acquis*. One such clue was given in the context of the Commission's propping up support for enlargement: 'While it is important that European Community legislation is transposed into national legis-lation, it is even more important that the legislation is implemented effectively through appropriate administrative and judicial structures. This is a prerequisite of the *mutual trust* required by EU membership' (European Commission 2001c: 8, my emphasis). During my fieldwork, I often encountered this curious trope called 'trust' – a trope I observed to run amok in Brussels concerning EU–Turkey relations – as my interlocutors from both sides lamented its absence time and time again. Following Karl W. Deutsch et al. (1957), scholars have argued that trust plays an important role in region-building, as opposed to the *realpolitik* school, which advocates no place for interpersonal feelings and perceptions like 'trust' in international relations (Carey 2017) (for more discussion on (mis)trust, see Chapter 5). Whereas my EU interlocutors seemed to follow Deutschean affective international politics, my Turkish interlocutors were keener on the *realpolitik* approach. Whether it makes sense from an international relations perspective, trust, or rather the lack of it, makes anthropological sense when one considers all the energy, time and money that went into instilling a 'sense of community', the 'we-feeling' Deutsch et al. (1957) talked about, between Turkish and EU policy workers and influencers, but that had ended up alienating these groups from one another – a theme I return to at the end of this chapter, after a brief look at how other candidates responded to the EU's accession pedagogy.

Comparative pedagogies

Critical pedagogy scholars have called attention to the difference between pedagogy (from the Greek *país*, genitive παιδός, *paidos* and άγω [*ágō*], literally meaning 'the leading of the child') and education (from Latin *educare*, 'to raise up' and 'to lead out') to explain how actors perceive and position themselves and others in this relationship. Capturing this difference, Too (1998: 5) argued that the concept of pedagogy changed in the twentieth century to include rather than exclude the pedagogue or the maker of the rules of education. Learning from best practices of one another invited the pedagogue to enter into the pedagogical network. To this, I add the active but not so voluntary participation of pupils, since the EU's accession pedagogy requires the active participation of candidate countries in this learning process, wherein power relations are, from the latter's perspective, recast to their inconvenience.

Studying a series of diplomatic exchanges between Hungary and the Commission early in the Hungarian accession negotiations, sociologist József Böröcz (2000: 871) concluded that the essence of the EU's strategy was 'integration without inclusion: participation in the production systems, and appendance to consumption markets of EU corporations without the attendant political, economic, social and cultural rights conferred by European Union citizenship'. As such, the accession pedagogy instituted an unmistakable hegemonic relationship. It conferred a trainee status on candidates, whereby the premise was that the EU and its 'best-practising' member states as instructors had much to teach. It dictated that candidates must provide quick responses to EU demands for reform and permit full disclosure to and detailed inspection by EU institutions, even after the candidate country acceded to the EU – indeed, the EU monitors Bulgaria and Romania well into their post-accession terms in the areas of justice and internal affairs, which these countries did not fulfil before joining the EU in 2007.

This performance measurement ultimately produces an unequal relationship of power between member countries and those seeking membership. One Commission interlocutor recounted a scene in a meeting during an enlargement round wherein a German (member state) representative undermined a Hungarian (candidate country) representative's account of past Hungarian practices that were clearly not best practices. The scene created a rather unpleasant situation for the Hungarian representative.

In terms of relations between them, the accession pedagogy put candidates in a race against each other. This created a deep sense of failure when progress was found wanting. Different candidate countries engaged with the accession pedagogy differently. Hungarian negotiators, for instance, tried to tame this political asymmetry by saying, 'if we want to develop a modern country, a normal country, then the implementation of European rules is not against our national interest. If our economy is absolutely integrated into the internal market, then their rules are our rules' (Gottfried & Györkös 2007: 205). According to Böröcz (2000), Hungary's tacit agreement with and internalisation of this power asymmetry was an important factor in its success in acquiring membership. Jacoby (1999) also argued that tacit agreement on the EU's pedagogy for the central and eastern European countries clearly depended on their confessions of weaknesses and failure, beginning as early as the screening phase.

Among those who sat through the accession experience, this sense of failure was more common than expected. It reflected the rift between being and becoming European (Bellier & Wilson 2000; Hudson 2000). Unlike their Hungarian colleagues, the Czech negotiators (Telicka & Bartak 2007: 144) openly reflected on this rift and the pedagogical management of negotiations by EU actors:

> It was psychologically difficult to become a pupil in the European classroom. The Czechs were not willing to assume the role of exotic tribesmen only recently accustomed to civilisation, which was attributed to them by some of the more ignorant commentators of the West. At the same time, many were unready to acknowledge that in several aspects that they badly needed to take some political lessons in democracy and economic policy, among other matters.

Czechs and Hungarians thus tried to domesticate the EU's accession pedagogy by analogising EU members' interests with their own.

Iceland, which is a member of European Free Trade Area (EFTA) and Schengen Area, applied, in July 2009, for EU membership. After three years of negotiating accession with the EU (2010–13), Iceland walked away from the negotiating table when the EU officials asked Icelanders to stop overfishing and to accept strict fishing quotas. Before they left the meeting, the Icelandic negotiators stated that Icelanders had 'more experience in fishing' than the European Union and that *they* 'could teach Brussels best practices' regarding fisheries policy (Euractiv 2013).

Defiant yet disengaging Turks

If the process of engaging with the EU carried its own pedagogy to discipline candidate governments – hastily dubbed as 'Europeanisation' – Turkey proved to be a difficult case, because its political, governmental and economic elites openly defied the EU's pedagogical approach. Nowhere did this more clearly manifest itself than in those parts of the accession process wherein EU bureaucrats presented some expected reforms as technicalities, while their Turkish counterparts tried to politicise them, and vice versa. Between Ankara and Brussels, the Turkish parliamentarians slowed down harmonisation with the EU *acquis* by keeping legislation at committee level and not passing it through parliament, which they had initially agreed to do. They also produced laws with wording and interpretation contradicting the EU *acquis*. Sometimes, after lobbying by business, those bureaucrats who drafted the text of the legislation left it ambiguous enough for its actual implementation to be counter to the *acquis* (Cebeci 2016). In the absence of proper instructions for implementation, lobbying had a greater impact than expected, as I discuss later in this book. In addition to regulatory, legislative and administrative defiance, Turkish actors discursively resisted the EU and defied its pedagogical approach towards them.

EU insiders recognised the Turkish response to the EU's accession pedagogy. As she reflected on Slovenia's negotiations with the EU, Sonja, a Slovenian diplomat, commented: 'When we were negotiating, we just accepted. We were always the first to make it [pass laws, meet benchmarks] even before the Commission had written it down. You [Turkey] can argue. They [Turkish representatives] sometimes say they are not happy with some things. Some member states are a bit nervous about it.'

A Commission official who worked on Turkish accession at a DG would have agreed. Using a rather grotesque analogy to compare Turkey's approach with that of previous candidates, off the record she confided: 'As if we [the EU] were the dog-jumpers at a circus, if we would have told some countries to jump, they would have jumped'. Her British colleague from another DG remarked that 'Bulgaria says, "come and please run our country because you do it better". Turkey doesn't say that. I don't think they ever will.'

Eliise, Sonja's Estonian colleague, compared Turkey and Croatia in terms of negotiating styles that refracted the technical-political dynamic I explained earlier:

> They [Turkish representatives] say there are countries in the Union that don't want Turkey in. Croats' approach is more technical. Turks don't understand that it's not an equal relationship, but that's the nature of the affair. People in the Union use the same approach [as Turkish representatives], so they don't like that. Sometimes it's about national interests: to take something, you give something.

The accession process is an exchange but not one among equals, for power is deeply embedded in the process, affecting the techno-bureaucratic relations of policy negotiators. The process does not add up to a real 'negotiation' for either party. Eliise further commented: 'I understand the Turkish way of thinking, but the *acquis* will not change according to Turkish legislation.' Yet, agents of Turkish accession tried to make this process a negotiation, and demanded that the EU recognise that Turkey was on a par with the Union, and that *the Union* 'give something to take something' from Turkey and acknowledge Turkey's failings only vis-à-vis its achievements in progress reports and during evaluations of whether the country sufficiently fulfilled benchmarks (see Chapter 6).

For the Hungarian policy-makers and negotiators, as sociologist József Böröcz (2000: 871) argued, what kept relations going despite 'drastic asymmetry' in power between their country and EU member states was 'the applicant state's tacit recognition of this strategy'. But what happens when a candidate country is unable or refuses to agree on certain key terms of its EU accession, as was often the case with Turkish politicians and their bureaucrats in accession negotiations?

Some Turkish officials politicised negotiations by spinning talk about their country's state identity. When I visited Merih, a Turkish diplomat, at her office inside the delegation and asked her how Turkey could demand 'equality' on a negotiating platform whose main premise was the maintenance of pedagogical relations, she responded:

> People from other representations [of new member states] tell us that they established structures [necessary for EU membership] easily. But they had none at all! What they did was to get out of a system, flatten it out and institute structures just like that [fingers snapped]! It's not the same for us. We have a *long-standing state tradition* [my emphasis]. They [the EU] demanded transparency; we opened ourselves all the way to our lungs. You know that decisions are made behind closed doors at home [Turkey]. Our job is much harder because we have to make reforms by integrating new structures with an existing system.

Whereas a demand for equality appears here as a trope of political psychology, Merih used state identity as a pretext for delaying EU reforms, that is, for reform inaction, affirming Turkey's difference from other candidates.

Turkish bureaucrats and politicians saw accession negotiations as a threat to their existing ways of governing, as they were deeply convinced that their governing practices worked. Sometimes existing laws and governing practices did indeed work best for Turkish society and an approximation to the EU *acquis* could cause social trouble. Acetone was a case in point. Unregulated in the EU, it is a popular substance of abuse among young people in Turkey, and the state regulates its sale. Turkish bureaucrats were reluctant to implement the EU *acquis* and secondary legislation (instructions on how to implement the *acquis*) to deregulate it.

At other times, Turkish actors' belief in the efficacy of their governing practices and their resistance to the accession pedagogy amounted to an anti-EU stance. They often evoked contradictory statements skewed between particularism and universalism in their resistance. A perfect example of this tension between Turkish difference from and commonality with European constituents was given by Şahin Mengü,[14] a Turkish politician and former deputy of the Cumhuriyet Halk Partisi (Republican People's Party) who summed up a sentiment that ran deep among the Turkish ruling elites across the political spectrum:

> The EU *cannot treat Turkey differently* to how it treats Romania or Bulgaria. It should treat us according to the *same criteria* it treats other candidates. It cannot make us the EU's social laboratory to test its emergent policies, like the policy on charitable foundations. The EU doesn't have a common Union policy on such foundations which it might ask us to comply with. We ask, which law on charitable foundations does it dictate we comply with? First, it should come up with a common policy, and only then demand that we comply with it. We say we have a *better policy* on

charitable foundations than that they impose on us. This is a subjective area; we have a policy which we argue suits us better. They should first *treat us equally*, then would we sit at the table to negotiate. The EU should *not see us like* Bulgaria. That country did not even have a law on trade, so the EU was able to open a blank page for them. It didn't matter to the Bulgarians which model they were asked to comply with. We are *different*; we have a practice of doing this business for seventy, eighty years. It *can't treat us like it treated* Bulgaria or Romania. ('Ankara Kulisi' ['Backstage Ankara]' CNNTürk, 23 May 2010, emphasis added)

This Turkish lawmaker saw accession negotiations as a threat to existing Turkish ways of governing, ways which he was deeply convinced work. In terms of the policy behaviour of lawmakers and diplomats like Merih, such resistance to EU reforms and accession pedagogy became two sides of the same coin. Inadvertently perhaps, their comparison of Turkey with EU member states and former candidates concretised the Turkish difference.

When I mentioned this Turkish 'exceptionalism' to Apostolos, a Greek diplomat who worked on energy issues at Greece's permanent representation to the EU, he pointed out the circular logic this exceptionalism bred in Brussels: 'Turkey presents itself as [if] they [its representatives] do a favour to the EU as they are already important. It doesn't work. It provides for those who are against [its membership].… Another argument that doesn't work is, "We're not like [them, other candidates]: special candidacy." The more you emphasise that, the more people think, "Let's move to some special relationship".'

The construction of that difference could also be quite instrumental but also unexpected and contradictory, unsettling established EU norms regarding a policy issue. After his participation at an informal meeting of EU energy ministers on 11 September 2010 in Brussels, the then Turkish energy and natural resources minister criticised the EU for holding back the opening of the energy chapter with claims that technical obstacles to further progress existed. Because of the division on the island, Cyprus's maritime sovereignty and rights to extraction of natural resources like natural gas, to which Turkey objects, remain contentious. Regarding the Cypriot reservations, the minister stated that energy talks were encumbered by politics and required a political solution. In his own words, the minister was quoted as saying:

Technically, we are already with Europe in terms of electricity and natural gas systems. In the field of energy, we have better facilities than most EU member states.… For that reason, it is not right to link the failure of not opening the energy chapter to technical reasons. The reasons are only political. Let me put it this way: they [the EU] have to come to a point where they can both heed the reservations of a small member state [Cyprus] and also find a solution. This is not our problem but the EU's … I think there is no option other than that we open this part of the chapter [on renewable energies], because Turkey is part of the solutions to the energy-related problems facing EU member states. So, this issue [about technical impediments] is not sustainable and it should certainly be solved politically. (*Today's Zaman*, 9–11 September 2010)

Once again, politicisation served the mutual interest of Turkey and the EU in the accession talks, whether they wanted to stall or advance membership.

Resistance to the EU's accession pedagogy manifested itself sometimes as a coping mechanism. Euroscepticism and pessimism about Turkey's future membership were common among Turkish diplomats in Brussels. Turkey intrigued many EU member state diplomats when they worked on its membership status, whereas their Turkish counterparts turned Eurosceptic. I asked Merih about this irony. She revealed that the issue came up during intra-staff meetings at the delegation.

When I met Hande, a colleague of Merih and a fellow diplomat, for breakfast at a café nearby the delegation, she observed that, as the reform process steadily slowed after the initial excitement in late 2005, Euroscepticism, blended with apathy, increased among Turkish diplomats in Brussels.

Hande liked to reminisce about her times in the Middle East before coming to Brussels. After a successful term in Cairo, where the locals and peers treated her 'like her eminence', Hande was posted to Brussels less than a year before when we met. Following her IR studies at our alma mater, she had earned two master's degrees on EU integration, one from Maastricht University and a second from the London School of Economics. During our talk, Hande mentioned a feeling of being barred from joining the EU not on technical but on identitarian grounds: 'When I was in the Netherlands, a twenty-two-year-old from Turkey, I was more eager to respond to stereotypes of Islam. But when you turn thirty, you feel exhausted [still having to do it] and you want to say to those people, "Get a life!"'

Turkish diplomats I spoke with found the EU accession a stressful process, which made working at the delegation a much-disliked job. Working on Turkey's EU bid taught them, in the words of Hande, 'how complicated things in the EU are [for Turkey]'. For them, accession presented them professionally with many problems beyond their ability to fix. Some asked themselves, as Hande had, whether Turkey should even join the EU. The perceived difficulty of the job sometimes led to a lack of motivation, Merih suggested: 'Due to the disadvantages of being a Turkish diplomat, we have to try 100 times harder than a Hungarian or a Croatian [diplomat].… [The work] is monotonous and thorny all the time.'

Murat felt like Hande and Merih. I met him when my fellow interns from the Committee and I visited the delegation. A mid-career diplomat, he was the delegation's spokesperson. Part of his job was to introduce his office and Turkey's EU membership bid to visitors like us. 'Turkey is a very sexy subject', he joked, adding that about 100–150 people visited the delegation weekly. Unlike Hande and Merih, Murat had received a Francophone education throughout his academic and professional life. When we met, he had been with the foreign ministry for twelve years. After his post at the United Nations in Ankara, he had been sent to the Congo. On his way back, he studied at College of Europe, a prestigious school for future Eurocrats, then had an appointment at the Turkish embassy to Belgium. After that he had a year at the ministry in Ankara, where he developed a good rapport with Turkey's future ambassador to the EU, and was posted to the delegation with the opening of accession negotiations. Murat envied his EU colleagues who dealt with issues like climate change, when his job was narrowed down to 'constantly explaining oneself [Turkey]' to his audience.

Turkish diplomats related the hardships of representing Turkey, an EU outsider, and of working in Brussels where Turkey's Europeanness, they felt, was constantly questioned by the technical procedures of the accession negotiations. Most supported the idea of Turkey's integration with the EU, especially those who had been educated abroad. Nonetheless, while their job was to facilitate Turkey's Europeanisation, many had profound doubts about its future in the EU. This partly stemmed from public opinion in Turkey but also partly from the very concept of 'Europeanisation'. This irked many: how could someone who grew up in modern Turkey and who already identified with Europe be made more European?

As human beings, diplomats were prone to identity discussions. They understood and responded to accession pedagogy as a mechanism that, echoing Fabian (1983), denied not only 'coeval-ness' but also co-location to Turkey and by implication to them. Instead of accruing a sense of equality between actors from both sides that were part of the same timescape and interconnected political geographies, accession pedagogy made Turkish actors feel extreme subjection. Eerily, Hande's weariness reminded me of a reader's online comments posted under a news article on Turkish Europeanisation: 'Why be a clown of the West when you can become the sultan of the East?'

The collective feeling of being an outsider yielded a new form of nationalism among Turkish actors. This neo-nationalism was highly Eurosceptic and aimed at mending the national ego bruised by Turkey's Europeanisation saga and its century-long 'loss of empire', as the AKP MP Zekeriya explained. Internalising such feelings of subjection and exclusion, some diplomats resorted to reproducing Turkey's difference from EU member states as well as other candidate states. When I asked Merih to comment on what I had heard regarding the friendly negotiation environment between the Commission and the Croatian officials, she became defensive: 'They excluded us! First, it is certain that the Croatians will join. Second, they [the EU and Croatia] have a culturally close relationship. We are different.'

Merih was not alone in this thinking. Hasan, a seasoned Turkish diplomat and a colleague of Merih, Murat and Hande, considered accumulation, private property and discipline to be the foundational values of European identity. Judging by these factors, he suggested, there were three different categories of people in Turkey who related to Europe: those who identified as European, those who were Europeanising and those who were against Europeanising. Judging by the same factors, Hasan went on, 'Turkey is European, but Turks are not.'

Earlier, I heard from Orhan a similar 'Europe versus Turkey' statement. Basing his comments on a spatial comparison, Orhan suggested that major European cities were built according to modern rules of urban planning, while major Turkish cities like Istanbul had a chaotic layout. Orhan's ahistorical account obliterated Istanbul's pre-modern history as world metropolis and the troubled history of urban planning by force in modern-day Europe (see Winner 1980), much like Hasan's essentialist discourse on state and nation formation in Turkey. Both their insights point to the diplomats' and lobbyists' increasing attentiveness to the discursive idioms of identity talk. In this way, a vicious circle was begun in which the various registers that took identity as a vector for political communication solidified said differences between Europe and Turkey.

By resorting to identity talk, Turkish politicians, diplomats and lobbyists like Zekeriya, Salim, Merih, Hande, Kerim, Murat, Hasan and Orhan defied the EU's accession pedagogy – albeit at the expense of delegitimising their country's EU membership. Euroscepticism, blended with increased apathy, among Turkish actors soon created an unspoken barrier in any attempted collocution between them and their EU counterparts; as a result, Turkish public and private interest representatives in Brussels would rather disengage from their EU colleagues than integrate with Eurocracy.

Conclusion

The accession pedagogy nurtured particular understandings of culture, power and policy. From a macro perspective, it arguably produced a new form of political and economic dependency wherein the norms and forms that governed the EU were expected to produce 'positive' developmental outcomes in its peripheries. Enlargement policy gave primacy to EU norms, which were presented as technical blueprints over which no contention need exist in European publics. But the processes of adjusting to EU norms in law, economy and society created tensions in both member and non-member countries, where its gradual effects were understood as relinquishing democratic sovereignty to a supranational order run by distant technocratic powers in Brussels.

In discussing the EU's accession arrangements as pedagogy and a technique of governance to 'prepare' or discipline candidate countries for EU membership, my intention has been to problematise EU accession as both a technical and a political procedure. I argued that Turkish bureaucrats and politicians recognised the EU's pedagogical engagement towards their country, but they chose to defy it, thereby showing agency.

A more important set of questions lingers. Why did Turkish politicians and bureaucrats defy the EU's accession pedagogy, despite the obvious cost of doing so (i.e. hampering Turkey's Europeanisation)? Was it because of Turkey's 'proud history and powerful nation', as Heather Grabbe (2006) – long-time senior adviser to commissioner Olli Rehn and later the director of Open Society European Policy Institute – rehashed the neo-Ottomanist argument? Or was it because of what EU accession and European integration meant for various constituents inside Turkey?

Evident from their internal negotiations and public statements, the EU actors considered their pedagogical approach necessary to 'integrate' European peripheries in a short period (Jacoby 2004). While the accession pedagogy was premised on minimal agency for candidate countries, Turkish politicians and bureaucrats as representatives of an 'unusual' accession state (Arvanitopoulos 2009) constantly attempted to widen their space for manoeuvring. In this way of resorting to a commonly available identity discourse, Turkish political and bureaucratic elites ultimately defied the EU's accession pedagogy, albeit at the expense of progress in Turkey's EU membership talks. But they did so to renegotiate significant terms and conditions of the EU's enlargement policy and accession framework, which established the EU's hegemonic power in key policy areas within the region. As human beings, they were affected by questions of identity at the personal level but, when deemed necessary, they did not shy away from using the identity talk tactically in their public negotiations with EU counterparts, as I discuss in the following chapters. Their 'de-Europeanisation', in other words, was strategic rather than fortuitous (cf. Aydın-Düzgit & Kaliber 2016).

Turkey is now entangled in the accession process, for the ending of membership negotiations, like their opening, requires assertive action, which in the EU's case would include a unanimous decision within the European Council. During negotiations, the EU's pedagogical management of Turkey's accession magnified the reality of being an outsider for Turkish diplomats and lobbyists. But the significance of the Turkish case does not lie with this growing Eurosceptic neo-nationalism; Euroscepticism, after all, is widely observed in most EU member states and candidate countries (Harmsen & Spiering 2016). Rather, the significance of the Turkish case lies with the fact that Euroscepticism, blended with new forms of nationalism, has never before led a country so consistently to resist EU reforms on the grounds of state identity and national interest. It is difficult to establish whether such nationalism among Turkish Eurocrats emerged as a response to the EU's accession pedagogy or simply as a factor in it. Here I argue that the design of policy negotiations structurally enabled the EU's accession pedagogy and Turkish Eurosceptic post-imperial nationalism to serve discursive frames in moulding EU and Turkish agents' actions, non-deeds and 'self and Other' narratives.

My aim in this chapter was not to reconstruct EU–Turkey relations from a governmentality perspective (Foucault 1991) that ascribes to the EU the role of the master teacher and to Turkey that of the unruly pupil in the European classroom. Nor do I wish to imply that Turkish actors are Giddens's (1991) 'reflexive subjects', heroically 'answering back' to the Brusselisation of their country. They defied this power because the accession pedagogy alienated them from Brussels' politico-cultural human tapestry. Their resistance came from the fact that the accession pedagogy placed them on the wrong side of the power divide – as outsiders in constant need of supervision. Otherwise, these policy elites had no problem with any pedagogy, since elites in Turkey have long practised pedagogy in matters of state–citizen relationships (Babül 2017; Kaplan 2006).

In the everyday life of EU policy negotiations, accession pedagogy served to redefine EU member states' and candidate countries' national interests. More commonly than admitted, such redefinitions yielded conflict and resistance. Whether such a conflict turns into antagonism or whether one interest prevails over others is always politically determined. I now turn to the European Council, wherein such political negotiations over sovereign interests and interstate bargains during Turkey's Europeanisation commonly take place.

Notes

1 The EU first enlarged in 1973 with the accessions of Denmark, Ireland and the UK. Greece joined in 1981. After German reunification in 1990, the eastern part of that country also became EU territory. Since the Turkish application in 1987, the Union enlarged with the addition of Austria, Sweden and Finland in 1995, and then Malta, Cyprus, Estonia, Latvia, Lithuania, Poland, Czech Republic, Slovakia, Slovenia and Hungary in 2004, followed by Bulgaria and Romania in 2007 and Croatia in 2013. Algeria left the EEC in 1962, when it gained independence from France, and Greenland left in 1985 when it gained greater autonomy from Denmark.

2 Presidency Conclusions of the 1991 Maastricht European Council state: 'the European Council recalls that the Treaty on European Union which the Heads of State and Government have now agreed, provides that any European State whose systems of Government are founded on the principle of democracy may apply to become members of the Union. The European Council notes that negotiations on accession to the European Union on the basis of the Treaty now agreed can start as soon as the Community has terminated its negotiations on Own Resources and related issues in 1992. The European Council notes that a number of European countries have submitted applications or announced their intention of seeking membership of the Union. The European Council invites the Commission to examine those questions including the implications for the Union's future development and with regard to the European Council in Lisbon [to be held in June 1992]' (Council of the European Union 1991: 2–3). Those European countries that had submitted their applications to which the Maastricht Presidency Conclusions refer were Turkey, Cyprus, Malta, Austria, Finland, Sweden and Switzerland. Among these, the last four, along with Norway and Liechtenstein, were at the time already members of the European Free Trade Association (EFTA).

3 Coining the term first in the 1990s to describe the reasons for the United States' world hegemony, Joseph Nye (2004: x) defined 'soft power' as 'the ability to get what you want through attraction rather than coercion and payments'. For Nye, a country's attractions arose from its culture, political ideals and policies. In his conservative politics, the hard power of a country (military force) should complement its soft power to maintain its local, regional and global hegemony.

4 In her study of good governance, human rights and Turkey's Europeanisation, Babül (2017) reached a similar conclusion.

5 Initially proposed in 2004 to engage with Algeria, Armenia, Azerbaijan, Belarus, Egypt, Georgia, Israel, Jordan, Lebanon, Libya, Moldova, Morocco, Occupied Palestinian Territory, Syria, Tunisia and Ukraine, the European neighbourhood policy aims at 'avoiding the emergence of new dividing lines between the enlarged EU and our neighbours and instead strengthening the prosperity, stability and security of all' (European Commission 2016). On 'policy cannibalism', see Burke (2012).

6 The screening reports on foreign security and defence policy and on energy had to be revised in mid-2016.

7 The open method of coordination is a much criticised policy tool. For a Foucauldean critique of the use of benchmarking and the open method of coordination as instruments of neoliberal governmentality, see Walters & Haahr (2005).

8 Though prepared, the Commission did not share its strategy and progress reports with the public in 2017, due to the 2016 coup attempt in Turkey. Thereafter, the Commission released its annual reports for all candidate countries in the spring.

9 By carrying to member states and their non-member peripheries the World Trade

Organization (WTO) rules on production and quality control measures, for example, the EU dictates trade terms and conditions to states that do business with EU member states and with non-EU regions and states (Duina 2007).

10 The Euro-Mediterranean Partnership (EUROMED) is an EU initiative that aims to enhance cooperation between EU member states and their Mediterranean neighbours. As a result of a push by the then French president Nicholas Sarkozy in 2008, EUROMED evolved into what is now known as the Union for the Mediterranean (UfM). When Sarkozy invited Turkey to join the UfM, Turkish diplomats and politicians took this as an attempt to sway Turkey away from EU membership. Turkey did, though, eventually join in the UfM.

11 Doris Pack, MEP from the European People's Party, speaking at the event 'Croatia: Next Member State and Challenges Ahead', jointly organised by the Croatian Business Council and EU Observer, 3 March 2009, Conrad Hotel, Brussels.

12 Olli Rehn speaking at the eighty-eighth meeting of the External Relations section of the European Economic and Social Committee, 5 February 2009, Brussels.

13 The mismatch of law/policy and practice has long concerned ethnographic studies of law and policy-making: see Latour (2010) and Moore (2000 [1978], 2016).

14 Real name.

Part III

Arts of diplomacy and lobbying in the EU institutions

Two hundred years ago, Napoleon conquered Europe on the battlefields of Austerlitz, Jena and Wagram. Today's battle for Europe is fought in committee rooms and conference halls. The weaponry has also undergone a significant change: instead of cavalry and cannon, the fate of nations is decided by administrative amendment and constructive compromise.

Derk-Jan Eppink, *Life of a European Mandarin* (2007: 26)

4

Enlargement, twice a week

Justus Lipsius

A notice under my door from the local police apologised for any inconvenience the upcoming traffic reordering might cause. The European Council meeting was imminent. I had been living in the *quartier européen* for some time and had already received several such notices warning residents about what was coming. These announcements always arrived weeks before the heads of EU member states were to meet so that local residents would have ample time to readjust their daily routines on that most important day in the Union's political life.

The Council, the Commission and the Parliament filled our neighbourhood with their concrete, wire and human presence. Once called *quartier Léopold*, after the Belgian King Leopold, the neighbourhood was soon labelled the European quarter after its transformation into the central executive district of EU affairs. Several of the landmark buildings in the neighbourhood curiously carried a Turkish touch. Unbeknown to most of the local residents, they had been designed by a well known Turkish architect-developer, the son of a retired Turkish NATO general who went native after his parents moved back to Turkey.

On the day of the meeting of the European Council, the highest political organ of the EU, the traffic of men and women dressed neatly in dark colours intensified the everyday dynamism in that part of the city. Some delegates arrived in black limousines; others poured out of the underground railway carrying heavy briefcases. Some simply stepped out of their offices surrounding the Schuman Roundabout only to enter Justus Lipsius, the main Council building since 1995. Named after the Flemish philologist and humanist Joost Lips (1547–1606), Justus Lipsius – 'just lips' – has been the punchline of much ridicule of the Council's work.

Sitting at the top of the EU's political hierarchy, the Council underscores the Union's intergovernmentalism. As in every intergovernmental organisation, negotiations between heads of state and governments require early preparation and careful negotiation of conflict and compromise. Scholars have long observed a shift away from high-level, on-the-spot deal-making by heads of government at the European Council, towards low-level preparatory negotiations conducted by their bureaucrats and diplomats long before Council meetings (Tallberg 2008).

Out of sight, mid-level diplomats from EU member states meet about 3,000 times in various Council committee meetings in a six-month period, with the Council Presidency providing administrative assistance to them, wherein 'common European interests' are *actually* negotiated.[1]

Whether their involvement in EU affairs was formal or informal, most of my neighbours were everyday actors in these negotiations. Assigned a diplomatic role, foreign service officers, who were posted to Brussels for three to five years, represented their countries' 'national interests' in the heart of Europolitics. They were 'Europeanised' through common schooling and socialisation, even though their primary responsibility was with their home country. Coming from an exclusive pool of human capital available in their countries, most exhibited a firm commitment to European integration – and a grave concern for its fate. Their job was to serve as a human conduit between their governments back home and Brussels. For that, they often acted like a 'permanent national lobby' (Geuijen et al. 2008; Spence 1993, 2002; van Schendelen 2010), influencing proto-policies and high-level political decisions taken in the EU. In this chapter, I map out the complex layout of this permanent national lobby in Brussels, based on accounts of diplomats from EU member states and Turkey. Here my focus is on diplomats' negotiations over sovereignty at the intergovernmental (interstate) level. Here sovereignty 'appears out of the practices of situated persons authorised to act in the name of the state' (Feldman 2019: 18), the nation or the Union. I problematise two vector concepts of sovereignty, which are essentially floating signifiers, devoid of agreed-upon meaning and difficult to contest, with which diplomats work on a daily basis: 'national interest', which constitutes diplomats' objective, and 'common European interest', which serves a vehicle for the relaying of national interests. I show how, faced with pressures from advanced neoliberal capitalism, the everyday (in)formal communicative practices of sovereignty by diplomats *cum* lobbyists behind closed doors shaped the 'common interests' of EU member states and of Turkey to oppose one another.

The complex machinery of national interests

For outsiders to the EU bureaucracy and policy-making, it may sound strange to consider public servants like diplomats as lobbyists. As agents of national interests, they know how to navigate the EU bureaucracy and how to push for the recognition of their governments' interests and positions better than their colleagues in the national capitals. In the Council, about 80 per cent of EU decisions are made by the qualified majority method. This method requires that 55 per cent of member states (but which have to represent at least 65 per cent of the total EU population) vote in favour of a proposal (van Schendelen 2010). The remaining 20 per cent of decisions include those over EU enlargement and accession of new states, which requires unanimous voting. Serving like a permanent national lobby, member state diplomats lobby each other, the Commission and the Parliament. Here lobbying, which requires personal industriousness, helps some EU members' interests prevail over others.

A complex machinery between EU member states and their diplomatic missions in Brussels facilitates these human conduits in their work and ensures the coordination of the national interests and their representation in Brussels with as little 'distortion' as possible along the national–intergovernmental axis. But the socio-spatial organisation of this setup looks more intricate than a simple transfer of national interests from state capitals to supranational Brussels suggests (Kassim et al. 2000, 2001). Diverse bureaucratic interests often reach the Council through policy or political competition among the government ministries of member states, or, in federalist systems, by powerful local or regional actors (van Schendelen 2010). Interest groups – ranging from national and transnational NGOs and their advocacy networks to multinational companies with complex board, tax payment and physical structures – have long cultivated exclusive access to the centres of power and politics in the EU and its member states with corporatist political cultures. Therefore, it would be most accurate to see the Council 'as more than simply the meeting place of national interests, but also the meeting place of different sectoral and bureaucratic interests[, which] thus exposes the complexity – and potential contradictions – subsumed by the concept of a "national interest"' (Christiansen 2001: 142).

Take the cases of France and Austria. In France, a comprehensive team of specialised bureaucrats work as policy experts in the office of the Secrétariat général des affaires européennes (SGAE, Secretariat General for European Affairs) in Paris.[2] Directly responsible to the prime minister's office, SGAE officers coordinate European affairs with assistance from ministerial colleagues. They operate in a much tighter institutional environment than those in other member states. Because SGAE also arbitrates, in the Court of Ministers, between ministers in negotiations where no agreement has been reached, it serves a further political function, monopolising access to expert advice to the head of government, the state at its highest level. It thus engages in a power struggle to 'produce more arguments to convince colleagues from other ministries to form a common European position', my contact explained. This intensified SGAE's political legitimacy. The ultimate objective of state agencies like the French SGAE is *at least* to ensure that France *appears* to speak with a single voice. Whoever has access to SGAE could thus claim to shape France's EU position (Lequesne 1996).

Like its counterparts in other EU member and non-member states, the role and weight of SGAE in drafting French positions suggested, at least as seen from Paris, that a common national position may be more likely to be drafted in the national capital. But when looked at from Brussels, the Paris–Brussels axis was more of a two-way street regarding the work of member state diplomats who sat in their Brussels offices and shaped common national and European positions – although the streets in some EU member states were narrower than others, to further the road analogy. The Paris–Brussels axis required that state organs in both capitals be responsible for coordinating with each other from a distance. SGAE and the French permanent representation in Brussels shared a similar division of labour on policy work. The French diplomat at France's permanent representation to the EU, in Brussels, had a counterpart who worked on same policy issue, say, enlargement, at SGAE in Paris. This way they could pass information – especially on 'sensitive' political matters like the Turkish accession – between the two offices seamlessly. During the 'Big Bang' enlargement, the ten new EU member states, as well as candidates like Turkey, had implemented the French model for nationally coordinating their EU affairs (Orban 2006; Peters & Wright 2001).

Ultimately, actors and the institutional framework for dialogue at the supranational decision-making level depend on the political culture of a member state and its cultures of bureaucracy in Brussels. In Brussels, even the socio-physical structure of the permanent representation offices can reflect how central this principle is in a country's EU policy-making. For instance, Austria's permanent representation to the EU in Brussels represents both the federal ministries and social partners like the *Länder*, Confederation of Austrian Cities, Austrian Federal Economic Chamber, Federal Chamber of Labour, Confederation of Trade Unions, Chamber of Agriculture, Federation of Austrian Industry and the Central Bank of Austria. The association between these groups and the Austrian state system is so strong that each of these groups receives copies of most internal communiqués sent from the permanent representation to Vienna. During the fieldwork I noted that the names of these social partners appear on the doorbell of the representation, which stood near the Schuman Roundabout in Brussels, where I walked daily.

One day I tagged along with a group of French-speaking Turkish high school students from Istanbul who were touring EU institutions in Brussels. Such school trips were more common during my fieldwork in Brussels than before or after, even though the number of Turkish people who believed that their country would join the EU went down during the same timeframe. The school administration's tour enquiry somehow found its way to Deniz's office in Brussels and to Esra. A dual Turkish-Austrian citizen, a graduate of the Austrian High School in Istanbul and an economist by training, Esra was married to Tobias, an Austrian official, who had been recently posted to Brussels. Soon after the couple moved from Vienna, Esra found herself working at Deniz's office, attending meetings as a Turkish lobbyist and writing weekly newsletters about EU–Turkey relations. When she received the high school's request, Esra used her insider connection to bring these young minds to meet their fictitious enemy face to face: successive Austrian governments publicly declared their opposition to Turkey's EU bid, which made the headlines of Turkish dailies, turning Austria into the target of Euroscepticism in Turkey.

The students turned up enthusiastic for this portion of their school trip, wearing ties with images of modern Turkey's founder or carrying books entitled *Sèvres*.[3] When the school party visited Oskar, an Austrian diplomat and enlargement officer in Brussels, on his own territory to challenge him, the excited young minds asked: 'What problem does Austria have with Turkish democracy? Is the EU a Christian club? Why does the Turkish army's influence over politics bother the Austrians so much, when, after all, the army protects people?' They recognised Oskar from the dramatic media coverage he had received in Turkey (he had also received similar coverage in the local Turkish-Belgian media). Oskar was well known for his government's (and his own) open opposition to Turkey's EU membership.[4] Later I learned of his long career in Brussels, serving at Austria's permanent representation for close to a decade before returning to home. His ability to represent his country was surely due to his exceptional skills as a diplomat and legal counsellor but also to his daily work at the Council, subtly carrying Austria's opposition to Turkey's EU membership.

Once we were inside the office of Austria's permanent representation, the liaison officers of each Austrian social partner greeted us. They worked in separate but adjacent rooms and could shape Austria's 'national interests' from Brussels as much as they did from Vienna. The students were too busy speaking up for their country to recognise pluralism at work. It was the day-to-day operation of EU–Turkey affairs through company and social partners' lobbying rather than the EU being a Christian club that affected the course of negotiations they were eager to learn about.

A complicated, contentious and at times contradictory political enigma (Christiansen 2001; Snyder 1989), national interest served a manoeuvring space wherein a multiplicity of public, private and corporate interests found representation and access through the communicative lines mid-level bureaucrats and diplomats of EU member states controlled. In serving as human conduits, these diplomats acted as formal participants in EU politics *and* its informal influencers behind the scenes. They turned Europolitics into 'undecidable geography' (Sidaway 2000), where one could never be sure whether those working in the diplomatic sphere represented those states and nations or produced them in the first place. The Council's confidential work contributed to it being an undecidable geography.

Europeanisation as obligation

Bureaucrats in Turkey and their diplomatic colleagues in Brussels, or 'Europeans by obligation' as Irène Bellier (2000a: 60) called them, used the space-time between Council meetings to secure their agendas. While heads of EU member states finalised negotiations, pre-settlement negotiations involved lobbyists in numerous encounters with lower- and mid-level bureaucrats and diplomats, who worked their concerns into 'common European interests'. Lobbyists or 'Europeans by interest' (Bellier 2000a: 60) cultivated a good rapport with member state diplomats and Council bureaucrats.

Take Lucas, for instance. A Swedish man with a long career at the Council, Lucas had previously worked on climate change in the Council before moving to enlargement. During the fifth ('Big Bang') enlargement, the Council, along with other EU institutions, underwent organisational proliferation, whereby new structures were put in place to prepare central and eastern European candidates for their EU membership. Attesting to the rising significance of enlargement as an EU policy and a space for governmental action, the Council established, in 1997, the Working Party on Enlargement, which became, in 2006, the Working Party on Enlargement and Countries Negotiating Accession to the EU (COELA; Gajdik & Schwarzinger 2008: 29).

This working group or working party (both terms were used in Eurospeak) sustained political dialogue between EU member and candidate states by supervising the fulfilment of the Copenhagen political criteria to which members had agreed during the Copenhagen European Council meeting in June 1993:

> Membership requires that the candidate country has achieved *stability of institutions guaranteeing democracy, the rule of law, human rights and respect for and protection of minorities,* a functioning market economy, and the capacity to cope with competitive pressure and market forces within the Union. Membership presupposes the candidate's ability to take on the obligations of membership including adherence to the aims of political, economic and monetary union. (Council of the European Union 1993; italics marking the political criteria are mine)

The Copenhagen agreement that candidate countries be(come) functioning liberal capitalist democracies required that the working group oversee EU reforms in all negotiating chapters in those countries. Until late 2009, Croatia and Turkey were the only accession candidates discussed at the working group level. Since then, Montenegro and Serbia have joined Turkey, Croatia acceded to the EU, and Albania and North Macedonia have become EU candidates but are not yet negotiating accession with the EU.

Lucas moved to the enlargement unit of the general secretariat of the Council's DG External Economic Relations, Politico-Military Affairs (now DG Foreign Affairs, Enlargement and Civil Protection). When we first met at the Justus Lipsius cafeteria, he was spending most of his days reading and learning about Turkey, revisiting this 'longstanding guest' in the EU, as he called it. Lucas organised the twice-weekly meetings of COELA, one of those low-level preparatory negotiating venues in the Council but perhaps the most crucial one in the political life of EU enlargement and the accession career of candidate countries.

Like other Council meetings, COELA meetings were access-restricted, closed to the public. During a visit to the Council Defne organised for a group of Turkish businesswomen, which I also attended, Lucas took his guests to where COELA meetings took place. I pictured EU member state enlargement officers filling this otherwise unremarkable room with their presence. At the time of our tour, I had already met more than half of the working group's regulars, who described the colourful conflicts and hard compromises this ordinary Council meeting room had witnessed twice a week.[5]

Every Tuesday and Friday at 10:00 sharp, Lucas and his boss welcomed the then twenty-seven EU enlargement officers to the meeting room in Justus Lipsius. Everyone took a seat, marked by the nametag of their member state. In the meeting room, they became Mr Germany, Ms France or Mr Poland. Crammed around a massive oblong table, they talked about reform progress, moulding candidate countries' future sovereignties and statecraft on their behalf.

Pascal, the head of Turkey unit of the Commission's DG Enlargement, also attended these meetings, along with the designated contact person between the working group and his DG. If required, Commission officials from other DGs like Daniela, who worked on Turkey's accession according to their chapter responsibilities, accompanied them. Their initial role in working group meetings was to provide 'technical facts'. Member state diplomats would, for instance, ask the Commission to comment on current candidate country progress, or, if none, provide assurance of future compliance. Lucas expounded this last point: 'Often the Commission [officials] would say, "Things are fine in this [policy] area", to which some Member States would respond by saying, "We have heard otherwise". The Council's legal adviser and expert on the EU *acquis*, who attended most working group meetings, told me that he would at that point step in and make 'a legal decision in a political house on whether a given problem [brought up by a member state diplomat] is part of the *acquis* or not'.

As one moved downwards in the Council decision-making hierarchy, one encountered less formalism because actor-participants had less authority to make and enforce decisions (Nedergaard 2007). Working group meetings and participants were a case in point. Their decisions were not formally binding. Yet the role these mid-level bureaucrats played carried great import, due to the need to reach consensus at lower-level Council configurations (Fouilleux et al. 2005). Technically, diplomats needed to find the best possible solution; politically, however, they needed to get everybody to accept their solution (Sannerstedt 2005). This dynamic was at the heart of EU decision-making, well justified by ever-pending political crisis and the constant need for a culture of compromise. Otherwise, 'the drawing of a clear-cut line between EU policy-making's technical and political aspects would lead to inter-institutional and intergovernmental stalemate' (Fouilleux et al. 2005: 611; see also Kleine 2014; Woll 2012). Actors' expertise in mediating the boundaries between the technical and political aspects of EU policy-making imbued working group participants with an ability to influence high-level decisions because their bosses lacked familiarity with policy perspectives in different EU member states.

Anyone who grew accustomed to the Council's work on EU enlargement and Turkish accession would testify to two facts on the ground. First, 'EU accession is a technical matter, but ultimately political', as Lucas observed; and 'with Turkey, everything is political', as Pascal remarked. These facts testified to why accession negotiations with Turkey have ultimately failed: if everything is 'open for contestation', one has to work much harder to build common ground before one can move forward with membership talks. And when all remains open for a discussion, other interests jump in.

Inside the working group

I met Sonja after she had recovered from her hard work preparing and running Slovenia's Council Presidency. She was one of the first from the working group to respond to my request for an interview. We agreed to meet after work hours in a bookshop not too close to her office. Though not openly objecting, she did not feel comfortable being recorded, which made me stop showing up to interviews with a recorder. Only when she warmed up to my 'hypothetical' questions did Sonja become more forthcoming.

Sonja had been working at Slovenia's permanent representation in Brussels for a couple years. As a diplomat, her main task was to mould common EU interests

according to her country's national interests. As a Council Presidency representative, however, she helped find ways to build consensus and compromise among
all member states. This new diplomatic task gave her a broader perspective on the
inner workings of the working group.

Besides her responsibilities at this working group, Sonja had to manage two
ad hoc groups during the Slovenian Presidency, both of which meet to this day:
the Ad Hoc Working Party on the Cooperation and Verification Mechanism
for Bulgaria and Romania, which continues to supervise progress being made
by those two countries regarding the EU requirements for justice and internal
affairs – requirements they had not fulfilled before they joined the EU – and the
Ad Hoc Working Party on the Follow-Up to the Council Conclusions on Cyprus
of 26 April 2004, which assessed improvements in the economic integration of
Cyprus and contacts between the Turkish-Cypriot and Greek-Cypriot communities with the EU. Both ad hoc working groups met once or twice per Presidency
and discussed regular reports of the Commission. When meetings happened at
the same time, as it did during Sonja's Brussels term, it posed a great challenge for
the Presidency. 'Because Romania, Bulgaria and Cyprus are now members of the
EU, they also sit at the table with others when their countries are being evaluated.
It thus becomes much more sensitive for representatives of other member states to
discuss and prepare these issues at the same time', Sonja explained.

At an ordinary morning meeting of COELA, Ms Estonia, Mr Malta, Ms Ireland,
Mr Germany and others sat down to talk about the nuts and bolts of progress
towards EU membership. During these meetings, no official notes were taken.
Nor were press conference headlines made. Participants informed those who were
entitled to know, such as their ministerial colleagues, the details of their discussion
through internal communiqués. Outsiders had to trust their good rapport with
enlargement officers to gain special access to what went on behind closed doors.

Sonja chaired the meeting, which opened with Pascal's presentation of the
current state of affairs and latest developments. After he had given his account,
member state diplomats noted their opinions and asked questions individually or
in twos or threes. The primary role of Commission officials like Pascal in working
group meetings is to persuade member state diplomats that a move forward in
accession negotiations is plausible. It was the Commission, for instance, that
convinced member states back in 2004 that opening negotiations with Turkey was
a possibility, since it had 'sufficiently' fulfilled the Copenhagen political criteria.
Whether they found the Commission's responses satisfactory or not, diplomats
agreed on the spot with recommended proposal for further action or inaction.[6]

Diplomats competed to shape the final wording of what 'common European
interests' should look like on a given issue. The Commission drafted the final
wording, in 'draft common positions' (DCPs). After interfacing with the candidate
country, the Commission presented this draft text to diplomats, who meticulously
debated over them; if agreed, the diplomats then sent the DCPs to higher levels in
the Council for approval and to be officially negotiated at an intergovernmental accession conference with the candidate country.[7] Otherwise, diplomats continued
to negotiate opposing interpretations of compliance at various Council levels.

Sonja's Estonian colleague Eliise recounted a meeting that revealed both how diplomats negotiated particular policy issues at the working group and how the Commission acted as a broker between EU member states and candidates like Turkey. Eliise recounted:

> There was an incident of opening a position paper on a chapter. The position had been communicated to Turkey beforehand so that they didn't object to it when they saw it. The Commission is very careful with that [to make sure that the Turkish side agrees]. [Member state] and [member state] changed [the position paper]. We got information that Turks agreed; then it turned out they didn't. So things on that chapter are blocked. It was terrible.

Eliise revealed that Commission officials at working group meetings acted to represent common member state positions *and* in the interest of the candidate country, whose representatives were not part of these 'internal' EU debates. As in this and other examples, the Commission officials often sought to build trust and confidence in the candidate countries on the part of member states.

Sonja reflected on how internal divisions barred Commission officials from acting categorically: not every official voiced the same opinion about candidates' progress; nor did they always agree on what counted as 'progress'. Unlike colleagues from other DGs, DG Enlargement officials, in Sonja's affirmation, were known to be pro-enlargement and in favour of the candidate countries, which were the object(ive)s of their work. Success in securing membership for a candidate country, according to Sonja, reflected well on them. Their opinion prevailed over those of colleagues sitting in the working group.

Though seen as essential, the Commission's presence in the working group generated an overall feeling of being watched among member state diplomats regarding their work on Turkey. As a result, they could not outwardly discriminate against any candidate because the norms of EU diplomacy rejected discrimination. Participants had to look *as if* they were acting fairly even when they might harbour prejudices.

The uninterested, the influencer, the competitor

Working group members regularly passed information *and* advice to their national capitals and received instructions from them on general policy frameworks on enlargement and on each candidate country. As soon as Sonja, Eliise and others left the working group meeting, they rushed back to their offices to report the meeting to a variety of state (and non-state) actors back home. In theory, bureaucrats from EU departments in Ljubljana, Riga or Valetta sent instructions to their auxiliaries in Brussels, and the Brussels-based diplomats then adjusted their representation at the working group by passing these instructions 'as is' or with minor modifications (Council 2002). In practice, however, member state diplomats participated in the production of common European positions *and* refined those national interests they were entrusted to relay (Geuijen et al. 2008; Geuijen & 't Hart 2010). EU member states' contributions to common member state positions greatly depended on their diplomats' diagnostic information and expertise in interpreting information to their governments back home on how other diplomats and EU actors in Brussels might behave. As in any act of interpretation, representatives of national interests had more flexibility and freedom to inform those interests they were entrusted with, rather than simply re-presenting them. Or, as the Maltese diplomat Giuseppe put it: 'Malta doesn't know everything we [diplomats] do'. But how much room did these diplomats have to influence their governments' national positions?

According to the German enlargement officer Paul, room to manoeuvre depended on several factors. Paul explained that a diplomat's flexibility hinged on the national position she or he was entrusted with representing; how hard it was to receive instructions from home (and 'if a coalition government is in office, it surely is harder'); how well colleagues from Berlin prepared instructions; how flexible the government was on a particular issue; and finally on the diplomat's individual competence.

Sonja suggested that there were differences between member states in terms of how much personal input diplomats could put into the national position. In comparison with Spain's 'relaxed attitude', she reflected:

> Many new member states such as the Baltic states, or even Slovenia, have more fixed positions. I think [Slovenia's inflexible position] is a remnant of socialism, communism.... But some old member states like Germany and France have also very fixed positions.... Maybe because older member states are more used to this environment, their approach to negotiations is much more difficult.

Whether a member state was more experienced than another in accession bargaining made a difference in meeting discussions. Ultimately, diplomats acted flexibly or firmly depending on whether their state had a 'keen' interest in the policy issue or in the candidate country under consideration. In Sonja's observation, not all member states were invested in negotiating an issue. Countries whose demands had already been generally satisfied 'acted on behalf' of candidate countries during the working group discussions. More significantly, Sonja observed, members with economic or political stakes in particular candidate countries took the working group meeting as a platform to push their own agenda onto accession negotiations.

Negotiations thus provided a space for member states to voice their economic, sectoral, social or political grievances against candidate countries. Here, bilateral disputes were couched as accession preconditions. Diplomats used legal-technical reasoning as a 'hook' to win arguments at the working group level – provided that the Council's legal adviser approved of its fit with the EU *acquis* (see Thedvall 2007). When an unresolved bilateral conflict was included in the EU *acquis*, it became a matter of technicality *and* politics at the same time.

Such bilateral disputes might not concern or involve everyone, which is why those who wanted to bring up the dispute as part of accession prerequisites had to strike a delicate balance in the working group. After all, as Sonja succinctly put it, 'what Croatia is to Slovenia is not the same [as what it is] to Germany'. Here, affect guided diplomats.

According to realist and *realpolitik* approaches, international politics excludes affect. Recent affective turns in anthropology (Davie-Kessler n.d.; Lutz 2017; Skoggard & Waterston 2015; Stoler 2007), political geography (Dittmer 2017; Kuus 2014) and political science critique this realist position (Clément & Sangar 2018; Demertzis 2017; Hogget & Thompson 2012). Similarly, I found that the working group meetings transformed diplomacy into an emotive domain and emotion work. Even when previously disinterested, diplomats may very well empathise with one side of a bilateral dispute, due to cultural affinity or historical memories of similar disputes.

Reflecting on the role of affect in political negotiations, Eliise recounted an empathic encounter she experienced during working group meetings when the Greek and Cypriot representatives spoke about Turkey: 'When one of your [Turkey's] neighbours is speaking, I understand them perfectly, because that's exactly how I feel about Russia.… We never side with them, but I see certain similarities and understand [their case]. Others either don't understand, or they don't care.'

As a diplomat, Eliise was conflicted about these emotions and what she perceived her job to be. She described other diplomat colleagues as 'emotionally involved' vis-à-vis her own 'objective' attitude yet marvelled at the 'power of history'. 'Between Greeks and Estonians, the goal is the same', she continued, meaning the EU enlargement, 'but interests and methods are different.' An emotionally charged case might not allow a member state to win an argument, but it certainly affected the messages diplomats relayed back home, as well as their attitudes towards the candidate country.

In cases of economic grievance – and those were dear to the EU – affect appeared less pronounced in my interlocutors' accounts but still carried import. One notable example concerned the taxation chapter and Turkey's demand to protect the interests of its privatised *rakı* industry vis-à-vis other producers and importers of alcoholic beverages, such as whisky, by charging an excise tax more than double the rate charged on *rakı*. Patented as a national drink in 2009, *rakı* is a favourite alcoholic drink, with a yearly consumption of 43 million litres in Turkey.

To fulfil one of the opening benchmarks for the taxation chapter, in 2009, the Turkish authorities proposed a timeline to eliminate the differential taxation of alcoholic beverages by 2018, while demanding an exemption for *rakı* similar to the Greek *ouzo*. When the Commission negotiated the Turkish request for derogation during one working group meeting, some found 2018 too distant and raised objections. A few noted that they had asked Croatia to fulfil a final condition on a similar case and asked that candidate countries be treated as equally as possible. The Commission tried to negotiate the opening of this chapter by assuring those who objected that, in case of non-compliance, final conditions would be applied.[8] In this case, a sense of fairness did the emotive work, even though 'fairness' as a trope was to mask political-economic interests.

Negotiations on taxation continue, however, and the chapter remains open. The European whisky lobby, led by spiritsEUROPE and the Scotch Whisky Association, continued to demand the elimination of the differential taxation on their exports to the Turkish market from the Commission and member state representatives in

Brussels, while the Turkish *rakı* producers lobbied the government in Ankara. Protesting against tax hikes which the conservative AKP government indiscriminately applied on all alcoholic beverages, Turkish brewers asked their pan-European partners, the Brewers of Europe, to help them lobby the Turkish government. Meanwhile, an interesting twist took place in Turkey's *rakı* sector.

As part of agreements with the International Monetary Fund and the World Bank, the Turkish government privatised the state-owned tobacco and spirits monopoly between 1999 and 2001. Mey, a Turkish LIMAK consortium partner with ties to President Erdoğan and one of the few builders of large-scale energy and transport infrastructure projects in Turkey, bought the production rights to *rakı* in 2003. LIMAK then sold Mey to American Texas Pacific Group in 2006, which sold it a few years later to Diageo, the world's leading Scotch whisky producer. *Rakı* had 70 per cent of Turkey's spirits market, worth $2.1 billion at the time (Fletcher 2011). But a far more significant advantage Diageo gained from this acquisition was the ability to market its spirits in Turkey, which was not feasible before, this time as an insider. Later in that year, the Commission assured EU member states: 'Turkey will be required to comply with the commitments in the Action Plan. Gradual elimination of discriminatory practices in taxation in line with the Action Plan is the key to making further progress in the accession negotiations under this [taxation] chapter' (European Commission 2011: 75).

Since it acquired Mey, Diageo has seen a significant sale drop. Some in Turkey objected to the 'British *rakı*' and instead consumed spirits produced by companies with domestic ownership. In May 2013, the Turkish government banned all alcohol advertising and sales after 22:00, alleging health concerns (Ozbilgin 2013). Many secular Turks took this ban as the last instance of the AKP's interference in their everyday lives. Three days later, their burgeoning concerns found expression in anti-government protests in the historic Gezi Park, which, lasting for a month, quickly spread all over the country and scared the Erdoğan government of the power of popular dissent (Evered & Evered 2016; Gürsel 2013; Temelkuran 2016; White 2014).[9]

Common European interests?

Typically, negotiations on a chapter with a specific focus on, say, commercial relations began with Paul, Eliise or Sonja informing industries in their countries that the working group was discussing an issue which may be of interest to them. Most enlargement officers gained a perspective on Turkey through their Turkey-based companies. These 'practitioners on the ground', as the Swedish enlargement officer Linnea described them, were tacitly asked to assess Turkey's reform performance.

Enlargement officers had otherwise limited personal experience with the Turkish state, bureaucracy and policy-making, as social institutions. Yet, most 'had to *imagine* how Turkey worked', as the Romanian diplomat Anton mused. Few had ever been to Turkey and even then only as tourists. The Turkish delegation sometimes arranged study visits for them to meet with (often cherry-picked) government and civil society representatives. Their limited engagement with

Turkey made their position as EU member state diplomats conducive to being lobbied from both inside and outside the Council. From makers of Portuguese port wine and Scotch whisky to Irish beef producers to multinational pharmaceutical, steel and finance companies – major economic players in Europe – lobbied the Commission and EU member state diplomats through their representatives and lobbyists in Brussels.

Many enlargement officers I spoke with suggested that there was a mutual benefit in meeting with professional lobbyists. The diplomats received valuable information (Bouwen 2002, 2004; Chalmers 2013), unavailable to them personally or professionally, while lobbyists channelled corporate interests through this open line of communication with diplomats, seeding 'national interests' with special interests they relayed in the form of information. Johan, my Dutch interlocutor, even suggested that being lobbied strengthened his central role in EU enlargement when he claimed: 'They must consider me and my work important enough to tell me what they do'. But how did these encounters with professional lobbyists occur? What did diplomats and professional lobbyists talk about? And what were the implications of these private meetings?

One morning, a man I shall call Jack visited Sonja in her office. Jack represented a multinational pharmaceutical company that had encountered problems in accessing Croatian markets. At the time, Slovenia and Croatia had an ongoing border dispute, which constituted a major impasse for Croatia's EU membership. The Slovenes wanted to solve this border dispute during Croatia's accession negotiations, thinking that, once Croatia was in, Croats would have fewer incentives to resolve it on Slovenian terms. Knowing about the border dispute, Jack thought there might be a mutual interest here. Sonja described her meeting with him:

> He presented their case on how Croatia did not implement the *acquis* correctly and asked me to raise this in the working group. I didn't bring it up because we [Slovenia] don't have an interest. But other members did! I think it was a general case that the Commission already knew about it. So it depends on the interest [of member states]. We have pharmaceuticals, but its significance is relative to member states. Some are more interested than others. But in this case, it was by a multinational company [that I was lobbied], and its case did not suit our national position. I mean, [our government] already knows our companies' interests, because it's a coordinated effort.[10]

Jack tried to persuade Sonja that the interests of the company he represented and Slovenian national interests matched. The lobbyist ultimately failed, but the Slovenian diplomat was one of twenty-seven. Jack continued to 'inform' other working group members, such as Paul, as Paul revealed to me. As with Germany, some diplomats found Jack's arguments congruent with their national interests. Corporate interests and national interests of EU member states did not always converge, however. So a lot of lobbying by people like Jack took place.

On another occasion, a lobbyist working for the world's multinational steel giant ArcelorMittal, whom I shall call Mike, paid a visit to Benoit in his office. With headquarters in Luxembourg, ArcelorMittal wanted to expand its presence in the Turkish market. It had its eye on buying the Turkish Ereğli Iron and Steel

Works (Erdemir). But there was one problem: publicly owned, Erdemir was the crown jewel of Turkey, bearing heavy industry's national developmentalist legacy. Above all, it was not (yet) for sale (Ağartan 2009). Mike asked Benoit to push for the privatisation of Erdemir at the working group. I learned about this case when I asked Benoit whether he was being lobbied. Benoit explained:

> Do we get lobbied? Yes. Do we lobby? Yes. Who lobbies us? Other member states, NGOs, special interest groups, our own industry, companies based in Luxembourg. I don't know how it is in Turkey, but big companies locate themselves in Luxembourg. They are so international in nature that they are not national. The interests of these companies are also our interests because we want them to stay where they are.

Benoit did not need much convincing, in other words. He agreed that Luxembourg had an interest in keeping ArcelorMittal where it was. In this case, the steel giant's corporate interests was 100 per cent in line with Luxembourg's national interests. Despite Mike's successful lobbying and Benoit's good efforts to lobby his diplomat colleagues at the Council, ArcelorMittal ultimately failed in its Turkey bid (see Chapter 5).

In these classic examples of advanced industrial capitalism's access and embeddedness in European political economic life, two multinational companies' corporate interests became the national interest of two EU member states. Through professional lobbying and further lobbying by diplomats, these interests found their way to the Council working group to mould 'common European interests'. Paul pointed out that there was virtually no difference between how commercial interests and more political issues, such as human rights, found their way to his office. The only difference might be that diplomats were more familiar with political issues like the protection of minorities and less so with steel trade, sugar production quotas or sanitary provisions in meat shipping!

Brussels' rule

Working group members across the board said that sharing information with their counterparts from Turkey and others made their job easier. Linnea said that her role was 'to communicate between Turks and Europe'. She shared information regarding the working group discussions with Turkish diplomats in Brussels – information that best suited her country's interests. Because of this 'open line', her Turkish colleagues found Sweden friendly towards Turkey and went to Linnea to relay their information and interests. The amount of information one could share with candidate country colleagues depended on the personal discretion of the member state representative. 'Otherwise they might use you', Eliise cautioned.

Turkish diplomats found the communication channels established with Linnea, Eliise, Paul and others vital. Merih explained the everyday job of diplomacy, with long hours in the office, at the Turkish delegation:

> Embassies are like feelers of the foreign affairs [ministry]. [Our job is to] reflect the air here [Brussels] in a clear and correct manner. Looking at it from here, we think

through what messages to give at a meeting [with the EU] and pass speech notes or suggestions accordingly. Ankara's mission is to work information and knowledge coming from Brussels into policy options. Such correspondence is, by [Ankara's] choice, shared with everyone, with us. A final decision emerges in Ankara from the ministry or rests at the bureaucratic level. The rule of diplomacy is that nothing remains in the dark.

But these communication channels were not always reliable. Merih explained:

Working on the EU is harder because you [Turkey/Turkish diplomats] are outside of the system: you cannot participate in meetings, even when they make decisions about you. You try to influence them from outside. You try to access information beforehand because channels [that are] open for communication [are not enough] so you need to keep on good terms with everybody. You need to cross-check the information you get because not everybody tells you everything.

Hande had a similar perspective:

[I communicate best with] Brits. [She pauses] It actually depends on the person, his/her style and how well equipped that person is. You may get information from someone who might not be supportive of you [Turkey's EU membership bid] … Some talk; some don't talk. You meet somebody, and that somebody tells you something. [But] You need to read between the lines of what you are told. The more you make them engaged with the subject, the better they reflect it positively.

Turkish diplomats informed member state enlargement officers of the EU reforms Turkey might have recorded, but their engagement did not amount to 'active lobbying, as one would expect', Paul found. Benoit suspected that the reason why his Turkish colleagues did not lobby his office was that they limited themselves to larger member states and paid no attention to smaller EU countries, be they Luxembourg or Malta – even though at the Council each member state had an equal voice and one vote.

Contrary to his EU colleagues, Murat did not see lobbying as part of his job description:

What we do here is not lobbying. We are a diplomatic representation. Our first duty is to defend the country's interests. In lobbying the task is to defend a person's or a private organisation's interests. You can't include state interests among these. When you say lobbying here, it is understood purely as economic lobbying or consultancy firms. For instance, somebody representing the Italian railway company visits the Commission when new legislation is to be passed. We have not exactly reached that level. [It's not lobbying because] We are not a full member yet.

From this Turkish perspective, diplomatic contact between Turkish and member state representatives remained within the classic confines of interstate diplomacy and could only mature into lobbying with Turkey's membership. But without lobbying EU member state diplomats, that membership remained unlikely.

Beyond classic diplomacy, what mattered, perhaps the most, in the world of EU representation was to demonstrate an interest in the EU's future and an active presence in Brussels' EU circles. At the bare minimum, EU lobbying demonstrated interest. Comparing the representational activities of past and present candidate country diplomats he had worked with in Brussels, Benoit suggested:

> Bulgaria never really made an effort to show they were getting ready. They never showed up here to have talks when they were still a candidate country. Romanians did. I would meet with somebody from the [Romanian] mission here. She would call me once every two to three months. We would meet and go over whatever I was working on. So they [the Romanian diplomats] made an effort to get to know things and people here. Croatians are active in that sense. They put in an effort. I have a monthly contact with my Croatian counterpart here at the mission. They would provide information on reforms and their negotiating positions. So, they *are very keen on or wanting to show* that they are preparing themselves. (My emphasis)

Here Benoit partially echoed commissioner Rehn, when the latter advised candidate countries to prove that they can achieve EU membership. To demonstrate interest, Benoit instructed candidate diplomats to engage in symbolic politics. Some (but not all) Turkish lobbyists have understood this symbolic aspect of Europolitics. Sibel, a younger-generation professional political lobbyist whom Deniz handpicked a decade previously to represent Turkey's Cumhuriyet Halk Partisi in Brussels, summed up what these EU actors convey here: 'Brussels has a rule: if you don't exist [through the corridors of power in Brussels], you don't exist!' This was a classic case for symbolic politics.

While we were standing next to one another at a party and talking about how my fieldwork was going, I mentioned to Esra Benoit's observations on the efficacy of symbolic politics in Brussels. Before she could say anything in defence of her Turkish diplomatic colleagues, Esra's husband, Tobias, confirmed that his Croatian counterpart gave him a call every other week and asked him whether he needed any information about any developments that have occurred in Croatia since their last phone call, which would help him do his job better. In a political field where competence in symbolic politics is the measure for diplomatic efficacy, the symbolic politics of EU accession presupposed a candidate's studious display of willingness to engage with accession demands. Many Turkish diplomats and lobbyists were generally good at symbolic politics, just not at performing it for their EU colleagues.

Bureaucratic politics inside the Turkish delegation

The institutional culture of the Turkish foreign service, power struggles within the administration and the organisational management of diplomatic relations with Eurocracy complicated Turkey's EU application and effective representation of its national interests at the supranational (EU) level. Inter-institutional struggles between various branches of the Turkish government over who got to steer Turkey's EU policy were common throughout the institutionalisation of Turkey's EU affairs (Keskin 2001). These factors turned the delegation into the most loved but also most hated diplomatic post.

After the 1999 Helsinki summit at which Turkey became a candidate country for EU membership, the same institutional pedagogy each EU candidate country had already gone through shaped Turkey's Eurocratic institutionalisation. In 2000, the European Union Secretariat-General (EUSG) was formed as the Turkish equivalent of the French SGAE under the office of the prime minister. During the next decade, the EUSG moved, figuratively speaking, back and forth between the prime minister's office and the foreign affairs ministry.

After much pressing from the EU and informal domestic actors, the Turkish government finally appointed a chief negotiator. Despite Deniz's advice to the contrary, Egemen Bağış[11] became Turkey's first EU minister *and* the new chief EU negotiator, at least 'freeing' the foreign affairs minister from the task of EU negotiations. By then, up to six EUSG personnel were stationed at the delegation in Brussels, four of whom were sent to work in pairs at Turkish diplomatic representations in future Council Presidencies, where they secured the EUSG's direct involvement in future negotiations.

In 2011, the government reorganised the EUSG into a separate ministry, headed by Turkey's EU minister and chief negotiator. As part of historical changes in Turkey's governance regime, in 2018, the Ministry of Foreign Affairs incorporated the EU Ministry by executive order akin to the DG NEAR's cannibalising of the DG ELARG a few years back.

Insiders suggest that Turkey's EU affairs have always been predisposed to 'bureaucratic politics', where different government offices act 'quasi-autonomous[ly] with their own purposive and reflexive goals' (Radaelli 1999: 38). Unlike the Weberian ideal-type bureaucrat, 'the most basic goal of any bureaucrat or bureaucracy [in bureaucratic politics] is not rational efficiency, but individual and organisational survival' (Herzfeld 1992: 5), suggesting that such politics are embedded deep in the make-up of bureaucratic systems. Bureaucratic politics can thus be described as self-serving or be 'concerned with the expansion of [bureaucrats'] own power, budget, prestige or reputation' (Radaelli 1999: 51n14) – a strange form of self-reflexivity in this case.

Bureaucratic politics and competition hardly remain specific to Turkey (Radaelli 1999: 38; Page & Wouters 1994; Page & Wright 1999). Yet the Turkish case scarcely went unnoticed by EU counterparts: 'When a new government takes over the office in Turkey', my SGAE contact noted, 'it completely changes the personnel responsible for European affairs'. Other EU interlocutors described Turkish bureaucratic culture as top-down. Nineteen of the thirty-nine Commission officials I interviewed, whose job description concerned Turkey's Europeanisation, observed this. The organisational hierarchy thickened as one moved upwards, creating a separation between the top and the bottom of administrations within and among public offices that were supposed to work together, which resulted in a vertically challenged communication. More significantly, unlike their EU counterparts, Turkish diplomats in Brussels had no central role in facilitating accession negotiations, except in the field of communication as outlined in Law No. 1173 on the conduct and coordination of Turkey's international relations, which gives the responsibility for conducting international negotiations on behalf of Turkey to the Ministry of Foreign Affairs. Even though EU interlocutors preferred to be in direct contact with their Turkish counterparts in Ankara-based ministries, they met with resistance from Turkish diplomats. Sticking to the chain of bureaucratic command and invoking Law No. 1173, Turkish diplomats insisted that all requests for information, appeals and complaints go through their office first.

Beyond the legal requirement, however, I found another reason for their reluctance: when diplomats were sent to Brussels, they risked being cut off from negotiations with the EU due to the institutional set-up of negotiations on the Turkish side. To prove public ownership of EU–Turkey relations, something demanded by President Erdoğan himself, they resisted relaxing Turkey–EU administrative communications: rigid formulas helped them (re)emphasise their otherwise diminished role in EU negotiations and also reinforced their part in Turkey's domestic bureaucratic politics.

Their degree of involvement in the negotiation process adversely impacted their public presence vis-à-vis their EU colleagues. With a diminished role in actual negotiations, delegation diplomats' main task increasingly became to arrange the visits of Turkish politicians and government officials in Brussels and to facilitate their high-level meetings with their EU counterparts, much like a travel agency does. As the ruling AKP increasingly blurred the boundaries between the state, the government and the party, many state offices abroad acted like AKP offices and advocated for the party's needs and wants.

Specialisation among Turkish diplomats was not well managed: 'Everyone is expected to be a specialist on everything', Merih bemoaned. By practice, the Turkish foreign office sent its diplomats to one or two 'developing' (read: non-Western) countries after a term in a 'developed' country and a term in the headquarters, regardless of their expertise and language skills. Turkish diplomats tended to favour two key foreign policy areas for their specialisation: NATO due to the Cold War and the EU due to the significance given to relations with this bloc. Each year, the ministry gave scholarships to two young diplomats to study at the College of Europe, one of whom would later be posted to the delegation in Brussels and the other to a European country. Turkish diplomats built lifelong friendships with other College of Europe alumni, many of whom would similarly be posted to Brussels and EU countries after their education. Merih, Murat and others were College of Europe alumnae, and their first appointment was to the delegation in Brussels, followed by one term in Ankara and another in a non-Western country, as foreign service commonly required.

Diplomats like Merih, Murat and Hande clearly had capacity to serve as human bridges between Brussels and Ankara. The problem was that their expertise was never made central to policy decisions. Instead of a specialised negotiating team, successive AKP governments wanted every state institution to get involved in the process and increase ownership of EU integration by as many actors from the public sector as possible, because the Turkish public sector showed the lowest support for Turkey's EU vocation.

Merih indicated another reason for lack of motivation among Turkish diplomats: work overload. During my fieldwork, the staff at the delegation numbered thirty-seven – including eleven diplomats from the Ministry of Foreign Affairs, six bureaucrats from the Foreign Trade Office, two from the Treasury and one each from the Ministry of Agriculture and the Ministry of Labour and Social Security. The remainder included a defence adviser, drivers, assistants, security personnel and other support staff. It was smaller than any other EU member state representation or candidate country mission, and even smaller than consultancy firms like Hill+Knowlton Strategies. In 2018, the delegation grew to forty-six staff.

Inside, a virtual wall separated diplomats from the Foreign Affairs Ministry and others from other Turkish ministries. Diplomats acted as if they ran, or were themselves, the delegation and called everyone else 'support staff'. Diplomat or not, no one – except the ambassador – enjoyed housing support or health insurance, which were available to their EU colleagues. Leaving their families behind, Turkish diplomats were sent to Brussels to build new lives with much blessing and three times their current public salary. They were advised to find accommodation 'suitable' to entertain EU colleagues and entertain them often and well.

The delegation operated like a black box compared with other representation offices I visited in Brussels, even from a native's perspective. While walking through it, I couldn't tell whether we were in Brussels or in Ankara. It took me a while to establish who was who in it. After the opening of accession negotiations, staff shortages turned acute. There were simply not enough bodies to work on individual negotiating chapters, leaving one administrator responsible for too many policy issues. Some policy areas received extensive (and extra) coverage, while others remained untouched. Dossiers frequently changed hands, badly affecting the working environment between Turkish diplomats and their EU colleagues. Work overload burdened many. Their daily routine included more deskwork, leaving them with less time to spend outside the office for networking.

I met Mustafa, a Turkish diplomat from the delegation, for the first time at a party. Intending to introduce the new art gallery and representation office of the city of Istanbul to Euro-circles, the gathering took place at the brand new Istanbul Centre in Brussels. The Centre promoted Istanbul as a global brand, in preparation for Istanbul's 2010 European Capital of Culture.[12] While Leyla became the media ambassador for the Istanbul 2010 project, Zehra, who was close to both Turkey's chief EU negotiator and the mayor of Istanbul, ran the Centre as its chairwoman. Pondering why the Centre was not at street level, those who knew Zehra mentioned her disdain for 'going down to the ordinary people' and her concern that 'those southerners [Turkish migrants in Brussels] might mistake the Centre for a community place, tourism office or a culture house'. A year later Zehra proudly received the best regional office award for the Istanbul Centre.

The Centre had prominent figures on its board. They included Bağış, one of the founding figures of the Istanbul 2010 project, back in 2000, and an MP from Erdoğan's AKP, who later became its first EU minister and (second) chief negotiator; and Joost Lagendijk, the Dutch politician and former MEP from the Greens, who at the time served as the co-chair of the EU–Turkey Joint Parliamentary Committee (JPC). A day before, Lagendijk showed support by appearing at a more modest event inside the EuroCities network, inaugurating the representation office of the city of Yalova, his Turkish wife's hometown. The following day and two blocks from EuroCities, the then enlargement commissioner, the mayor of Istanbul and Zehra cut the ribbon inaugurating the Centre. Everyone moved to the galleries and conversations continued over drinks and hors-d'oeuvres – a variety of dishes from around Turkey. While in the background Zehra was trying to convince the Turkish-Cypriot ambassador – a title Turkish diplomats bestowed on him – to hold future meetings of the Turkish-Cypriot president at the Istanbul Centre, Mustafa was joking with a well known British journalist about how boring life for European diplomats would have been without the Turkish EU bid to bicker about.

Unlike his colleagues, Mustafa had a job with a clear focus. He was to follow relations with Greece and Cyprus. He never made himself available to me for interview. He explained how a meeting with me was impossible since he could not talk about his job. I pressed and suggested that we could talk about his personal views on EU–Turkey affairs, but he did not bow to my persistence: 'My personal view is the same as the state's official discourse; *realpolitik* dictates it this way, it has to'. Though we never sat down for a one-to-one talk, on occasion Mustafa and I attended the same meetings, seminars, talks, cultural-political events or press conferences. About a year after the event at the Istanbul Centre, between a press conference and a party at the European Parliament, I managed to chat with him.

The occasion for the press conference was to raise awareness about the Varosha district of Famagusta/Gazimağusa, a port city under Turkish rule with historical significance for Mediterranean commerce. It featured the Greek mayor-in-exile. Positioned south of the city's port, Turkish forces have sealed off Varosha since 1974. With the accession of Cyprus to the EU in 2004, the Famagusta Refugee Movement, which represented Greek-Cypriot refugees, now EU citizens, from Varosha, petitioned the European Parliament to visit the area. The petitioners sought 'the assistance of the European Parliament to ensure that the Commission's initiatives to stimulate the economic development of northern Cyprus include the return of the closed area of Famagusta', according to the Parliament's *Report on the Fact Finding Visit to Cyprus* of 2008 (European Parliament 2008: 2). A delegation of four MEPs tried to visit Varosha in 2007, but failed. Instead, they peeked through the barbed wire: 'It [Varosha] is entirely fenced off by a decaying length of wire fencing and rusty oil-drums, by concrete barricades.... [T]he sea-front hotels, apartment blocks and restaurants are no more than decaying concrete skeletons – massive urban gravestones standing resolutely against the march of time' (European Parliament 2008: 4; see also Navaro-Yashin 2012; Papadakis 2005). About a year later, Famagusta's Greek-Cypriot mayor-in-exile travelled to Brussels to meet with EU politicians. He pushed the EU leaders to pressure the Turkish government into reopening his city to maritime traffic with the outside world. The press conference and photo exhibit, titled 'A European Ghost Town', was meant to garner sympathy for the demands. During my fieldwork, I attended many events organised by both Turkish-Cypriots and Greek-Cypriots. Island residents from both sides had one common affliction: while the southerners criticised the Turkish occupation in the nouth, the northerners criticised the almost-universal embargo they were under, although, ironically, that had been imposed as a consequence of that same occupation.

During the press conference held inside the Parliament's Anna Politkovskaya Pressroom, named after the assassinated Russian journalist, Mustafa scribbled down notes recording who said what to whom. After leaving such meetings, he would return to his office to crypto-message his notes to Ankara. Much like anthropologist Catherine Alexander's study of Turkish bureaucracy in Ankara revealed, this encryption and other communications were nothing but 'materialised activity ... proof of productivity, of adherence to the official charter of obligations' (Alexander 2002: 97). Mustafa proved to be a tough statesman, but less a company- or a party-liner, unlike some of his other colleagues, such as Hasan.

An expert diplomat, Hasan was a typical Turkish modernisation success story. Born and raised in a central Anatolian town, he went to Ankara to study economics and continued his studies in France and later in Britain on government scholarships. Hasan was an idealist. He volunteered for active duty in politically volatile countries. This earned him the respect and recognition a diplomat needed to rise through the ranks of the Turkish foreign service, which has been difficult under Erdoğan's rule, which rejected several key diplomatic customs. Following his 'One minute!' outburst during a panel discussion on Gaza directed at Israeli President Shimon Peres at the World Economic Forum in Davos in 2009, Erdoğan showed contempt for his diplomatic advisers, who cautioned him to act moderately regarding the Israeli–Palestinian conflict. Returning to Turkey after his now famous flare-up, which had made him a hero among his supporters at home and abroad in the Middle East, Erdoğan scorned his diplomats' 'timidity'. Labelling them *monşer* (a term derived from the French *mon chère*), he showed much dislike of the well educated, well mannered, Francophone agents of Turkish diplomacy (Aras 2011).

By all accounts, Hasan fell outside of this category. His posting to Afghanistan brought him a choice between Paris and Brussels for his next destination. Diplomats usually had no say where they were going to be posted, but this was going to be his reward for outstanding performance. He thought, 'If EU membership talks are going to open, I'll go to Brussels'. When accession negotiations were opened, Hasan moved to Brussels. In fact, this was his second posting to the delegation. When I got to know him, Hasan had been with the Ministry of Foreign Affairs for twenty years, the last three of which he had served at the delegation.

Both Mustafa and Hasan came from class backgrounds too simple for the old establishment diplomacy to allow them to rise through the ranks.[13] Both men joined the Ministry of Foreign Affairs around the same time and worked on the Balkans and the EU. Unlike Hasan, Mustafa was known for his Middle East expertise. After their service in Brussels, both men were sent to Iraq. Hasan had a successful tenure after Brussels, proving his diplomatic skills to Turkey's EU minister and chief negotiator, Bağış, to the foreign affairs minister and later prime minister, Davutoğlu, and finally to prime minister and later president, Erdoğan himself, especially after the kidnapping and later release of sixteen Turkish construction workers by ISIS in Iraq in 2015. I watched Hasan on television presenting the brave workers to Erdoğan in his presidential palace. Unlike Hasan, after his brief stint advising the prime minister, Mustafa's diplomatic career dramatically faltered. The Turkish government took 101 days to save him from his ISIS captors inside Turkey's Mosul embassy, where he was held hostage along with his staff in 2014. Whereas Hasan later became Turkey's EU ambassador and deputy minister for foreign affairs, Mustafa left diplomacy for politics and was elected to the Turkish parliament on the opposition ticket in 2015, assuming the role of foreign-policy adviser to the party leader and later deputy chairman.

While still in Brussels, Mustafa received an e-mail from Elena, a parliamentary assistant to a liberal Bulgarian MEP, which exposed the black box of Turkish diplomacy in an unexpected way. That morning, a Turkish actor had revealed during a television show a potentially incriminating incident regarding events that took place during his military service in the north of divided Cyprus. The Greek-Cypriot media picked this up quickly and uploaded his testimony onto YouTube. Cypriot MEPs circulated the YouTube video through Brussels' EU circles. Elena wrote to Mustafa, informing him that the video had gone viral around the European Parliament. Mustafa wanted to respond to Elena when an awkward technicality barred him from doing so: YouTube was at the time banned in Turkey and Mustafa had no access to the video from his work computer. The delegation was a black box even to its own people!

The problem of collocution and a fix

Since she was overburdened by deskwork, only on rare occasions did I spot Merih in public. Once I did so at an event promoting Croatia's EU membership, hosted by the Croatian Business Council, at the luxurious Conrad Hotel (currently Steigenberger Wiltcher's). Located in Brussels' upmarket shopping district, the Turkish government and business society organisations, too, favoured this hotel. About a year previously, I, along with three Turkish ambassadors, their diplomats and journalists, had attended a lunchtime event there on Turkey's economic potential and EU membership, where the Turkish minister for trade was the guest speaker. The earlier event had been organised by Mehmet, who represented the Confederation of Businessmen and Industrialists of Turkey in Brussels. A conservative version of the Turkish Industry and Business Association, Deniz's organisation, and well spoken of by Erdoğan himself during its heyday, the Confederation was banned following the 15 July 2016 coup attempt, due to its alleged links to the Turkish Muslim cleric Fethullah Gülen, who lives in self-exile in the United States and who has been accused of masterminding the unsuccessful putsch. Before the Confederation was banned, however, a British think-tanker, who wrote a column for a banned, Gülen-affiliated Turkish newspaper and who occasionally lobbied for British Petroleum, tried to bring Deniz and Mehmet together to collaborate. Deniz stayed away from Mehmet as far as possible, considering how politically unsavoury such a collaboration could be, even before the coup attempt.

A year after that high-level lunch, I was back at the Conrad. The air in the room this time was calmer than a year ago. I recognised the faces of interlocutors from EU member states and the Commission. While we waited for the speakers, the projector showed still images of Croatian and EU leaders shaking hands or talking to each other in a friendly manner. Pictures from the Croatian seaside appeared next. Croatia had one simple message to the EU: if it were to join the EU, the Western Balkans would follow. During negotiations, Croatia was presented as a candidate country that held the key to solve the conflicts in troubled Western Balkan countries and would facilitate their eventual EU accession. Croatian diplomats appeared to know their EU counterparts well; Merih seemed to know them all.

During coffee break, I mentioned to Merih how much the Slovenia–Croatia border dispute reminded me of the Cyprus conflict. She berated me for not raising the issue during Q&A. Since I was a student, she suggested, I could have (and, as a Turk, should have) asked about it. Merih essentially asked me to act like an 'immigrant ambassador' (Hess 2009) or a 'citizen diplomat' (Conley Tyler & Beyerinck, 2016), a role many Turkish expats gladly performed in Brussels. A Turkish friend who worked at the Commission publicly expressed his disappointment in Turkey's (and his) Europeanness being questioned ('Only after coming to Europe [Brussels] did I learn that I might not be European'). Acting like a citizen-lobbyist, a position which calls for action, more so than that of a citizen-diplomat, he wanted to fix this 'mistake' by contacting Commission libraries to correct their cataloguing of Turkey as an 'Asian' country. On another occasion, Murat compared Turkish-Belgians with Belgians of Greek and Armenian origin. He shared his frustration with the 'failings' (sic) of Turkish-Belgians in mobilising to lobby the EU for Turkish accession. The citizen-lobbyist remained a powerful subject position, celebrated equally by white-collar expats and diplomats.

To ask questions about Turkey's fate in the EU was not something the diplomats themselves felt they could do. Merih could not do it herself, she lamented, because, as a diplomat, people would think she was delivering a 'political' message, giving the state line in a public meeting. Both Merih and Hande felt that when they said something in public, the audience took it 'like the state is talking'. '[But] when the lobbies talk, it is the voice of civil society', as Hande and Murat put it, agreeing with the Commission's deep lobbying, expressed by a Commission official who suggested that some things are better said by others.

Another reason may be, as Hasan later suggested, that, as representatives of Turkish public interests, he and his colleagues from the delegation felt more 'listened to', or influential, at EU institutions like the European Parliament. This indicates at least a mismatch between parties to Turkey's EU accession dialogue, a problem of collocution. Turkish diplomats in Brussels found it much easier to communicate with politicians and their staff than EU member state diplomats, who were of similar aptitude.

In a world of fast communication, rules of communication change and quick responses are now demanded, which threatens to make diplomacy's traditional agents obsolete. To prove their significance for the accession process, then, delegation diplomats strove to monopolise communications, at least, between EU partners and government institutions between Brussels and Ankara. They demanded that all information and communication pass through their office and the Ministry of Foreign Affairs before being distributed to stakeholders in the country. They thus further bureaucratised communication between Brussels and Ankara. This bureaucratisation contributed to a conflict of interest between different state institutions – hindering the much-needed collocution between Turkish and EU actors.

Conclusion

Formal and informal communicative practices such as intergovernmental negotiations, diplomacy and lobbying created channels of information, interest and influence between EU member states, aspiring members and corporations that were invested in the ways member states and candidate countries related. Closed to public scrutiny, internal Council meetings on EU enlargement provided a pertinent platform to that end – and an exceptional vantage point to observe how sovereignty was exercised in today's Europe, confirming Eppink's insider revelation with which I opened Part III of the book.

In this chapter, I laid out the complex machinery of how corporate, institutional and bureaucratic interests influenced the construction and conveyance of 'national interests' during Turkey's Europeanisation. Those interests then moulded 'common European interests' and investments in Turkey's future sovereignty and statecraft. I mapped out how diplomats and lobbyists from both sides navigated the terms and conditions of Turkey's EU accession responsibilities at the Council level. Whereas EU member state diplomats enjoyed greater flexibility in diplomacy and lobbying, Turkish diplomats participated in the construction of Turkish national interests less (than their potential), due to how Ankara managed Turkey's EU policy. In this tight environment, Turkish diplomats enhanced the wedge between Turkish and EU policy fields, instead of facilitating their integration, to make their services useful.

The emerging conclusion is that 'national interest' is a fabricated representational instrument whose monopoly and legitimacy as a unitary category are lost to diplomats from both sides, for different reasons. Today, the national interests of EU member states and Turkey are very much shaped by intra-governmental (bureaucratic) and extra-governmental (corporate) interests. This is undoubtedly not a new development. Economic globalisation cum Europeanisation allowed new political and economic actors, whose accountability is not determined by democratic mandate, to take over matters that affect the lives of others. Europolitics enables the moulding of common member state interests by private interests (held by individual bureaucrats or corporate entities) via the vehicle of national interest, turning the interest of a few into the interests of millions. The Commission is the most important platform wherein private interest representatives from both sides effectively influence the terms and conditions of Turkey's Europeanisation to a greater extent than they are able to in other EU institutions, however. I now turn to that EU institution.

Notes

1 When a member state assumes the Council Presidency, it sends additional staff to Brussels from the national capital to help coordinate and manage Council Presidency activities and agenda (Elgström 2003).

2 In 2008, I visited SGAE as part of my EESC internship.

3 Signed in the French city of Sèvres on 10 August 1920, the Treaty of Peace Between the Allied Powers and the Ottoman Empire, the Treaty of Sèvres, marked the partitioning of what was left of the Ottoman Empire at the end of World War I. For many patriotic Turks, Sèvres represents the breaking-up of their homeland by international powers. Many fear that EU integration might do the same (White 2014).

4 Oskar never responded to my requests for an interview.

5 Because the working group was closed and I had no direct access, I cross-checked my interlocutors' accounts with one another. I interviewed thirteen enlargement officers; two members of the Council secretariat; diplomats from non-member Norway, Switzerland and Armenia, who followed the Council's work on EU enlargement from a distance; various Commission officials from DG Enlargement; and Turkish and Croatian diplomats in Brussels. I also had access to notes of the working group's meetings taken by two participants during two separate sessions, describing in detail what went on in those meetings. In one instance, I gained access to a memo that was meant for internal distribution. Thus, my account portrays both the ideal and the actual workings of the group.

6 As of January 2016, fifteen out of Turkey's thirty-five chapters had made it to COELA. The rest of the chapters remained at the Commission, awaiting the willingness of EU institutions and actors to deem Turkey's reform performance 'sufficiently qualifying' and to move the negotiations further.

7 Meanwhile, the Council Presidency and Commission met with candidate countries on issues related to the supervision of their compliance with the Copenhagen and Maastricht criteria but only after they informed member states in advance, which meant that member states closely monitored what the Presidency and Commission were doing in this regard.

8 Internal meeting notes of the EU Council Working Party on Enlargement, 5 June 2009.

9 Meanwhile, Turkish regulators fined Diageo for breeching competition rules in 2014 and again in August 2015. The Turkish Competition Authority put the company under investigation for 'abusing its market dominance' (Finkel & Buckley 2015).

10 DG Trade's Market Access Database keeps an online database of trade barriers that EU companies encounter with their main trading partners.

11 Real name.

12 The Centre was taken from Zehra soon after Istanbul 2010. The European Cultural Capital project, despite being embroiled in corruption scandals, on the whole contributed to the cleaning up of urban façades in Istanbul and to it becoming of a regional conference city.

13 For more information on the role of bureaucrats' class distinction in the Turkish diplomatic profession, see Alexander (2002) and Babül (2017).

5

Dramas of statecraft, mistrust and the politics of non-membership

Failed promises

Diplomacy and lobbying are often considered to require mutual trust and common understanding, because these underpin effective communication (Coen 1998, 2007; Woll 2012). Turkish–EU relations, however, are marked precisely by an absence of mutual trust between officials, economic actors and interest representatives on both sides. As relations were marked by mutual suspicion, mistrust and wariness on both sides, Turkish actors engaged in a curious politics of *non*-membership in order to manage the political and economic costs associated with Turkish Europeanisation. This new negotiation style pushed the politics of economic integration towards prioritising markets in Europe and Turkey instead of accession. This chapter investigates how bureaucrats, diplomats and lobbyists performed bureaucratic and symbolic politics during economic negotiations over the EU–Turkey customs union and Turkey's steel trade with EU countries – two strong pillars of EU–Turkey economic integration. The negotiations over industrial goods, manufactured agricultural products, steel, livestock, tomato paste and other sectors illustrate how actors negotiated economic integration through the prism of bureaucratic cultures that reflected and reinforced unequal and competing political economic interests.

Here, I take bureaucratic encounters between bureaucrats, diplomats and lobbyists during both formal and informal meetings, such as meetings of the EU–Turkey customs union, the Commission's expert committees, the EU–Turkey Steel Contact Group or over dinner, as symbolic performances constitutive of cultural and political relations. Participants influenced economic integration negotiations and the definition of economic interests on both sides through these and other communicative channels that I discuss in this chapter.

Contrary to neo-functionalism, which valorises meetings between national- and EU-level bureaucrats, experts, representatives of organised interests and elected politicians for their capacity to foster socialisation (March & Olsen 1998; Suvarierol 2009; cf. Shore 2000), my analysis of transnational encounters between Turkish and EU actors during technical, sectoral and social meetings reveals a disjunction between actors' politico-cultural imaginaries of what common interests would look like. The larger politico-economic context and its associated fissures that surround such encounters eclipse further bureaucratic work on ways to enhance economic integration and make cultural encounters during EU–Turkish meetings undesirable.

Customs union and the lobbyists' success

Customs regimes impact a state's sovereignty, in that they reduce its ability to make economic policy in its own territory. Not only are customs a source of revenue but they also eliminate outside competition for the country's economic claimants (Tilly 1985: 181). Inspired by a model of economic cooperation that resolves political feuds – feuds that resulted in two devastating wars in the region – the six states that ultimately founded the EU first formed a community based on coal and steel cooperation when they signed the Treaty of Paris in 1951. In 1957, the Treaty of Rome established the European Economic Community (EEC). Partially modelled on the German Zollverein (Henderson 1981), it prescribed a common customs regime whereby goods and services could circulate among member states without tariff or customs duty barriers. This 'pooling of sovereignties' (Keohane 2002; Ong 2006; Sassen 1996, 2006) at the EU level (also known as 'exclusive competence' in EU-speak) means that the Commission alone proposes policy in matters of: customs union; internal market and competition; and economic, monetary and commercial affairs. It also enforces EU decisions that prevail over the interests of individual member states in these policy areas. The EU has thus become a super- or a supra-state, not by collecting taxes as classical states do (Sassen 2006) but by the Commission instituting and managing a customs regime common to all EU member states, British Overseas Territories, and Monaco, Andorra, San Marino and Turkey. Because of its roles in policy-making and enforcing of common member state interests, the Commission has become the hub of economic diplomacy and lobbying over these policies through the exchanges of information, interests and influence between EU bureaucrats and lobbyists. Such exchange relations are magnified in the negotiations over EU–Turkey economic integration.

Following the Treaty of Rome, Turkey applied, in 1959, for association with the Community, which led to the famous Ankara Agreement of 1963, the only international agreement ever signed by the EU and Turkey in their long-running relationship. The Community and Turkey signed an additional protocol in 1970, provisioning the launching of a customs union whenever the parties were ready to do so. Developmental inequalities between them resulted in Turkey's gradual lifting of tariffs and customs duties on EU imports over two decades, while the Community unilaterally abolished customs duties on industrial goods and manu-factured agricultural products imported from Turkey in 1971 – except for textiles. By 1981, textiles represented 15 per cent of Turkey's total exports to Europe, leading the Community to apply quota restrictions to Turkish cotton yarn. The Turkish government retaliated with import restrictions on European steel products. Textile quotas remained a major problem between the Turkish government and the Commission for many years, until Turkish textile exporters took negotiations into their own hands by opening a representation office in Brussels, with Altan as their EU representative. Problems in the steel trade endured, however.

Political integration between Europe and Turkey was hardly an issue when the customs union was envisaged in the 1960s. By the time the customs union went into operation in 1996, European economic and political cooperation was maturing, with enlargement through the accession of former socialist countries. By then, Turkey had been experimenting with free market mechanisms for over a decade, having launched a transition from import substitution protectionism to export-oriented industrialisation in the early 1980s. The country had also launched its application for full membership of the EEC, in 1987, in response to which the Commission in its opinion to the Council two and a half years later offered instead to enhance preparations for a customs union.

At the onset of customs union efforts, Turkey's deepening economic integration with the EU meant more than simple regulatory changes and short-term economic benefits for Turkish power and policy elites but a step towards EU membership, which they valued highly (Kramer 1996). Political rhetoric back then suggested that further economic integration with the EU could eventually bring membership. Major theories, projections and promises of EU integration pointed that way. Functionalist Ernst Haas (1964: 65) suggested that 'the indirect penetration of the political by way of the economic' is a necessary evil because '"purely" economic decisions always acquire political significance in the minds of participants'. After the Commission's negative response to Turkey's membership application, the Turkish governmental and business communities decided not to wait for the famous 'spill-over' effect to kick in. They actively engaged in efforts to make the customs union happen, which they saw as the last chance for full membership (Atan 2004). The Turkish government hired lobbyists from prominent multinational public relations (PR) firms to run campaigns in Brussels, Washington, DC, Paris and Berlin. The Turkish business community began its own campaign of economic diplomacy through its counterparts in Europe. It also called on large Turkey-based German, Italian, French and other firms to lobby the EU on Turkey's behalf (Atan 2004).

The campaigns succeeded and Turkey entered a customs union with the EU on 1 January 1996, fulfilling the decades-old promise of the Ankara Agreement. In that year, Turkey also became a party to the European Coal and Steel Community with a free trade agreement (FTA) on steel, effective in 1999. The EU and Turkey signed another FTA, pertaining to agricultural goods, in 1998. While the customs union anchored Turkey to the EU through trade and economic cooperation, accession negotiations were to safeguard this economic integration with political integration, guaranteeing the participation of Turkish citizens in decisions made at the EU level.

During the PR campaign, consultants from the Brussels office of the New York-based Hill+Knowlton reached out to MEPs via EU member state diplomats for their parliamentary support. Helen was one of the campaign lobbyists. During our interview in her office several blocks from the Commission and at a time when problems with the EU–Turkey customs union were being voiced more loudly than ever, Helen explained that during the campaign she was to convince MEPs that a customs union with Turkey was 'safe' for Europe.[1] She reminisced that German Christian Democrats supported the initiative, contemplating that the customs union would be enough for Turkey. Signifying a nightmare scenario of turning their country into an EU colony in the Turkish mind, the German proposal of 'privileged partnership' (instead of EU membership) and the Turkish emphasis on 'full membership' originated in those days.

Hill+Knowlton was trusted. Having maintained an office in Turkey since 1989, the firm worked for the Turkish government before the customs union campaign, and after. Later, its lobbyists campaigned for the opening of EU–Turkey accession negotiations and Istanbul's candidacy for the 2010 European Capital of Culture. Turkish governments since the 1990s have contracted major multinational PR firms like Hill+Knowlton, Burson-Marsteller, APCO and others. Since 2002, AKP governments have displayed a particular appetite for foreign consultants. Hill+Knowlton developed strong ties during the customs union campaign with Turkish governmental and business community representatives in Brussels. The lobbying campaign made careers for a handful of Turkish diplomats and lobbyists who were at the time among the negotiators of the customs union deal in Brussels. Some of these diplomats joined the private sector as economic lobbyists after the deal was consummated.

A decade after the customs union campaign, Turkey's economic integration with the EU looked like it would come to fruition. Subsequently, Helen from Hill+Knowlton met with Deniz. The two talked about launching a campaign 'to change the hearts and minds of the people' in Europe about Turkey. Their goal was to show support for the accession negotiations from a non-governmental, 'civil society' angle. That campaign lasted from October 2005 to March 2007, during which Deniz and members of the Turkish business community travelled EU capitals to meet with their counterparts.

Daniela was then an intern at Hill+Knowlton, working with Helen on the case. When I visited Daniela many years later at her office in DG Internal Market, she was working, again, on the Turkish case, this time as a Commission official. Before moving on to talk about internal market issues like public procurement and their implications for Turkey's EU accession, Daniela reflected on the complexity of the task in front of her during that PR campaign:

> It was not a normal campaign whereby a company would lobby for legislative changes in, say, health issues. Was there a product to sell? Turkish industrialists realised that there were a lot of misconceptions about Turkey and that they had to be changed. The campaign went well. The name of Turkish industrialists became known.

As an insider, Daniela measured the success of that lobbying campaign vis-à-vis the satisfaction of Hill+Knowlton's then client, which represented Turkey's most powerful companies. The real measure of efficacy, according to Daniela, however, was that the campaign helped Deniz and his association become more visible in Brussels' Eurocratic scenes. During the customs union negotiations, Deniz advised the Turkish delegation in Brussels in an unofficial capacity. His role during those negotiations helped him become known among Eurocratic circles in Brussels. That PR campaign and Hill+Knowlton's lobbying later helped Deniz become the coordinator of the representation offices his organisation maintained around the world and, later, the chief executive officer of his organisation.

Other Turkish lobbyists – Altan, Orhan and Biray – organised similar lobbying campaigns in Brussels to deepen EU–Turkey integration. They sometimes enlisted paid help from lobbying firms or think-tanks, the latter of which worked like PR firms during the campaigns – much like the Croatian business event at Conrad Hotel I reported in Chapter 3. Their agenda varied from the modernisation of the customs union to the lifting of trade quotas and the visa restrictions with which Turkish service-providers often grappled. They scheduled appointments with MEPs and commissioners; organised press conferences, seminars and other public meetings at EU institutions or their premises; screened films and exhibited art; and held other kinds of social activities. The campaigns made Turkish interest representatives known in Brussels, and gained them recognition in the eyes of their employers at home, ultimately leading to contract renewals and job retention.

For decades, Turkey's EU lobbying has been closely associated with its business community representation in Brussels. This metonymical relationship was not always clear to Eurocratic minds: Did Turkey stand for its business community/ lobby, or did its business community/lobby stand for Turkey? While the EU– Turkey economic integration did not mature into political integration, throughout Turkey's EU saga the customs union has been a historical marker in building this supportive yet ultimately metonymical relationship between Turkey and its business community.

'The China of Europe'

Despite strong domestic dissent often couched as anti-globalisation sentiments, many in the country were ecstatic when Turkish and EU politicians sealed the customs union agreement, thanks in part to the lobbying campaign (Eder 2001; Ülgen 2006; Ülgen & Zahariadis 2004; Yılmaz 2007). An EC–Turkey Customs Union Joint Committee (CUJC) was subsequently tasked with providing a common platform for officials and experts from both sides to ensure the smooth functioning of the customs union.[2]

The customs union with the EU, in the main, implied free movement (elimin-ation of customs duties and quantitative restrictions) for goods either wholly produced or put in free circulation after their importation from third countries in either Turkey or the EC. It covers industrial products and manufactured agri-cultural products but not agricultural goods and steel products, which are covered by separate FTAs. For services (free movement of labour) and public procurement (government contracts), no common regulation exists, even though efforts to modernise the customs union include provisions for them.

Because of trade liberalisation in the neoliberal 1980s and the customs union in the mid-1990s (Öniş 2004), Turkey's economic integration with the EU accelerated, quintupling Turkey–EU trade volume between 1996 and 2016. Today, Turkey is the EU's fifth largest export market and sixth largest provider of imports. The EU exports machinery, transport material, chemical products and manufactured goods to Turkey, while Turkey exports to the EU mostly machinery and transport equipment, followed by manufactured goods (DG Trade 2019). Between 1996 and 2016, the share of agriculture, textiles and clothing in Turkish exports to the EU fell dramatically, while the share of automotive sector, machinery, and iron and steel exploded (BKP Development and Research Consulting 2016).

EU–Turkey trade volumes were popular statistics among AKP politicians and AKP-supporting businesspeople. They provided favourable figures to support Turkey's EU integration. Visiting Brussels, the AKP politicians I watched give talks at public forums proudly announced that their country was the sixth largest economy *of* Europe.

Turkey's growing share of manufactured goods exported to the EU led analysts to acclaim the country as 'Europe's BRIC' or 'the China of Europe' (*Economist* 2010). Participants at high-level exclusive economic gatherings enjoyed Turkey being called the China of Europe, as they hoped it would attract more foreign investment; successive neoliberal AKP governments based their economic 'miracle' on this investment.[3] While guests were sipping the instant Turkish coffee Zehra's team served during a European business summit panel on Turkey which Zehra organised for Turkey's largest telecommunications company, Turkcell, and which Deniz moderated, Turkcell's chief executive officer told his audience about the potentials of Europe's fourth largest labour force, whom he described as 'driven, educated, skilled, innovative and hungry!'

But not everyone agreed. A chemical engineer who owned a small pharmaceuticals company and supplied the steel sector explained the inequalities disguised by this new alias:

> They [potential buyers from the EU] come to us and tell us to produce such-and-such product according to such-and-such regulations and product model. They tell us how much they will pay us for the product. They impose their own experts [on us] as controllers during the production process. They even demand that their own lorries transport the finished products to designated addresses in the EU. There is greater industrial production in the EU but no one to drive the lorries [to transport goods around]. For the EU, Turkey is the Near East [China being the Far East]. They need human labour; skilled human labour; labour of those who are like them.

In short, the cost to Turkish suppliers of becoming Europe's 'China' came with disciplinary market measures.

These market measures caused problems that spilled over to other sectors, like logistics. With the help of Deniz and Orhan (though they did not get along well), the International Freight Forwarders Association, representing Turkey's logistics industry, campaigned for a quota-free Europe. The Association also hired Osman, one of Turkey's few expert lobbyists. Representing the interests of Turkey's freight transporters' union, Osman would speak at seminars organised by EU think-tanks in the morning and meet with the Commission officials in the afternoon. During one of his visits to Brussels, Osman revealed his lobbying strategy to 'clear the ball' away from the Turkish goal: if the Commission did not want to hurt the EU economy, it needed to get rid of export quotas and visa restrictions on Turkish lorry drivers, who drove 'European goods' manufactured by Turkish factories fuelled with EU capital for EU consumers. Despite Osman's well calculated lobbying, the visa issue continues to be a problem for Turkish service providers.

'Living in sin'

According to the terms set in 1996, Turkey agreed to join the EU's common customs area, which already existed at the time, with established rules and norms, including past, present and future FTAs the EU has signed and may sign with third countries. The difference between a customs union and an FTA is that the former disciplines the signatories' external economic relations with third countries, while an FTA is a strictly one-to-one relationship and does not concern others not a party to the agreement (Ahearn 2011). By implication, within the FTA framework, states are free to apply instruments of trade protection to third countries. As part of its customs union obligations, Turkey has to apply the EU's common external tariff regime on non-EU imports. According to the FTA principle, when third countries' goods enter the EU market paying no customs duties, they also enter the Turkish market with the same provisions. But the same does not hold for Turkish exports to those markets, unless those third countries with which the EU has signed FTA agreements sign additional FTAs with Turkey, which they rarely do. Turkey thus has to apply EU trade rules while trading with third countries even though Turkey had no say in making the rules. Turkey's enduring powerlessness regarding EU decision-making troubled Turkish actors the most.

Usual EU practice suggests that candidate countries enter a customs union with the EU when they become Union members; that is, political integration precedes or goes hand in hand with economic integration. In that regard, the Turkish case remains an anomaly because, even though Turkey has become a de facto part of the EU's common market (except for agriculture, services and public procurement), Turkish legislators and businesspeople have to abide by the EU *acquis* without having a say in its making. In addition, a customs union falls short of the intermediary stages of common market and economic and monetary union (the euro as the common currency) before complete economic integration. Turkey remains the only country that entered the Union's economic zone before it even gained EU candidacy (Eder 2001: 33). This situation led an early critic to describe the EU–Turkey customs union as 'living in sin' (Peers 1996).

As per the recommendation of the 2002 Copenhagen European Council that the customs union with Turkey be 'extended and deepened', Turkish representatives to the CUJC asked the Commission to consider Turkey's interests while negotiating new FTAs with third countries and to inform Turkish authorities about common EU positions before and after their signing (Ülgen & Zahariadis 2004: 7–8). According to my copies of the CUJC meeting transcripts from 2008 to 2016, Turkish representatives recommended that the Commission add a 'Turkey clause' to future FTAs. They repeatedly sought the Commission's intervention as a go-between for Turkey in trade matters discussed between EU member states and third countries, which put the Commission in an awkward position. The Commission did not reject Turkey's calls for help. Various commissioners had helped solve such matters for Turkey in the past, but this was exactly when a technical matter of economic loss turned into a matter of political representation, requiring the Commission to act on Turkey's behalf. But back in 2008, the Commission chose not to intervene when it took the following position: although any FTA the EU signs with third countries are by default extended to include Andorra and San Marino, Turkey is a major competitive power, unlike those two countries, and the EU could not negotiate FTAs on behalf of Turkey with third countries within the existing institutional structure – that is, without EU membership. Until Turkey becomes a member of the EU, then, companies from both sides trade in uncharted territory, and the issue remains unresolved.

Wars and weapons of diplomacy and trade

From the Commission's perspective, the customs union brought both rights and obligations. Turkey is expected to harmonise its trade laws with EU legislation and eliminate technical barriers to trade. Contrary to EU prescriptions, this turned out to be a massive problem with great cost for Turkish bureaucrats and lawmakers (for actual cost estimates, see Togan 2015). Fred Misrahi, an official who had worked at the EU delegation in Ankara for several years and had first-hand access to and knowledge of the negotiations, suggested that the problem was more of a political nature than an economic one:

> Turkish authorities were arguably not encouraged by a number of other factors that negatively affected their ability to effectively align their technical legislation with the EU's. For political reasons the EU, which had taken more than a year to communicate the list of instruments to Turkey, did not deliver the aid announced as part of the political deal surrounding the CU [customs union], whereas Turkey lacked expertise and needed technical assistance to adopt, implement and enforce *acquis*-compatible legislation. (Misrahi 2010: 196)

This should not come as a surprise, however, when even the EU *acquis* itself can become a means of politicising Turkey–EU relations.

The most serious problems were in the areas of metrology, calibration, quality certification, standardisation, testing, inspection and laboratory accreditation. A decade into the customs union, Misrahi (2010) complained, Turkey continued to lack the technical capacity and infrastructure to meet the needs of the testing and certification processes of traded goods. Such lack of infrastructure in turn translated into a lack of confidence in Turkish processes and procedures. The burden for Turkish exporters became significant, as they needed to certify their products with foreign laboratories and institutes, which created trade barriers for Turkish exports to the EU and increased transport and administrative costs (Ülgen & Zahariadis 2004: 16).

To protect its economic interests, Turkey came up with its own trade protection instruments, some of which were quite imaginative. For instance, Turkish customs officials did not recognise existing trade certificates for certain categories of EU exports to Turkey and required duplicate procedures for imports already certified tradable or put restrictions on imports of third-country goods already freely circulating in the Turkey–EU common customs area.[4] To this day, Turkish customs authorities require duplicate testing to shifting categories of imports. The practice remains high on the agenda of the CUJC.

In the absence of trust and confidence, both parties used 'technical' means to protect their interests (European Commission 2009; Misrahi 2010; Ülgen & Zahariadis 2004). Such weapons of diplomacy, lobbying and protectionism are common phenomena from an international political economic perspective (Eckhardt 2015; van Apeldoorn 2002), which anthropologists and ethnographers have begun to document (Abélès 2011; Garsten & Sörbom 2017, 2018; Niezen & Sapignoli 2017). The problem with trade protectionism from the perspective of the EU, as my Commission interlocutors suggested, is that it ran against the spirit of the common customs regime, the bilateral trade agreements as well as 'trustworthy partnerships'. Their Turkish counterparts could not agree more.

As attested by both anthropologists and political scientists, the establishment of mutual (mis)trust and (non-)confidence are socio-cultural matters (Carey 2017; Cook et al. 2009; Gambetta 1988; Kalb & Tak 2006; Keating & Ruziska 2014). 'Just like interests', Kalb and Tak suggested, trust and mistrust 'are involved in the production of [the] knowledge of daily experience, which in this sense [is] naturally strongly determined by earlier experiences. Trust is real but constructed, and of course contested' (Kalb & Tak 2006: 197). Trust and confidence also require different cultural strategies. The apparent distortions and mismanagement in the EU–Turkey customs union that became manifest served as a form of latent economic protectionism in trade relations, and also as a means for both sides to manage the political and economic costs associated with Turkey's EU accession process. Such protectionism was evident not only in issues related to the customs union but also in other EU–Turkey economic and trade relations, for example in the steel trade. More significantly, protectionism was not just an economic or political matter. It had important implications at the individual bureaucratic level, manifested in the cultural behaviour of the actors and agents of this process.

The 'T. file' on steel

Alessandro welcomed me to his office, of just six square metres, in the Commission's DG Enterprise and Industry (now DG Grow) – one of many nearly identical small offices I had visited in many other Commission buildings. Before sitting with me to talk about EU–Turkey relations, Alessandro pulled from a nearby shelf a green file with a 'T.' for Turkey on it. An economics professor who besides his job at the Commission taught at a university in his native Italy, Alessandro had been working on the 'T. file' for fifteen years when we met.

In the aftermath of World War II, France, Germany, Italy, the Netherlands, Luxembourg and Belgium signed the Treaty Establishing the European Coal and Steel Community in 1951 – a precursor to the founding treaties for what evolved into a political union at the close of the twentieth century. Envisioning greater economic integration between the German coal and the French steel industries, this treaty was originally signed for fifty years and expired in 2002. Turkey became a party to it in 1996 with a special steel FTA. Once one of the two main pillars of economic integration in Europe, along with coal, today steel is the most important import-sensitive sector in the region (and globally) and is highly protected across EU markets, attesting to the influence steel interests enjoy among EU policy-makers and decision-makers (Galgóczi et al. 2015; Grünert 1987; Sedelmeier 2002). And until recently, Turkey was deeply integrated with the EU through the steel trade.

With thirty-two steel plants, Turkey is the eighth largest steel producer in the world and the third largest in Europe, after Russia and Germany (World Steel Association 2018). The EU has been by value the largest exporter of steel to Turkey; in quantity, however, Turkey has been the largest exporter to the EU. Turkey produces twice the quantity of long steel products (mainly rebar and beams supplying its booming construction sector), which require less sophisticated production technologies (Ülgen 2008: 6) than the highly engineered flat products used in making ships, cars, consumer durables, and oil and gas pipelines.[5] The demand for flat products is high, and Turkey imports from France, Germany, Russia, and the Ukraine in Europe. Investments in flat products has gradually increased, and their production (as well as export) has tripled since 2001 but so has output of long products (Ministry of Science, Industry and Technology 2018; World Steel Association 2018). These factors brought Turkish producers into yet another unequal trading relationship with their EU counterparts, who have been reluctant to share their technology, due to fears about the consequences of rising Turkish competitiveness in world markets.

There are three key reasons for Turkey's competitiveness in steel. First, Turkish steel producers commonly cut costs by importing cheap raw materials from Russia and the Ukraine, which sell their surplus to Turkey at a lower price than in the EU, while the EU applies a quota to Russian and Ukrainian steel (Pleines 2005). High domestic demand put Turkish companies in an awkward position: they could ignore EU quotas and buy as much as they needed from Russia and the Ukraine or face financial difficulties by paying higher EU prices (Ülgen 2008: 12–13). Second, Turkish labour costs continue to be much lower than those in EU member states (Günay 2008: 222) – Turkish steel workers earn about one-fifth of the wages of steel workers in Germany or Belgium (Ülgen 2008: 8). Third, Turkish steel's competitiveness in EU markets benefits from recycling. Between 1999 and 2017, Turkey increased its scrap imports threefold; it has been the world's top scrap importer. Turkish producers buy scrap metal from domestic and international markets, remanufacture and sell it as long products to domestic and foreign markets. Unlike raw steel, scrap metal is abundant. As the director of a major Turkish steel company, Sedat, explained to me with great satisfaction, when we met for an interview in his Istanbul office in 2011: 'Scrap is produced both during the making of machines' at, for instance, primarily export-oriented automotive manufacturing plants that run on cheap Turkish labour and expensive European capital and technology, and 'once those machines become scrap; there is, hence, plenty of scrap to export and plenty to buy'.

Alessandro was convinced that Turkish producers sold their steel (unfinished bars and wire rod) at lower prices than the EU average, therefore disturbing traditional purchasing practices in steel-intensive sectors like French or Italian automobile producers, which favoured French or Italian steel producers. He pointed out that if Turkish producers were to export their products evenly between traditional and new markets in Europe, the Commission would have had a hard time detecting it. But instead, cheaper Turkish steel poured into the well-protected markets of France, Italy and Spain, which remained, in practice, 'national', threatening the EU's 'common market'.

'Common interests'?

I mentioned my interest in the EU–Turkey steel trade to Mesut, who, as Alessandro's counterpart, followed steel sector-related problems (among many other things) at the Turkish delegation. Chitchatting during at a nearby pub, Mesut mentioned that that morning the Commission had launched a new anti-dumping complaint, upsetting delegation diplomats and Turkish steel producers.

Mesut and his colleagues suspected the European Confederation of Iron and Steel Industries (EUROFER) of being the culprit. Representing the collective voice of European steel producers, EUROFER had special access to EU policy-makers (Grünert 1987: 266–8). It pressured the Commission to investigate anti-dumping complaints by big European and Europe-based transnational steel companies, most notably by ArcelorMittal, a multinational conglomerate and the world's largest steel producer. If dumping were substantiated, DG Trade would recommend that the Commission refer the case to the World Trade Organization for further investigation. Even at this early stage, such a recommendation would disgrace the alleged perpetrator. Even if found unproven, anti-dumping investigations might damage the market value of the companies under investigation.

With headquarters in Luxembourg, ArcelorMittal actively lobbied both the Luxembourg government and the EU to influence EU steel policies and practices, as the Luxembourgian diplomat Benoit revealed to us in the previous chapter. Benoit explained:

> They [ArcelorMittal] are in contact with us for legislative proposals that affect them directly. Normally, it's not a confrontational relationship. The interests of these companies are also our interests because we want them to stay where they are [in Luxembourg]. From our side, the lobby[ing] we do is the kind that is more directly involved in the legislative process. So, it's either people from the Commission or member states to whom we try to get our view across.

Benoit mentioned a specific privatisation case involving ArcelorMittal that had taken place a couple of years earlier in Turkey. Towards the end of the privatisation of Erdemir, according to EUROFER's director for trade and external relations, Matthias, the Commission suggested that Erdemir take a Western partner and recommended Arcelor. A formerly state-owned Turkish steel company, Erdemir provided about half of Turkish domestic demand in flat steel at that time. Its privatisation was a long anticipated, yet often protracted, outcome of the neo-liberal restructuring of Turkey's state-owned enterprises. Between 1987 and 2005, Erdemir was privatised in piecemeal fashion (Ağartan 2009). Final negotiations for its public tender took place the day after the EU opened accession negotiations with Turkey. Two years before Erdemir's privatisation, ArcelorMittal successfully bought Poland's state-owned steel company (Trappmann 2013); buyouts took place also during the privatisation of the Spanish steel sector. To EU counterparts' dismay, the Turkish Armed Forces Pension Fund (OYAK) became Erdemir's largest shareholder. Meanwhile, Arcelor and Mittal together bought about 14 per cent of Erdemir's stock. After winning the bid, OYAK began looking into foreign partners and briefly considered Mittal and Arcelor. In 2008, Arcelor and Mittal merged and increased their joint shares in Erdemir to just under 25 per cent. ArcelorMittal sold half of its shares in Erdemir after Erdemir's world status declined (Eryilmaz 2012).

When Matthias lobbied DG Trade on behalf of EUROFER, he used the curious trope of 'common European interest'. Anthropologist Marc Abélès and his colleagues said 'common European interest' functioned like a 'floating signifier' (Abélès et al. 1993: 62) – much like 'national interest' or 'the Community' as insiders refer to the EU (Abélès 2000: 42–3). Inspired by Claude Lévi-Strauss (1987 [1950]), Abélès et al. (1993: 62) defined the 'common European interest' as 'an idea which is essential but at the same time sufficiently vague that merely invoking it has a powerful effect'. Much like 'national interest', 'common European interest' as a floating signifier served a particular function in EU negotiations: member states invoked it when outsiders posed an economic threat (Abélès & Bellier 1996). In this classic example of advanced industrial capitalism's access and embeddedness in political-economic life, one multinational company's corporate interests became the 'common national interest' of an EU member state, which then moulded 'common European interests'. As a result, market competitors were successfully thwarted by means of lobbying the Commission and EU member states.

Domestic lobbying and state aid

Meanwhile in Turkey, the leading steel companies and the venerable Mahmut as their collective voice from Turkish Steel Producers Association lobbied the Turkish government to initiate its own anti-dumping investigations against EU competitors (SteelOrbis 2015). On their part, EU steel producers argued at the Commission that Turkish companies were successful because they received state subsidies, an argument that was not at all unfounded and a fourth factor in Turkish steel's competitiveness (Günay 2008: 212; Ülgen 2008: 6): Turkish steel producers received state aid in the form of low-interest development loans, export credits, insurance and tax relief benefits and the provision of low-cost inputs to suppliers.

In addition, 'Turkish steel producers that generate power with their own coal-fired or natural gas power plants benefit from state-controlled pricing schemes, resulting in artificially low energy costs for such producers' (Price et al. 2016: 19).

Between 1983 and 1994, Turkish steel production exploded, due mainly to the state's generous aid regime, which was traditionally given to selected companies, making public money highly prone to political influence. On the eve of the signing the FTA on steel with the EU in 1996, the Turkish government agreed to stop helping specific companies, sectors and regions, but the country negotiators also requested a five-year transition period. Meanwhile, the state continued to subsidise its steel industry, increasing the sector's growth between 2000 and 2014 by 150 per cent (Price et al. 2016: 2). The construction and automotive industries were key sectors in which Turkish steel enjoyed a comparative advantage domestically.

According to the current EU state aid regulations that now bind Turkey, too, EU member and candidate states can give state aid under strict conditions relating to environmental protection, research and development, and social measures taken in connection with plant closures (such as lay-offs or complete privatisation). Following the opening of accession negotiations, the European Commission (2006b: 6) recommended that the Turkish government establish a monitoring and supervision authority for state aid, and prepare a national plan on restructuring the steel sector and a comprehensive state aid inventory identifying companies that have received state subsidies since 2001. It also recommended that companies refund subsidies before any derogations could be granted. The Commission objected to the 2009 draft national restructuring plan on steel, which had no individual business plans. But the EU executive agreed that the Turkish government could continue subsidising its steel industry on the condition that the state would help the development of *flat* steel, where Turkey faced a disadvantage. Instead, Mesut explained, some Turkish steel companies that received state aid to build new capacity for flat products used it to increase their capacities for long products for emergent buyers in alternative markets from the Middle East and Commonwealth of Independent States.[6]

Individual business plans remained a major point of friction in the EU–Turkey steel trade. In 2010, Sedat was reluctant to open his firm's records to a British consultancy's Spanish auditors that had won a Commission bid to audit the Turkish steel sector's adherence to restructuring. He indicated the deep rivalry Turkish producers had with Spanish steel producers, some of the largest of which were acquired by ArcelorMittal *en masse* in 2006. Sedat and his colleagues from other Turkish steel companies fiercely competed with Spanish and other European steel producers in regional forums like EUROFER, the OECD Steel Committee and the EU–Turkey Steel Contact Group.

Steel interests face to face

Since 1998, Alessandro recounted, Turkish government officials from various public offices had met their counterparts from the Commission once a year within the framework of the EU–Turkey Steel Contact Group. Providing an exclusive space conducive to regional (and global) steel interest competition, forums like these revealed what was most important to steel traders. By nature, the bilateral Steel Contact Group was an exclusive platform for people who had known each other and had done business together for a long time. The EU–Turkey FTA on steel nurtured these business relations but the accession process added another layer of discipline to them.

During an ordinary meeting, Alessandro recounted (and other interlocutors who attended these meetings confirmed), Turkish and EU officials would gather to exchange opinions and the latest sectoral information. In a meeting room next door, Mahmut, Matthias, Sedat, who also sat on the board of Mahmut's Turkish Steel Producers Association, representatives of Erdemir and ArcelorMittal and other private steel firms and their lobbyists met. The Ankara-based national umbrella organisation of steel producers represented private Turkish interests, while the Brussels-based EUROFER represented private EU interests. The eight Turkish steel companies and their umbrella organisation were also associate members of EUROFER. To outsiders, who represented whom was hard to discern; to insiders, it was crystal clear. Powerful industrial players, meeting away from EU and Turkish negotiators, battled over competing private interests.

The atmosphere would dramatically change with the entrance of company representatives and lobbyists, who wished to brief their government officials. They would bring conflicts from next door into the official meeting, which would then become an arena with lobbyists and company representatives arguing. Alessandro suggested that each meeting turned into a fierce battle between the Turkish and EU representatives. If at the end of the meeting the Steel Contact Group failed to reach a common position satisfying both sides, participants blocked further negotiations. Interest battles then took the form of publicity attacks. The next day, newspapers would report different versions of what might have happened behind closed doors. Turkish and EU business and bureaucratic cultures were well attuned on this occasion.

Short-range passes on a narrow field

Customs union and steel trade negotiations played out in a narrow field, wherein actors brought in varying skills and competence from their cultures of governance, statecraft and bureaucracy. Meetings between EU and Turkish negotiators brought about mutual learning and understanding (but not necessarily agreement). During accession negotiations, negotiators from both sides devised ways to 'manage' each other. We cannot think of such learning outside of the pedagogical framework that emphasises mutual learning and teaching, wherein participants negotiate with each other as much as they learn how to negotiate, but fail to achieve common interests. For instance, the Turkish government initially sent high-level bureaucrats to meetings with the Commission. This changed, I was told, as soon as the government realised that the primary objective of such meetings was simply to exchange technical information – albeit 'technical information exchanges' are never as simple as that, as I show later in this chapter.

Other than technical and sectoral meetings, such as meetings of the CUJC and Steel Contact Group, the Commission invited Turkish representatives as observers to expert committee meetings, such as those on cars and textiles, of which Turkey was an important producer and exporter to the EU. In EU jargon, expert committees refer to proto-decision-making platforms that assist the Commission in executing its implementing powers by giving an opinion on draft implementation measures. These meetings were to provide a channel of communication and an informal forum for discussions on implementing measures. Turkish representatives went to these meetings without voting on texts that carried the Commission's opinions. Part of Mesut's job was to follow these meetings as the Turkish trade representative:

> It is like an intra-family meeting. You feel like you entered their bedroom. Twenty-seven [before Croatia's accession] of the member states sit in these meetings. Twenty-seven of them are speaking to each other calmly and properly. It affects me a lot. They call each other Mr Germany, Ms UK. They have a serious tradition of consensus and cooperation. Twenty-seven people sit down and talk about issues down to minute detail, and they talk openly, freely.

Mesut's immediate thoughts and feelings as he recounted his encounter with the EU bureaucracy triggered embarrassment. He felt like an outsider in a place where he thought he was a guest, as if the gathering were for family members only. Here were two processes of Othering, operating in tandem: Othering the EU bureaucracy vis-à-vis the Turkish bureaucracy and internally Othering the Turkish bureaucracy as the anti-character to itself.

Courtier versus college

Talking about each other, Turkish and EU officials frequently used stereotypes – stereotypes they refined over many years of encounter. Such stereotypes prove bureaucracy to be a social institution. Much like Mesut's account above, John, a British Commission official, invoked several stereotypes during our talk at his DG's cafeteria. Relaying his expertise and experience with the courtly world of power politics, John described the culture of governing and statecraft in Turkey as he perceived it. When exposed to Turkish interests and arguments, he thought of incoherence. Negotiating with Turkish counterparts, he would often ask himself: 'Is Turkey very clever, in which case you can manage incoherence? Or is there a method in its madness?' Like Mesut's account, John's includes portrayals of both self and Other. Unlike Mesut's latent comparison, John's account below is transparently comparative because, bred by accession pedagogy, comparison is deeply embedded in the very logic of EU governance and membership negotiations.

Prompted by my question on working with Turkish counterparts, John began his account by reflecting on two distinct administrative structures and negotiating methodologies in the EU: courtier and college systems. Both systems, John argued, long existed in Europe. 'Courtier' was a term first used in fourteenth-century Renaissance Italy to describe those who practised flattery at a royal court to win favour. In the college system, government ministers sat around a table and talked about problems in a policy area, where each had an equal say. From John's viewpoint, the main objective of ministerial meetings in the college system was to solve problems through public policy. Officials attending these meetings compromised on working plans. In the college system – and John gave Germany as an example – between governmental and political actors the common cause effected 'compromise' and 'cooperation'. The courtier system, to the contrary, depended on high concentrations of power and authority in individuals who sat at the top of the political structure. Here, elite outsiders could manipulate the system – even exploit it to their advantage – without a seat at the negotiating table, if they could access these individuals at the top.

True to countries with strong state traditions, John concluded, France and Italy used a courtier system rather than a college system, as did Turkey and Russia, which were 'still imperial powers', he observed. The difference between the French and the Italian courts, and the Turkish court, according to John, was that President Erdoğan was the sole decider on policy, without resorting much to technocratic expertise. In his court, no trade-offs and no functioning central staff to make compromises to balance out the courtier system existed between ministers and his personal advisers. John suggested that those countries which used the courtier system and had an imperial past adopted 'revanchism' as a negotiation style in their talks with the EU: 'Your concession today, my concession tomorrow'. I could picture Zekeriya (see Chapter 3) advising President Erdoğan in exactly this manner. In the absence of 'lateral contact' (Alexander 2002: 98) and a mechanism for compromise the different departments of government to reach a compromise (the absence of such a mechanism was commented upon by John as a result of his experience of meetings with Turkish cabinet members), President Erdoğan decided what needed to be done and who should do it. But how did all this courtly talk affect everyday negotiations between EU and Turkish representatives in Brussels, I wondered. What were the implications of the Turkish courtier system on the individual bureaucratic level?

Bureaucratic inertia, state tradition or sheer size matters?

John observed (and other Commission interlocutors confirmed) that technical meetings with the Commission were attended by a veritable crowd of Turkish negotiators. The size of the Turkish team varied, but no less than forty and up to eighty people were present in technical meetings held with the Commission, representing all governmental ministries and state agencies, especially if the meeting took place in Turkey. Meetings with the Commission provided a learning experience for Turkish delegates. Some saw these meetings as a rare opportunity to travel abroad, as Mesut explained and added: 'In Turkey bureaucrats think that attending a meeting is itself an action [eylem]'

When meetings were held in Brussels, Turkish delegates were welcomed by a Commission delegation typically of only five or six officials. During their meetings, group membership was obvious; so were the interests each group represented.

EU and Turkish officials sat facing each other. John and other Commission inter-locutors suggested that candidate country representatives usually had leeway to influence the atmosphere in which technical negotiations took place. The Turkish team chose to boost the meetings with their bodies. The sitting order gave clues about the ensuing style of negotiation and ultimately what the 'culture of com-promise' (Abélès & Bellier 1996; Bellier 2000a; Sideri 2005; Telesca 2015) was to look like between officials from both sides, something my Turkish interlocutors also mentioned.

Unlike the Croatian diplomats and bureaucrats, who tended to socialise during technical meetings, Turkish officials sat together as if they were lining up for an upcoming battle or a penalty kick in a football match. Considering that the intra-group communication between (the mostly male) Turkish diplomats and lobbyists in Brussels was infused with football terminology, the football analogy is pertinent. In this predominantly macho environment, Turkish actors told jokes and teased one another about the football clubs they supported and built alli-ances through football vernacular. There were lots of women administrators in state offices that dealt with EU accession. Many were based in Brussels or travelled there to attend technical meetings with the Commission. They were well educated and well versed in the EU system; many spoke better English than their male colleagues. But their presence did not change the gendered environment of nego-tiation. Some actively participated in it.

After I learned of an especially thorny issue in Turkey–EU trade, I phoned up the Turkish economy ministry to get fresh information about tomato paste quotas. Following many calls to enquire about who dealt with this curious topic at the ministry, I reached the Turkish negotiator, who had followed the controversy for two years. During our conversation, I asked him to comment on the behaviour of Turkish and Croatian bureaucrats I had heard about from my Commission con-tacts. The Turkish official on the phone suggested that it was wrong to compare the two and explained: 'We [Turkish bureaucrats] have a state tradition. We would never become buddy-buddy [*kanka olmak*] with the Commission [as Croatian officials do], even if Turkey might become a member state.' His colleagues at the Turkish delegation couldn't agree more. Three out of seven Turkish officials I interviewed in Brussels explicitly referred to Turkey's 'state tradition', which distinguished it from other candidate countries. My interlocutors used 'state tradi-tion' as both a value and a trope. As a value, 'state tradition' referred to 'experience in statecraft, respect for the state, the importance of the state in Turkish culture … endowing it with a degree of political gravitas' (Mango 1977: 265). As a trope, however, 'state tradition' was used to signify Turkish bureaucrats' unwillingness to concede to Brussels regarding Turkish national interests; as such, it impeded the country's progress towards accession not because it was a distortion of reality but because it was often used as an alibi to stall EU demands. More recently, 'state tradition' has served as a salutation to neo-Ottomanism.

Because so few Turkish officials actively participated in the EU negotiations, despite their high numbers in attendance, my Commission interlocutors com-monly assumed that there was widespread inertia in the Turkish bureaucracy.

Some of their Turkish colleagues agreed with this interpretation. Because the lower-level bureaucrats had little authority in decision-making – hence heavily depended on higher-level officials' policy decisions – they appeared to act as simple conduits, implementing policies designed, defined and decided elsewhere.

In a geographically distant but bureaucratically familiar context, anthropologist Yasushi Uchiyamada (2004) made a similar point. Lower-level Japanese officials, whom he described as 'beautifully decorated surface matters', acted like 'sub-alterns, who are not allowed to express their views, [but] are nevertheless expected to be present to show their corporeal and collective conformity' to Japan's imperial history and its reflection in Japanese bureaucratic culture (Uchiyamada 2004: 7). The same could be said of the passive presence of Turkish bureaucrats in meetings with the Commission and the dynamics of the Turkish bureaucratic culture and how it responded to power inequities in its relations with the EU.

Turkish bureaucrats' mere attendance and non-participation appeared as one of many 'traditional' aspects of the Turkish bureaucratic culture, to which many self-reflecting Turkish officials in Brussels added lack of institutional memory, absence of accumulation of knowledge, bureaucratic inertia, lack of systems of accountability, and power struggles between and within state organs – all of which Mesut perfectly summed up: 'In the Turkish state bureaucracy, one should act to be able to do something, not to be somebody. But to do something, you need to be somebody.' According to his insider's definition, a bureaucrat's capacity to do something preceded bureaucracy as the administration of rules and regulations, or 'red tape'. Displays of bureaucratic entrepreneurship through last-minute organising of meetings with members of the Commission or of the European Parliament attested to solid competence, whereas failure to do so might lead to a reprimand.

Lower-level bureaucrats might not be forthcoming with their opinions, despite holding necessary technical information, for fear of being sanctioned, John suggested. Bureaucrats worried that their unit heads or other seniors in Ankara, who might or might not be present at these meetings in Brussels, would view their comments as inappropriate. Surely, officials from both sides ran critical accounts of each meeting, and those accounts were circulated and further circulated from one state office to another, which may provoke rewards or sanctions.

Mesut suggested considering those aspects of Turkish bureaucratic culture that may result in inertia and other 'bureaucratic abnormalities' as indicators of the potential malleability of Turkey's bureaucracy. He confidently concluded: 'When something needs to be done, it gets done!' But how could such malleable bureaucratic potentialities turn into bureaucratic realities? Any attempt in that regard, it seems, had to address other aspects of the courtier system, manifest in more informal channels and spaces of politics and politicking, such as lobbying.

A more productive way to conceptualise bureaucratic stereotypes is to view them as 'one of the currencies of social life', as anthropologist Michael Herzfeld (1992: 72) suggested in his seminal work on Greek administration. Stereotypes provide a means for those involved to make sense of each other. Bureaucratic stereotypes such as inertia or the college and courtier systems 'emerge from situated actors' relationships with the sources of power' (Herzfeld 1992: 77). In my case, these stereotypes are even more interesting because those using them were at the centre of power.

A more persuasive argument to counter that of bureaucratic inertia, then, is that which anthropologist Josiah Heyman posited:

> The results of bureaucratic action are not idiosyncrasies or failures but in some way reflections of the combination of various internal and external power relations surrounding the organisation, often crystallised into patterns of organisational routine. We should pay particular attention to the way bureaucrats go about their work, especially in the zone between official policy and unofficial routine and discretion, as clues to wider political arrangements and governing ideologies. (Heyman 2004: 489)

From this perspective, I argue that Turkish bureaucratic 'inertia' was a reaction to lateral pressures by power-holders at the top and lobbyists from Turkey. A deeper look at the Turkish and EU negotiators' communicative practices during technical meetings in the Commission supports my argument.

Wariness, uncertainty and mistrust

Trade negotiations provide an insight into the everyday workings of the Turkish courtier system. Before working on Turkey, the Spanish Commission official Rosalia worked on Poland's accession. When offered a move to the Turkey desk, she accepted without hesitation. Rosalia felt comfortable in this new position, at first, thinking her previous expertise in negotiating would easily translate to the Turkish case. Turkey quickly proved Rosalia wrong. When we met, Rosalia had been working at the Commission's DG Enlargement Turkey unit for five years. She communicated a deep sense of frustration:

> I feel very lonely in doing my job. I am only a facilitator, but you need two to argue. It's not that Turkey is more complicated. I don't have a clear message and clear definition of my job. I think they [Turkish colleagues] like me but don't understand my job. They want me to see [things] through their eyes but it's not reality. I need to show Turkey as it is.

Mesut had already ranted about how 'the Europeans' (be they working at a Swedish NGO or at the Commission) saw Turkey's problems through 'their own lenses'. 'Come and live in Yozgat [a not-so-well-off city in central Anatolia]', Mesut channelled his imaginary European colleagues through me, 'and see yourselves [how hard life is, how hard it is to live there]!'

Yet, Rosalia's frustration had an extra, temporal dimension, related to the forces of politicisation during the EU–Turkey negotiations. Rosalia explained diverging temporalities of negotiation at the everyday level between national and EU administrations (Ekengren 2002) and the ramifications thereof when timing was not closely observed, which, according to her, was often the case with Turkey:

> If the French permanent representation came to us with a ten-page set of questions and wanted a response by the next day, and if we could provide them with answers

by nine the next morning, they would say they know what we are talking about, that we are at work, and that they can trust us. But if it takes three months to get an answer [from Turkish colleagues], you need to ... become credible again.

In other words, when it took Turkish colleagues a long time to respond to relatively routine requests – where other member state colleagues might take as little as a day – they and the Commission lost credibility. Mesut confirmed the slow bureaucratic communication between the Turkish delegation in Brussels and Ankara and the difficulties it created to gather information in a timely manner. He had experienced this problem when he had been tasked with compiling a list of state-aid derogations other candidate countries had been granted.

Becoming 'credible again' was a political process. When the temporal order of supranational negotiations was disturbed, the very terms of the agreement had to be opened to renegotiation, and hence politicisation. If the current agreement was renegotiated, there was no guarantee that the existing terms would remain in place. Nor was there any more room for informal manoeuvring by existing actors, as new actors would try to push their way into the negotiations. In the Turkish case, divergent temporalities helped politicise accession negotiations by other means.

Rosalia suggested that the negotiation tactics of Turkish colleagues like Mesut impeded her work:

> They [Turkish colleagues] don't give me sellable arguments. They say something to me and something else to a Permanent Representation. You don't have to surrender; you find and accept a generous solution ... stay calm and concentrated; just give the data. Be cool on debates. [But] they lose their temper. Don't go to the poetical game, because you [Turkish officials] are going to pay there! It's not free of charge to get tomato quotas; you [need to] give us fiscal data.... The European Community is not a heaven; consensus is not without a cost. Generosity, welfare ... you [Turkey] need to care about others, respect others.

Rosalia's implicit juxtaposition of the cool Commission Eurocrat with temperamental Turkish bureaucrat might seem like classic Orientalism, yet would misjudge the actual dynamics of the negotiating table. From Rosalia's perspective, and true to Turkey's 'state tradition', her Turkish colleagues saw negotiations as an opportunity to give less and take more, without surrendering points to the opposing team. Concession-makers risked at best looking weak in the Turkish bureaucratic hierarchy or at worst losing control of negotiations altogether. Per sociologist Erving Goffman's (1959) frontstage–backstage performances, Mesut recounted an incident when a colleague who, returning from a technical meeting with the Commission, bragged to his seniors in Ankara about his 'victory over the Europeans', once again in football terminology. While the backstage behaviour of this bureaucrat may also be his frontstage performance, disguising his other interests and vulnerabilities, I suspected whether Rosalia's Turkish colleagues often used frontstage displays of 'temper' as a negotiating tactic.

Hajjis, tomatoes and the beef ban

I met Rosalia's direct counterpart at the Turkish delegation, the person responsible for trade and customs union relations, about a week before my meeting with her. A seasoned bureaucrat, Fikret was the second in command at the delegation and Mesut's immediate boss. He was posted to Brussels from the Turkish Foreign Trade Office, which was created back in 1935, where Fikret had worked since 1971. During the political turmoil and military coups of the 1970s and 1980s, Fikret was exiled to Pakistan and then Saudi Arabia because of his leftist political views. After his second exile, Fikret left state employment, only to come back in 1999. He was not a typical AKP bureaucrat but was an agent and a product of Turkish bureaucratic culture.

Rosalia's frustration with Turkey's EU negotiations made sense to me only after I considered it in light of my meeting with Fikret, who shed light on the seemingly divergent negotiating tactics he and his Ankara colleagues used. Before he shared those tactics with me, however, Fikret had to explain the troubling tomato quotas!

This particular problem originated in fact from difficulties in trading another commodity. In 1996, mad cow disease affected Turkey and some EU member states. Turkish farmers saw an opportunity to boost domestic production and they collectively lobbied the Turkish government to halt imports of livestock (beef and bovine) from Europe as a 'precaution' – a case known as the 'beef ban' in Turkey–EU vernacular. To retaliate, the EU reintroduced duties and reduced quotas on imports of Turkish tomato paste (and watermelons) in 1998 and has not allowed Turkey its full export quota since.[7]

After much pressure from the Commission, Turkey, now a net exporter of beef, opened its borders to EU beef and bovines in 2010, but only fifteen selected member states were granted access, a counter-common-market practice. Subsequently, the negotiating chapter (Chapter 12) on food safety, veterinary and phytosanitary policy was opened in Brussels. Meanwhile, import duties decreased considerably, due to tariff protection for livestock being contingent on prices in Turkey. Within a couple of years, Turkey had become the largest export market for EU beef (World Bank 2014: 73).

On the flip side, the EU did (still does) not allow exports of any livestock of Turkish origin to EU markets. With thirty years of experience as a legal adviser on the common European food safety, veterinary and phytosanitary policy, my contact at DG Sanco (now Sante) Martin began to explain the complex set of problems behind this EU ban on Turkish livestock: 'You have the Sacrifice Feast'. This holiday honoured Abraham's willingness to sacrifice his son, one of two Muslim holidays celebrated worldwide. Was this French EU officer making a statement against Islam? What could Islam have possibly to do with veterinary policy? It turned out that the Turkish troubles with common food safety, veterinary and phytosanitary policy of the EU had a great deal to do with Islam and its associated practices – just not the kind that the Turkish and EU publics had heard repeatedly from their representatives who propagated the 'too Muslim' argument of the triple mantra.

A large volume of livestock was smuggled into Turkey every year from its eastern borders with Iran, Iraq and Syria. This uncontrolled animal traffic increased especially during the days and months leading to the Sacrifice Feast, which created a surge in demand for red meat in Turkey. Local Commission experts found live animal markets unsanitary, though this was changing, they noted. From a sanitation perspective, the more mobile an animal is, the more likely it will contract a disease. Not all animals traded between Turkey and its eastern neighbours carried disease of course, but since much of this trade was unsanctioned and border inspection controls were difficult, the Commission argued, the Turkish authorities had no way of controlling animal disease inside Turkey. In addition, Turkish laboratories performing health checks on livestock lacked EU accreditation. There was a perceived risk of uncontrolled animal disease spilling over the EU territory by way of animal interactions between the eastern (Turkish) and western (Greek, Bulgarian and Romanian, read: the EU) parts of Thrace.[8]

Aside from sanitary risks, this essentially unauthorised trade between Turkey and its eastern neighbours caused alarm for the Commission because those neighbours were not authorised to export to the EU. Since inspection and control in Turkey's eastern borders were challenging, due to size and topography, the EU wanted Turkey to cease any trading of livestock with its eastern neighbours, which, according to Fikret, was politically unfeasible. Livestock smuggling primarily took place in Turkey's economically distressed eastern border provinces, which are mainly populated by the Kurds, the largest ethnic minority in Turkey and a stateless nation divided between Turkey, Iran, Iraq and Syria (Bozcalı forthcoming). Moreover, Turkey does not recognise Kurds as an official minority and deprives them of critical fundamental rights such as freedom of education in their mother tongue, causing problems in its EU accession negotiations regarding negotiating Chapter 23, on judiciary and fundamental rights, and Chapter 24, on justice, freedom and security.

Cross-border trade historically constitutes a significant economic activity in border regions around the world. A considerable part of this trade takes place informally. Trade across Turkey's eastern borders is no exception. To compensate for the devastating effects of decades-long underdevelopment and armed conflict between the Kurdish armed movement and state forces in the region, the Turkish government has turned a blind eye to illicit trade on its eastern borders. Fikret hypothesised that if the Turkish government were to halt livestock smuggling in the east at the behest of the EU, it risked uproar among Kurds and the loss of their electoral support. Although government control of smuggling has increased, the state and the army showed poor judgement in distinguishing between cross-border guerrilla fighters and ordinary smugglers when they killed thirty-four smugglers during a targeted aerial attack in Şırnak province in south-eastern Turkey in 2011 (Letsch 2013).

Reverse trade has also been a cause for concern for the Commission. During the EU army's occupation of Iraq between 2003 and 2011, Turkey served as a transit point for American shipments of meat to troops in Iraq, which the United States first exported via Turkey's Mersin port on the Mediterranean. According to Martin, this transit trade constituted another form of unauthorised trade, increasing the risk of EU markets and consumers being exposed to unauthorised competition from third countries.

After explaining the complicated picture of tomato paste quotas, mutual beef bans, cross-border trade security, state terrorism and military logistics, Fikret had eloquently addressed his and his colleagues' negotiating tactics with Rosalia and her co-workers at the Commission:

> When we work with Orientals [şarklı], we do business with 'Okay, hajji. Let's do this, hajji. If we don't do it, they will hurt us, hajji. [Otherwise] Kiss the death, hajji!' During coffee breaks [when] we discuss [issues] I hold his hands, hold his with both of my hands and I'd say 'Don't do this, our country has an interest in this.' Sentimental words would work with them. They would work with me, too. But with Westerners, we cry, 'You don't want to understand us. Your standards are not just double, but multiple!'

Hajji refers to someone who has made the pilgrimage to Mecca. In addition, the term is often used as a term of endearment among Muslim men. Fikret seemed to use the term to strike up brotherly camaraderie between him and his male colleagues in a self-Orientalising fashion. Self-Orientalising, as we have already seen, was not uncommon among Turkish diplomats and bureaucrats (Alexander 2002, 2017; Turem 2011).

Fikret described bureaucratic interactions he had during and after one CUJC meeting, which I found illustrative of his negotiating. True to any bureaucratic interaction, Turkish and EU bureaucrats negotiated in both formal (the Commission's technical rooms) and informal (during coffee breaks or at nearby restaurants) settings. During his first CUJC meeting, the Commission bureaucrats criticised aspects of the Turkish legal system, which very much upset Fikret. After the meeting, core members of the two teams had dinner together at a nearby Turkish restaurant, Sublime Porte. Surrounded by lavish decor and exquisite food, they continued their conversation in a more informal manner. The name of the restaurant aptly translates into English as 'Ottoman imperial seat', a synecdoche for the central government of the Ottoman Empire. The significance of the chosen location of the dinner revealed more than its usually dimly lit, cosy ambiance would have otherwise disguised.

In light of his Commission colleagues' critical comments on Turkey's legal system during the CUJC meeting, Fikret began his dinner talk sarcastically. He singled out his Belgian Commission counterpart for a reference to an ongoing murder trial of a prominent Turkish businessperson: 'You are right about being unable to understand the Turkish legal system, especially in consideration of your coming from a country that still debates whether to prosecute a terrorist who killed a businessman in Turkey.' The Belgian police had just arrested one of the three alleged assailants with suspected ties to a Turkish radical left terrorist organisation.[9]

As I came to understand over the course of my conversations with Alessandro, Rosalia, Fikret, John, Martin, Mesut and others who sat at the EU–Turkey negotiating table, my interlocutors perfectly understood each other's negotiating tactics – not least because they commonly socialised together outside the Commission's formal meeting rooms at nearby restaurants for example. But Fikret deprived his Commission colleague of a handshake (with all its symbolic associations) in technical meetings while they sat at opposite sides of the table and negotiated the nuts and bolts of Turkish entry, and accused Rosalia of discriminating against his country. It was part of his team's negotiating technique.[10]

From a purely technical point of view, a touch of hands does not translate into policy documents in the Commission's techno-bureaucratic universe, especially when the Commission has to consider twenty-eight member states with a multitude of cultural approaches in bureaucratic negotiations. Yet, bureaucratic negotiations at the Commission, much like those at the Council, are foremost human interactions (Herzfeld 1992; Heyman 2004). Commission officials quickly interpreted such physical-symbolic tactics as lack of self-confidence by their Turkish counterparts. During our interview, Rosalia said: 'Turks do not even trust themselves.... There are people [in the Turkish administration who are] against EU accession. I believe in the EU enlargement towards Turkey more than they do.' Commission officials equally interpreted such tactics as Turkey's awkward misunderstanding of European community, consensus and solidarity. Rosalia again echoed: 'You come to consensus and win something because you believe in belonging in the Union. Turkey needs to decide what it is, what it wants to become, and what it really wants from Europe!'

It is not a handshake, I would suggest, but its symbolically loaded absence that perfectly translates into diverging bureaucratic attitudes and negotiating techniques – as well as information, impression and influence – the exchange of political economic interests have left behind, as they are channelled out of the technical meeting rooms. This partially explains how and why Turkish and EU diplomats grew apart from one another. As we wrapped up our interview, Fikret's last remarks, in terms suited to contact sports, were telling: 'You should not stand bruised. You should attack back. You have got to keep hitting them in the eye', he coached; 'you should not behave with Oriental courtesy'.

Several months after my meetings with them, Alessandro, Martin and Fikret had happily retired, while Rosalia had moved, with gratitude, to a different unit. John was still in office, but Mesut had left state employment for the private sector despite his candid belief in public service. Matthias still represented European steel producers, while his Turkish counterpart, Mahmut, took a brief pause from his duties at the association of steel producers for a high-level governmental position in the very office he once lobbied from the 'outside'.

Political economy of *non*-membership

Under such conditions of failed promises of economic integration and alienation at the individual bureaucratic level, bureaucrats, diplomats and lobbyists have been negotiating with each other with an understanding that Turkey might *not* become an EU member. According to Sinan Ülgen, a prominent Turkish EU expert and economic consultant who participated in the steel FTA negotiations as a career diplomat during the early 1990s in Brussels, this was all too reasonable, because Turkey's EU membership depended on how soon EU members were to be ready for it. It was thus logical for this diplomat-turned-lobbyist that, unlike in past enlargement practices, Turkey requested longer transitional periods to cover its (companies') economic interests in the interim (Ülgen 2005: 57). This change in the negotiating position turned Turkey's EU bid into an anti-case. And when wariness, uncertainty and mistrust clouded the sky, companies from both sides, seeing each other at the opposite, competitive end of the spectrum, turned to lobbying their own governments and tightened the grip over their own state agents.

Turkish business elites had developed clientelistic, paternalistic and corporatist relationships with the public sector since the beginning of Turkish capitalism (Bianchi 1984; Buğra 1994; Heper 1985, 1991; Öniş 1991; Seufert & Vorhoff 2000). Through such relationships, they first tried to use EU integration to discipline the bureaucratic apparatus (Yılmaz 1999). With the beginning of membership talks, however, many also realised that 'support for accession would come at a price' (Ülgen 2006: 2). Some welcomed the deepening of economic integration with the EU, hoping for political integration; others feared increasing levels of competition and the loss of generous state aid, and lobbied the Turkish government for domestic sector protection (Uğur 2000). The politics of *non*-membership emerged as a viable negotiating position after this experience, but it took a decade before it became a de facto negotiating strategy shared by many of those on both sides.

Peak organisations representing business, labour and other corporate interests from Turkey learned how to instrumentalise the EU agenda to boost their domestic legitimacy vis-à-vis the Turkish state.[11] In return, their power and proximity to political authority at the national level diminished their need to lobby the Turkish government via the EU. A new politics of *non*-membership of a symbolic-political nature was at play.

Even though Turkish and EU negotiators now discussed the terms and conditions of Turkey's *non*-membership, that is, access but not accession, lobbyists and interest representatives like Orhan, Deniz and others still pretended that business was as usual and continued with their normal work. While waiting in the lobby of the Commission's Charlemagne building for my interlocutor to take me through security, I would occasionally greet Orhan when he was there for an appointment with a Commission counterpart. Each time I tried to glance over the registration book to see whom Orhan was waiting to meet, zealous security staff would stop me. But he was there to do his job, lobbying the Commission on behalf of his organisation.

On another occasion, I joined Deniz, Sibel and the Brussels-based Turkish correspondent Kaan for dinner with Eurocrats from the European Investment Bank (EIB) and DG Enlargement. Son of a former diplomat, Kaan had attended a Francophone school in Turkey and later studied in France, before he became a foreign news correspondent for Turkey's first news channel in the mid-1990s. Besides media, Kaan's parent company was active in construction, energy, tourism and cars. At that time, I was interning with Adem, who, as the head reporter of the EU–Turkey News Network, asked me to attend. The dinner invitation had come from the EIB on the Bank's opening of its Istanbul office. The Bank wanted to meet with Brussels-based Turkish interest and media representatives to discuss its ongoing operations and lending strategy in Turkey, including special support measures in response to the 2008 financial crisis, for the year ahead.

The Turkish representatives had not much to add to the EIB's macroeconomic talk, but they encouraged the Bank, which had been doing business in the country since the mid-1960s, to increase its visibility in Turkey. After all, the Bank is an EU institution and a lender of EU money to ongoing infrastructure projects in Turkey (see Firat 2016). Kaan declared: 'The EU doesn't change people's lives [in Turkey] but the EIB does, say, with Marmaray' – the first railway connection between Europe and Asia that crosses the Bosphorus underground, which the EIB heavily financed. Four decades previously, the Bank had helped finance the construction of the Bosphorus Bridge – the first bridge connection between Europe and Asia. Then the EIB organised PR events, highlighting its contribution to the bridge. Precedents to Kaan's recommendation existed, in other words. Even though Kaan's idea was not novel, Deniz piggybacked him and suggested: 'If EU flags would cover roads and street billboards in Turkey, it would have a political effect'. 'Which would make our [the Turkish representatives'] job [of selling the EU integration to the Turkish public] easier', Kaan chimed in. Despite much enthusiasm, the EIB officials did not respond to Deniz's billboard proposal. My take from that evening was that the enduring success of these representatives as 'effective communicators' did *not* come from their actual lobbying of EU actors and offices but from their skills applied elsewhere.

With no full-time representative in Brussels, the Turkish flat steel producers, who supplied the automotive industry in Turkey and in Europe, constituted another case in point. Deniz, Zehra and Zehra's right-hand staff member Elif represented Turkish steel interests in Brussels. Another Turkish reporter known to associate with Zehra was also involved, as she amateurishly enquired about the automotive industry during the EIB dinner. The next time I heard of this reporter, she had become a newsreader at a government-supported private news channel. Later she donned a diplomatic cloak and was posted as press secretary to a neighbouring country. Her closeness to Zehra paid off well.

Turkish lobbyists had long provided their EU counterparts with much-needed information that was deemed impartial, often simply because it looked like the information came from the non-government circles (Ülgen 2006). Their involvement gave a certain legitimacy to the negotiation process and added to the symbolic dimension of this political bargain. But how could I be sure that the lobbyists' effectiveness was not the result of their actual lobbying of EU institutions but due to their skills in symbolic politics? For the unconvinced, here is another tale.

Spirales of lobbying

When I met her for an interview at a café near her house on a Saturday morning, Camille, a Flemish-Belgian Commission official, had been working on the competitiveness and innovation programme at DG Enterprise and Industry for several years. Throughout our conversation that morning, I detected a certain irritation in Camille's voice. She felt that when her people learned that she was working on the T. file, they thought of her as 'working for Turkey', and she mentioned the scepticism of those around her (family as well as colleagues in the Commission) about Turkey's EU membership.

Camille told me that Turkish representatives did not lobby her office. Similar to John's remarks about why he did not receive much lobbying, she hypothesised that lobbying must have been more important vis-à-vis other sectors, such as the automotive sector, where sectoral issues were more 'political' rather than related to policy-making.

With Camille's hint, I contacted Thomas, her colleague from the same DG who worked on issues related to the automotive sector. The automotive industry constituted a backbone of EU–Turkey trade. Several European car companies had production plants inside Turkey, serving both the Turkish domestic market and the EU market. Thomas stated that the Turkish car industry did not lobby his office, perhaps because it solved its problems elsewhere, in pan-European business federations such as the European Association of Automotive Suppliers (CLEPA). I was not convinced and was determined to dig deeper.

I followed Thomas's lead and met up with Valter, the Swedish secretary general of CLEPA. Valter had been to Turkey many times to hold CLEPA meetings and knew the country perhaps better than his Turkish colleagues would have wanted. We spoke about Istanbul's drastically changing urban scenery that accompanied Turkey's grave socio-economic inequalities. When his Turkish colleagues wanted him to see the beauty of the Bosphorus, the 'other Istanbul' caught Valter's attention. He observed Istanbul's grand boulevards morphing into poor neighbourhoods a few blocks down from the finance and business hotspots.

Valter told me that his organisation had an associate member from Turkey but that neither this member nor anybody else from Turkey lobbied his office because its work was not 'political'. Instead, Valter suspected, the Turkish associate member used its CLEPA membership like a badge to 'show off to his government friends'. In meetings with the government, members of the Turkish organisation bragged about how well they were integrated into the EU.

In short, Turkish economic lobbying was targeted elsewhere: its attention and energies were directed to political lobbying in Ankara, instead of lobbying policy processes at the Commission or the related pan-European business community. Since many Turkish bureaucrats and economic elites 'believed in' their lasting presence through the corridors of power, the efficacy of the Turkish economic lobby had a symbolic quality to it. Whether they played along with the politics of non-membership or not, they maintained a curious monopoly over who could represent Turkish economic interests in Brussels. When it was raised as a negotiation strategy, non-membership, along with their spinning of it by means of symbolic politics, helped them keep their jobs in Brussels.

In sectors the EU heavily regulated, such as the steel and automotive industries, the existing practice of government 'consultation' with industry justified domestic lobbying during the transposition of the EU *acquis* into Turkish law. Some laws that were passed with minimum consultation with members of industry, Sedat explained, contained technical errors caused by mistranslations of the *acquis*, which, once done, took a long time to undo, due to bureaucratic procedures and politics in Turkey. These laws were thus considered to be irresponsive to industry needs, as Elif explained. Some even transgressed the general outline provided by the *acquis*. Under such circumstances, further modifications were required – hence more lobbying was needed.

A common sentiment among certain business groups, in the words of Sedat, was that the Turkish government's approach during the transposition was symbolic, 'to look like they were consulting with business', but no substantial consultation existed in reality, as John also observed. Make no mistake, large companies like the one Sedat worked for made themselves heard during interest-framing and legislative processes, through their government contact in Ankara and international contacts in Europe, including Brussels. But the Turkish interest representatives' symbolic presence in Brussels, the Turkish government's looking like consulting with business, and legislative misinterpretations or mistakes all opened an even bigger space for politicking and for further lobbying.

Turkish companies hired consultants and lobbyists to gather information about legislative changes in the EU and to calculate the feasibility of changes to domestic regulatory and company behaviour, which EU-level requirements might demand, or to provide interest and influence brokerage when they desired no such change. While Deniz and Zehra were mostly busy with politicking at the top, their agents, primarily the many talented women who worked for them in Brussels, followed draft EU laws, directives and regulations as they were being prepared at the Commission with an objective to assess how these texts might affect Turkey's business environment. A Turkish-Belgian expatriate, Elif was one such lobbyist; she had worked for Zehra for five years when we met. They knew each other through family. Unlike her boss, who was busy shuttling between Brussels and Ankara, due to her unofficial position as consultant to her close friend EU minister Bağış, Elif worked as deputy director in the Brussels office, where she and her colleagues received clients from a wide range of business sectors (from the automotive to telecommunications) in Turkey.

Elif explained that following directives and regulations in their initial form required a good knowledge of EU law and economy and good connections in Brussels and Ankara. One needed a good knowledge of EU law to evaluate whether the proposed text was drafted as a directive, in which case member states had some leeway in implementation. Directives were particularly important for those Turkish companies with EU partners, in which case those Turkish companies could try to influence the EU law as it affected them through their partners in the Union. Knowing economics helped consultants forecast the extent to which proposed changes in EU legislation might affect relevant public and private sector actors in Turkey and individual companies.

Once individual companies were to see the micro- and macro-effects of proposed changes, they could directly go to the Turkish government with this knowledge, which the government might or might not have, or send their lobby-ists to do the relaying. Together, they lobbied the government, and increasingly President Erdoğan, due to the ongoing centralisation of power at the very top. Regarding official positions over derogations, Turkish officials like Mesut and Fikret bargained with the Commission during further negotiations in Brussels. Economic actors and their representatives also initiated public awareness campaigns as another way of influencing public sector decisions in line with their interests.

When Mesut and Fikret attended technical meetings with Alessandro, Rosalia, Martin or John in Brussels, whether these meetings were on individual commodity exports, third-party free trade agreements or energy security, they felt they could say nothing definitive to their Commission counterparts because they lacked clear instructions from those on whose behalf they spoke during the meetings. Mesut and Fikret thus participated in these meetings without being able to say much on any 'open' issue that was being lobbied at the national level by Elif, Zehra, Sedat and their associates – except that *'all is under study'.*

Conclusion

In this chapter I documented the process of how a politics of non-membership conditioned Turkey's objectives with EU membership. The chapter moved from diplomats' and lobbyists' negotiations, which made the EU–Turkey economic in-tegration possible on several fronts: within the framework of actions and practices that centred on the European Commission to actors' encounters with one another in technical, sectoral and social meetings to lobbyists' and diplomats' negotiations that led EU–Turkey economic integration to mutate into a troubled relationship. On the one hand, I discussed the work of a supra-governmental bureaucracy, making regulations and representing European capitalists. On the other hand, I presented a peripheral nominee for EU accession whose economic interests increasingly came into conflict with the people with whom it was negotiating membership. In such an unbalanced power situation, it is no surprise that proudly post-imperial AKP governments would try to balance out Turkey's economic power deficit by dramatic displays of state power (sending more delegates to meetings than the other side, playing the opponent discursively and so on). Con-gruent with the courtier system, dramatic expressions of state power only made Turkish negotiators appear more peripheral in a setting where the EU marketed itself as working largely on the college model. However, what appeared to EU actors as Turkish bureaucratic inertia, as I uncovered, was due to intense lobbying in Turkey, which left Turkish bureaucrats participating inexpertly in technical negotiations of governance, sovereignty and statecraft. While Turkish negotiators increasingly reoriented themselves domestically and disengaged from Eurocracy, Turkey lost on important economic matters such as the customs union, FTAs the EU signed with third countries and other sectoral disputes.

Crystallised in the customs union, steel and other sectoral arrangements since 1996, deeper economic cooperation between the EU and Turkey did not fulfil

Turkish expectations of enhanced political integration with the Union. Decoupled from a commitment to the country's prospective EU membership, arguments and practices based on 'common interests' failed to convince either side of the future viability of the existing terms and conditions of Turkey's economic integration and its itinerant politics, especially in a context where those interests competed. In this chapter, I argued that problems in managing economic integration were due to unequal power relations between the EU and Turkey. Turkish and EU lobbyists and diplomats capitalised on this inequality to broaden their influence and advance their interests. Techno-bureaucrats and lobbyists have historically been the main engineers and promoters of economic integration in Europe. But their actions are both reflections of and constitutive of the wider political economic realities in which they live and operate.

In the end, the negotiation process that was supposed to move Turkey from limited economic integration to full political integration with the EU laid bare the shrinking of EU–Turkey economic cooperation. Diplomacy and lobbying once made EU–Turkey economic integration possible. While its actors and agents had displayed their skills in effective negotiation for two decades, diplomacy and lobbying this time made economic integration difficult. I found that the efforts of diplomats and lobbyists for Turkey–EU political integration in the European Parliament followed a logic similar to how negotiations over economic integration with the Commission were framed. But the media they used were quite different. The next chapter examines lobbying efforts inside the European Parliament.

Notes

1 The Turkish government hired another lobbying company in Washington, DC, to lobby the US government so that it, in turn, would lobby EU publics. The Turkish government's efforts resulted in the US mission to the EU in Brussels and US embassies in big member states mobilising their support for Turkey at the EU level.

2 Co-chaired by Turkish and EU bureaucrats, the CUJC met once or twice a year during my fieldwork, although it was initially envisaged to meet once a month. Its meetings were exclusive gatherings with restricted access. I gained access to transcripts of CUJC meetings between 2008 and 2016 through my private sector contacts. The committee held its twentieth meeting in 2008 and its thirty-third in 2016.

3 Süreyya Cılıv, the then chief executive officer of Turkcell, and Tuğrul Kutadgobilik, the chairman of the Turkish Confederation of Employer Associations, both spoke at the 'Opportunity of Enlargement to Europe: Turkey', a high-level working session during the European business summit in March 2009 in Brussels. Egemen Bağış, Olli Rehn, Alpaslan Korkmaz, a Turkish-Swiss national and then president of National Investment Support and Promotion Agency of Turkey under Erdoğan's auspices, also spoke. Zehra's husband, a fellow consultant with work experience in Arthur Andersen and Cisco Systems, was later appointed as Turkcell's chief executive officer, replacing Cılıv.

4 For a discussion of some of these trade restrictions, see Misrahi (2009).

5 This ratio was four to one in 2000 and three to one in 2012 (Ministry of Science, Industry and Technology 2018: 10).

6 In 2012, 43 per cent of Turkey's steel exports went to the EU, while the remainder went to Middle Eastern markets (Ministry of Science, Industry and Technology 2018).

7   See 2006/999/EC: Decision No. 2/2006 of the EC–Turkey Association Council of 17 October 2006, amending Protocols 1 and 2 to Decision No. 1/98 on the trade regime for agricultural products.

8   See 'Turkey Draft Common Position, Chapter 12: Food safety, veterinary and phyto-sanitary policy', referred to by the General Secretariat of the Council to the Working Group on Enlargement and Countries Negotiating Accession to the EU on 26 June 2010.

9   The alleged assassin was later acquitted of this charge and was given political refugee status in Belgium.

10 For another bodily gesture (laughter) used as technique of negotiation, see Ballestero (2012).

11 For an analysis of Turkish labour unions and their instrumentalisation of the EU agenda, see Alemdar (2009).

6

Political documents and bureaucratic entrepreneurs

The marketplace at Place Lux

Imagine a busy marketplace in the middle of Brussels, bustling with vendors displaying their goods with much dexterity and determination. You are trying to find your way through this marketplace, roaming around, watching those who offer their products and sales skills. In this marketplace, money, for the most part, won't get you what you are looking for. People come here to shop for information, interests and influence. A web of concrete, glass and wire in the middle of Brussels, navigable only through large atriums and wide corridors connecting meeting rooms, this marketplace is the European Parliament. Within this political labyrinth, diverse interests strive to gain representation in a common European framework. Let me introduce it to you in the way I came to know it.

But first a secret: in my late twenties, I had never been inside a parliament before! Even though I lived for many years in Ankara, where the Turkish parliament stood in much grandeur, I never felt that being a citizen or paying taxes was reason enough to enter that building. So, when Hasan suggested that I visit the European Parliament, I was intrigued.

Wearing a dark-blue suit with thin stripes, a uniform-like outfit for men in bureaucracies, Hasan greeted me in front of the offices of the Turkish delegation, where he worked and where we said we could meet for lunch. Hasan handled relations with the European Parliament. He was part of the small group of people who represented the 'Turkish public interest' in the EU. 'Public' retains an unresolved ambiguity in the Turkish language: the concept emically comprises an amalgam of the public (as in 'the people') and its administration. I could see Hasan rushing from one MEP office to another, cornering administrators from political groups and committees along the corridors to channel official correspondence, information notes and position papers that came from Ankara to relevant parliamentary offices and contacts in the European Parliament. He was the most well known and well respected Turkish marketer from the state side in Brussels.

During our talk, it came up that the European Parliament's Committee on Foreign Affairs (AFET) was to convene in two days to talk about Turkey – the 'sexiest' topic on the Parliament's agenda ever, attracting a lot of interest and

Figure 6.1 Documents of the European Parliament. Source: European Parliament/Pietro Naj-Oleari

exchanges from all over Europe. I knew better than to miss Hasan's offer to facilitate my attendance at that meeting. Hasan wrote to a colleague from AFET; next, I found myself in the Parliament's accreditation centre! There, several receptionists greeted me in our common mother tongue. Inside the Parliament, MEPs, diplomats and lobbyists carried colour-coded badges. To enter, visitors needed to be registered and accompanied at all times by a parliamentary insider, even though, once in, many found their way by themselves to MEPs' offices and committee meetings through the networked corridors.

Although the Commission initiated the terms and conditions of EU membership, the Parliament then moved to the centre of accession negotiations in its close following of Turkey's progress in instituting the internal reforms (e.g. in democratisation) the EU required for its accession. The Parliament's annual reports on political and policy matters constitute the bulk of this work. Since 1985, the European Parliament has prepared over twenty parliamentary reports – and numerous opinions and questions – on Turkey–EU affairs. Their content varies according to the EU's changing priorities regarding Turkey. Initially, the Parliament reviewed Turkey's democratic performance on its own initiative and independent from the accession process. After initiating Turkey's candidacy, the reports became a regular means to assess the country's reform performance. Whereas earlier reports mostly concerned human rights, later ones focused on Turkey's eligibility for EU membership. Open yet opaque, the actual parliamentary work of negotiation and compromise over the Turkish bid is inscribed in the sequential drafts of these documents.

Derived from the French *parle* (to converse), parliaments throughout the political history of western Europe came to refer to a formal conference for the discussion of public affairs (Richardson 1928). In these socio-physical spaces, parliamentarians represent and negotiate the public's affairs and interests (Abélès 1992; Bayley 2004; Crewe 2015, 2017; Rai 2010). Unlike the Council, which consists of representatives of member state governments and bureaucracies who together make EU legislation, or the Commission, whose members (commissioners) are political appointees, who draft laws and propose legislation together with their expert staff, eligible member state voters have elected MEPs since 1979, transforming the Parliament from a mere consultative body to a 'parliament' in the classic sense of the term.

Out of 500 million citizens from twenty-eight EU member states, 213 million elected their representatives to the European Parliament in the 2019 elections. Groupings of political parties within the Parliament ('political groups' in EU-speak) that formed anew ranged from the far right to the far left, to more centrists like the Christian Democrats, the Socialists, the Liberals, to the non-aligned like the Greens. Along with the chairperson, each political group decides on the division of labour within its political stratum, known as the 'bureau'. At its nucleus, the bureau consists of the chairperson and elected vice-chairs responsible for political and policy agenda. Managed by a secretary general, a large secretariat assists the bureau. Members of the secretariat address bureaucratic, organisational and administrative aspects of running the political life of the Parliament.

Thirty years after its first elections, the Parliament gained more powers with the 2009 Lisbon Treaty, which put it on an equal footing with the Council on an extended number of issues such as migration, police and judicial cooperation, aspects of trade policy and agriculture, the EU budget and international agreements signed between the EU and third countries. Most significant for our purposes, the Lisbon Treaty mandates that the Parliament give its assent to the accession of new members.

Although the plenary session meets in Strasbourg and its general secretariat is in Luxembourg City, the bulk of the Parliament's work takes place in Brussels. Members generally spend their political time in Brussels from the Monday afternoon to the Thursday evening of the first two weeks of every month. From Thursday afternoon, the Parliament gets quieter. Trains take off from Brussels-Luxembourg train station next door, carrying MEPs back to their constituencies. By Friday, only the permanent occupants of the Parliament remain: members of political groups and committee secretariats, MEPs' assistants, security personnel and other service staff.

Since they commute between Brussels, Strasbourg and their constituencies, MEPs have no *real* time to engage in public discussions in the meeting rooms or in front of the public. Unlike parliaments that are 'about talking' (Crewe 2005: 192), little formal debate takes place here. As a result, the actual parliamentary work of negotiation and compromise do not take place in public, prompting enduring accusations that the Parliament suffers from a 'democratic deficit' (Andersen & Eliassen 1996b; Caporaso 2000; Shore 2004). If there is a 'democratic deficit', diplomats, lobbyists and other experts offer their services to fill the shortage!

MEPs negotiate for their constituencies' interests both directly (face to face) and indirectly. Assistants and advisers, political group and committee secretariats, country and policy advisers, diplomats and lobbyists from member and candidate states help in negotiations before, during and after the parliamentary meetings of political groups and committees. One might find them talking quietly (or heatedly) along the Parliament's corridors, in each other's offices, at the legendary Mickey Mouse Bar inside the Parliament or in the restaurants and cafés surrounding

Brussels' famous Place Luxembourg. Located a few steps from the Parliament and run by a Turkish-Belgian owner, Café Le London became the place for Turkish representatives and journalists to meet with MEPs and other parliamentary very important persons (VIPs).

Over lunch, dinner or coffee, through e-mails, personal chats or official appointments, MEPs communicate competing policy intentions, interests, acts and actions through parliamentary channels in this highly bureaucratised environment. In these in-between spaces and times, diplomats, lobbyists or NGO workers from within and outside the EU inform MEPs, whose elaborate deals – be they on traffic rules (McDonald-Walker 2000) or employment policies (Muntigl et al. 2000) – can have region-wide effects.

Much like the Commission, the Parliament considers all activities to be lobbying if 'carried out with the objective of directly or indirectly influencing the formulation or implementation of policy and the decision-making processes of the EU institutions, irrespective of where they are undertaken and of the channel or medium of communication' (*Official Journal of the European Union* 2014: 12). This broad definition blurs the nuances involved in the in-house and extra-parliamentary lobbying regarding Turkey's Europeanisation.

Those who lobby the Parliament act as human conduits as they channel information, influence and interests through this EU institution. Those in need of compromise often find materiality in documents, such as the reports and opinions that the MEPs draft. Lobbying plays a vital role in the production and dissemination of MEPs' draft documents. These documents exhibit the finesse of complex parliamentary negotiations. This highly securitised system is difficult to penetrate from outside by commoners. Lobbying turns the Parliament into a big, encapsulated *agora* in the classical sense of the term, much as Marc Abélès (1992) described it: a marketplace where interests, information and influence frequently exchange hands.

Most market rules apply here, including barter exchange. Like in the Moroccan marketplace (*suq*) Clifford Geertz (1978) eloquently described, reliable information (in and out of the institution) lies at the heart of the Parliament. In this marketplace, information and influence are commoditised – not so much in exchange of monetary value, though that, too, happens occasionally, but for further influence. Paradoxically, as Arjun Appadurai (1986: 43) reading Geertz (1978) suggested, the institution and its culture make reliable information 'hard to get, [while] also facilitating the search for it'. Advantages in exchange stem from superior communication skills (Appadurai 1986: 31).[1]

In this chapter, I hone in on the Parliament's textual repository on Turkey as a site and medium where EU actors and their Turkish counterparts negotiated interests invested in (or disinvested from) Turkey's bid for EU membership. I follow the Parliament's annual Turkey reports and the Turkish responses they elicited as these documents passed between actors through policy-making processes and institutional structures embodied by the EU and Turkish bureaucracies. I focus on these political documents because the majority of the Parliament's work and the lobbying it attracted were crystallised in these bureaucratic artefacts. By following the Parliament's Turkey reports and their Turkish responses literally as they passed from one hand to another through the rooms and corridors of EU and Turkish bureaucracies, I trace here the textual repository of Turkey's Europeanisation as both an ethnographic object and an artefact of social relations as they were reflected in texts and real life (Riles 2006). Here I argue that, as political documents, these reports contributed to bureaucratic politics in both the EU and Turkey. Those who drafted, circulated or influenced their writing increasingly relied on them to sustain communication between otherwise reluctant parties. In return, political documents served as the means through which actors maintained an enduring demand for their expertise.

Political lobbying and the Parliament's T. file

Parliamentary political groups encouraged political parties and interest groups from all over Europe to join them for information-sharing, networking and campaigning purposes. Turkish public and private interest representatives usually worked with all political groups, except with the far right, which commonly objected to Turkey's EU membership; the far left, because of its position on the treatment of Kurds in Turkey and the large number of Cypriot MEPs in it; and Christian Democrats, who were reluctant to grant Turkey accession. Indeed, both the Kurdish Halkların Demokratik Partisi (HDP; People's Democratic Party) and the Cumhuriyet Halk Partisi (CHP; Republican People's Party) have long been members of the pan-European social democratic centrist Party of European Socialists (PES). Turkey's ruling AKP became an associate member of the conservative centrist European People's Party (EPP) in 2005, only to leave it in 2013. The AKP then joined the Eurosceptic Alliance of Conservatives and Reformists in Europe, where it enjoyed full membership, until 2018, when it was pushed out by the growing far right elements in that group. As full members of these pan-European political alliances, all three Turkish parties participated in their political group work and contributed to their positions. The HDP opened a representation office in Brussels in 2005 to gain greater influence during accession negotiations; the CHP and AKP followed in 2008 and 2013, respectively.[2]

Even though, on the phone, we had arranged to meet at his office in Schaerbeek, Bayram sounded suspicious when I rang the doorbell. Ayhan, a Kurdish lobbyist who worked at the Parliament, had given me his number. After I dropped Ayhan's name, Bayram eased up, and we began our conversation. Bayram's account showed how familiar and mundane the work of a Turkish political lobbyist in the European Parliament was – apart from the added troubles of the political context he had to work with.

Born in Turkey and Kurdish by origin, Bayram had lived in France for many years before moving to Brussels. There, Bayram represented Turkey's Halkın Demokrasi Partisi (HADEP, People's Democracy Party), which the Constitutional Court of Turkey banned in 2003 on the basis that the party supported the Partiya Karkerên Kurdistanê (PKK; Kurdistan Worker's Party), the outlawed organisation fighting for Kurdish rights in Turkey. The Kurdish politicians then regrouped around Demokratik Halk Partisi (DEHAP, Democratic People's Party). Demo-kratik Toplum Partisi (DTP; Democratic Society Party) was formed as a result of a merger between DEHAP and the Democratic Society Movement (DTH) founded by Leyla Zana. The DTP thus replaced DEHAP in 2005, until it was banned in 2009. The Barış ve Demokrasi Partisi (BDP; Peace and Democracy Party) followed, until it merged with the HDP in 2012. When we met, Bayram still represented the DTP, managing his party's EU and the Council of Europe (in Strasbourg) portfolios. His job was to make the DTP's opinions prevail in Europe. He brought delegates of DTP MPs, members of the party assembly, local and regional politicians and civil society organisations to Brussels to lobby their counterparts in Europe on issues that ranged from the Kurdish cause to self-governance of natural resources in their regions. His office organised conferences, seminars and press meetings in EU institutions. He also followed committee and political group meetings at the European Parliament and publicised his party's declarations on whatever the agenda was at the time. By informing the EU about the DTP's policies on Turkish reforms, he aimed to pressure Turkey and the EU to work together on solving Turkish–Kurdish conflict within an accession framework.

Bayram attended PES meetings; through him, his party took part in the PES's organisational decisions, too. That the DTP was a full member of the PES meant that Bayram could vote in PES platforms on matters with region-wide significance. Bayram mentioned the CHP's PES membership and joked about how Sibel, whose professional role included representing the CHP, did not attend the PES meetings Bayram attended, reflecting, in Brussels, Turkish political conflicts.

Besides the PES, the DTP kept good relations with the far left European United Left/Nordic Green Left (GUE/NLG). Bayram pressured this political group to change its notorious anti-Turkey position and become supportive of the Turkish accession, 'due to its potential to bring more democracy to the country', as the GUE/NLG adviser on European enlargement and Turkey had explained to me. Bayram worked with all political groups from the Parliament, except the Conserva-tives, who, he explained, 'would like to use us [Kurds] as a trump card for their Turkey-opposition, thinking, "The enemy of my enemy is my friend"'. Bayram ob-served that 'sometimes Christian Democrats would say things regarding Turkey's Kurdish issue much more progressive than others'. Yet he was convinced that they did this 'to keep Turkey out'.

Even though neither the far right nor the far left carried much voting weight, their positions on problematic Turkey issues garnered sufficient attention to keep those issues alive in the Parliament. As for larger political groups, like the Socialists and the Liberals, they pledged support to Turkey's accession on many occasions. However, parliamentary assistants who followed Socialist and Liberal MEPs into internal group meetings told me there were important frictions within these groups over the T. file. These frictions surfaced only in intra-group meet-ings and did not make their way to the plenary. Reluctant MEPs kept parts of the T. file debate solely in the Parliament. This gave the benefit of the doubt to those MEPs from majority political groups who remained reluctant to support Turkish accession, even though their parties might support it.

All political groups had a Turkey adviser, who was sometimes additional to the staff who worked on enlargement and the accession of new countries within the political group. Political groups' special advisers and staff working on related policy issues jointly followed the work of the parliamentary committees, which were the main platforms where parliamentary work took place.

Political groups appointed members to twenty or so parliamentary committees, wherein MEPs debated and proposed amendments to EU directives and regulations drawn up by the Commission. Parliamentary committees usually met once (or twice) a month in Brussels. Each committee elects a chair and four vice-chairs for two and a half years and forms a secretariat.

The AFET committee has been long-standing and is the largest parliamentary committee, with a fifth of MEPs (149 of 785) serving as members or substitutes during the sixth legislature (2004–9). AFET members deliberate on EU enlargement and accession. Christian Democrats, the largest political group in the Parliament since the 2000s, chair this important committee.

According to its priorities, each parliamentary committee delivers its opinions on Commission proposals and communications in committee reports. Regarding EU enlargement and accession of candidates, the Commission prepares a strategy report on enlargement and annual progress reports on each candidate country, to which AFET drafts Parliament's response. Representing each political group within the parliamentary committee, coordinators entrust the drafting of each committee report to rapporteurs according to a point system. Political groups with more MEPs nominate rapporteurs according to their interest areas. The committees choose rapporteurs to work on an issue for two and a half years. Rapporteurs may choose to resign at any time, or to continue in their role if re-elected. Parliamentary reports become official when they are adopted at the plenary by a simple majority vote. Until then, they are referred to as 'draft reports' in the Parliament's vernacular, but are technically 'motions for resolution'. The parliamentary committee in charge of drafting the report and its rapporteur consult the whole body politic to come up with agreed solutions to contentious issues. A decade into accession negotiations, no one doubted that every bit of the Turkish EU bid remained as contentious as ever.

Besides the work in the AFET, the Subcommittee on Human Rights and the Committee on Women's Rights and Gender Equality and other parliamentary committees did minor but significant work on Turkey's Europeanisation. Making the T. file an agenda item in parliamentary committee meetings was contingent upon committee members' interests. And there were plenty of those in the Parliament! For instance, in 2010, Turkish diplomats lobbied the Turkish-Bulgarian Liberal (or 'Bulgarian Turk' as his community self-identified) MEP from the Internal Trade Committee to draft a report on EU–Turkey trade relations, which, considering Turkey's then economic success, recommended modernisation of the customs union.

Until the elections in 2014, AFET's Turkey rapporteur came from the Christian Democrats. An MEP from the Liberals drafted the 1999 and 2000 reports. In practice, MEPs chose a rapporteur from among 'not-so-radical' members, in order not to jeopardise relations with Turkey, but the rapporteur always came from an EU member state known for strong opposition to Turkish membership, such as Germany or the Netherlands, as Luisa, the PES's adviser for foreign affairs and enlargement, explained. Turkish diplomats often did their best to influence the choice of rapporteur. Murat bragged about how his office lobbied to block MEPs who were particularly unsympathetic to Turkey.

The weight of a political group and its members' interests in particular committee work determined the choice of rapporteur. For instance, an Austrian member of the Socialist group drafted AFET reports on Croatia during the sixth legislature to make Croatian accession happen.

True to the political nature of this marketplace, MEPs institutionalise a careful balancing of influence and interest by adopting a point system, where political groups are assigned points according to their size. Reports are then auctioned off between political groups, which literally place bids on them. 'Turkey report has high points', as Canan, the Turkish-German assistant of a Turkish-German MEP from the Greens explained to me. This meant that members of smaller political groups like the Greens never got to become rapporteur for Turkey. So their members bid for the second most important position: the shadow rapporteur. Appointed by their political groups, one (or two) shadow rapporteur(s) monitored the rapporteur's work and prepared their groups' position. Shadow rapporteurs brokered amendments between the rapporteur and their own political group during the Strasbourg plenaries. For this, different political groups allied over specific amendments.

I observed AFET meetings between 2008 and 2009 (Figure 6.2), when the rapporteur released ten- and twelve-page Turkey reports for 2007 to 2008. At that time, the AFET's Turkey rapporteur, Ria Oomen-Ruijten,[3] a Dutch MEP from the Christian Democrats, newly assumed the task. The most successful rapporteur in the Parliament's history, she drafted seven Turkey reports from 2008 to 2014. Her parliamentary assistant did most of the intellectual work in the office. Like other parliamentary assistants, his work on reports, opinions, questions and amendment requests appeared under the rapporteur's name. When not accompanying the MEP to Strasbourg or to Turkey for study visits, the assistant worked in Brussels, along with parliamentary secretaries and interns. Most parliamentary assistants I met in Brussels were young graduates of political science, international relations or law. Massive workloads and long working hours spent in the Parliament burdened many. They shared common EU citizenship and nationality with their MEPs, although employment in the Parliament did not require EU citizenship, to the advantage of young Turks.

Turkish parliamentarians and governing elites viewed the Parliament's (often critical) opinions as interference in their domestic affairs. Advising their bosses and other politicians back in Turkey, Hasan, Murat and others often argued that MEPs were unaccountable to their constituencies in their contribution to non-legislative acts on issues of enlargement and the Turkish candidacy, and that they targeted Turkey for their domestic political success. Each report caused a public backlash, with heightened nationalist undertones. Turkish political and bureaucratic actors stoked public outcry against the European Parliament, often by deprecating its reports in the media. One Turkish politician once threw it into the trash; others proclaimed that the Parliament had become 'overtly politicised' (Tisdall 2012). Since June 2015, the Turkish government via its ambassador to the EU has been, figuratively speaking, sending these reports back to Brussels, an important gesture for its political symbolism. Turkish politicians and bureaucrats have long recommended that the European Parliament adopt a constructive attitude towards Turkey by looking at its good and bad deeds together – more praising and less badmouthing, or 'positive pedagogy' as I call it here. They communicated such recommendations to their counterparts from the European Parliament through lobbying and bureaucratic entrepreneurship.

At a time when membership talks collapsed into a death spiral, I often observed actors and agents resolve contention among competing interests only when they could tame political interests by technical will. Nit-picking by parliamentary and extra-parliamentary actors over the use of terms, such as 'accession', in the parliamentary reports I analyse in this chapter, reflected this tension and ultimately actors' differences over Turkish membership. Both my Turkish and my EU interlocutors tried to make political issues 'technical' (and vice versa) by bureaucratic entreneurship. Both the Parliament's work on Turkey and the responses it triggered among the Turkish governing elite, communicated through these political documents, I argue, contributed to self-serving, enhanced bureaucratic politics.

'And now the Turkish delights!'[4]

During meetings when a draft Turkey report was up for debate, the meeting room would overflow with MEPs, member and candidate country diplomats, lobbyists and anyone else curious about EU–Turkey affairs or who wanted to watch a heated debate. There was no space left to sit or stand.

While few members from political group secretariats were in attendance, policy and country experts and advisers of political groups and parliamentary committees were almost always present at AFET meetings, as were Commission officials from DG Enlargement's Turkey unit, which was responsible for political criteria.

Turkish diplomats and lobbyists would enter the room only when the AFET debate approached the draft Turkey report. Diplomats had reserved seats at the back of the room; lobbyists sat in visitors' rows away from the diplomats. Distancing themselves from one another in front of the EU actors, they tried to obscure their cooperation with representatives. In each AFET meeting I observed, the moment the chairman (most chairs were men) announced the next issue on the agenda, the debate ended and the meeting room cleared as quickly as it had filled.

Initially, meetings on draft Turkey reports always closed with the rapporteur's announcement that the deadline for tabling amendments would end within a month. Until the next meeting, intense negotiations over amendments took place between MEPs' offices, with regulars making frequent amendments. Of all parliamentary reports, those on enlargement and individual candidate countries received the most amendments, and the Turkey reports received the most among

Figure 6.2 European Parliament AFET meeting in session. Source: European Parliament

all AFET reports. In fact, Turkey attracted more attention than any other subject on the Parliament's agenda. Each amendment reflected different interests invested in (or divested from) its EU accession.

Extra-parliamentary interests often wrote some of these amendments. In fact, supplying MEPs, political groups and parliamentary committee secretariats with fully developed amendments was a common practice among EU lobbyists (also see Hoedeman 2007). Industry and business lobbies, political parties, women's NGOs, human rights groups, minority associations, cities and regions, the Commission (including its Ankara representation, which sometimes considered matters differently from Brussels), the governments of EU member states and Turkey – all intensively lobbied relevant parliamentary offices to shape the Parliament's final report according to their investment in Turkey's EU prospect.

The existence and intensity of such lobbying suggest that the Parliament provided the best platform and means for diverse interests to seek representation during accession negotiations. For groups that felt most discriminated against, membership negotiations provided means to force the Ankara government to resolve problems through negotiation. From the perspective of the 'pro-Turkey lobby', the most famous of the former were the 'Armenian lobby', which wanted the European Parliament to recognise the Armenian genocide, and the 'Rum [Greek and Cypriot] lobby', which wanted Turkey to pull troops out of Cyprus. These 'counter-lobbies' (karşı lobiler) lobbied the Parliament from within and outside and organised public campaigns and street demonstrations with seemingly 'anti-Turkey' messages, a label the pro-Turkey lobby issued to maintain its own *raison d'être* in Brussels. None of these groups publicly campaigned on keeping Turkey out of the EU, however. A more accurate reading of their shared objective suggests that they worked towards Turkish compliance with their demands via the EU's brokering.

After the deadline, the rapporteur assembled amendments and constructed her compromises. Her parliamentary assistant, who often drafted the main text of these reports, put the arithmetic of compromise this way: 'Opposite amendments cancel each other out; even though in the end the actual wording might not make any sense, the remaining amendments are put together'. The rapporteur then edited the report one last time.

At the next meeting, MEPs voted on the compromises one by one, each in a few seconds. They kept their eyes on the electronic tally board and ears on the chairperson. Their assistants walked around with lists, putting pluses against each accepted amendment and a minus for each rejected one. At the end of the vote, sighs and clapping filled the meeting room. MEPs hugged and congratulated each other on their good work. Some shared the good news with their Turkish colleagues by shaking their hands. Others drew up critical accounts of which alliances had failed, for future reference; still others accepted defeat with mute disappointment. It usually took half a year and numerous political group, parliamentary committee and one-on-one meetings between MEPs, diplomats and lobbyists before the Parliament adopted the report. During this time, other parliamentary committees also submitted reports and opinions. The rapporteur's political skills at compromise determined how long a report took to finish. The diplomats' and lobbyists' cultural competencies, on the other hand, determined the shape of her reports.

Gender(ed) diplomacy and lobbying

Diplomacy is as much a gendered and classed vocation as any other profession (Bilgic 2016; Kuus 2014; Neumann 2012). Public administration in Turkey is governed by rampant gender inequality in wages, recruitment and retention. In 2018, only 38 per cent of all Turkish public servants were women. In the same year, out of 2175 career diplomats, deputy directors and directors, 709 (less than 31 per cent) were women (Yüzbaşıoğlu & Baykan 2018). As expressions of gender identity, a complex semiotics of hair and clothing has inscribed diplomatic bodies, across sexes, since the founding of modern Turkey. These markers of status, ideology, identity, class and group allegiance have helped members of modern Turkish bureaucracy gain access to influence, power and authority. When Erdoğan's AKP came to power, male bureaucrats exhibited their loyalty to his party and its president by sporting facial hair, reversing the post-1980 coup ban on male public servants having either a beard or long hair (Alimen 2018).

Emulating high-ranking party officials beginning with Erdoğan himself, many male bureaucrats wore a clipped, almond-style moustache (Tuğal 2009). This Erdoğan-style moustache was more common among local- and regional-level officials; diplomats still adhered to the post-coup 'no facial hair' policy and were always clean-shaven. But their dress code followed the changing politics of clothing in Turkey. When male bureaucrats visited Brussels, most donned a red tie on a white shirt, recreating the Turkish flag effect, showing allegiance to the country. Diplomats based in Brussels toned down such expressive identity markers.

Much like diplomacy, lobbying had been a gendered profession. With more women negotiators coming on to the political stage since 2005, the EU–Turkey negotiations became more democratic on the gender front – a common trend within the lobbying communities on both sides of the Atlantic (Benoit 2007; Izadi 2013). Even though women appeared in their ranks, Turkish diplomats and lobbyists who strove to participate in accession negotiations were mostly men; nonetheless, women were found to be better communicators. Referring to the role of gender in diplomacy and lobbying, 'Women are better lobbyists', Canan observed: 'When men lobby, they say: "Do this, do that!" – it has no wit. When women do it, they want things to be more flexible.' My parliamentary interlocutors recognised Hasan as a powerful marketer, but they also found his (and some of his colleagues') methods of persuasion less 'flexible', to put it mildly.

Even though gender identity and equality were less problematic in the Turkish diplomatic and lobbying communities, diplomats and lobbyists still needed to address them during accession negotiations because they remained problematic in Turkish society at large. When I went to her office at the Parliament one early morning, Luisa, the Socialist group's adviser on enlargement, shared with me a press release. A few weeks earlier, the Turkish parliament had established a committee to supervise gender equality in Turkey. Since 1998, women's groups have been lobbying the Turkish parliament to form such a committee and had called for the Commission to monitor the Turkish government on that issue. Under Commission pressure to align with the EU *acquis* on gender equality, the Turkish government established a committee to fulfil a benchmark that would satisfy the social policy and employment chapter. Before the committee became official, however, several AKP MPs tabled a last-minute amendment to change the planned committee's mandate by changing its name from one to supervise 'gender equality' into another that was to guarantee 'equality in opportunity', which the women's organisations interpreted as part of the government's anti-women stance. Defne explained later that women's organisations knew of the internal debate on 'gender equality' and 'equal opportunity' among members of the government but were not prepared for 'equality in opportunity'. The next day, Defne and her Istanbul- and Ankara-based colleagues drafted a press release in response to the tabled amendment and asked other women's organisations for their endorsement. In a few days, two platform organisations and thirty-one associations, cooperatives, foundations, solidarity centres, human rights and LGBTQI+ rights organisations signed the press release. Defne then sent it to her contacts in the Council, Commission and Parliament, including to Luisa.

Although the press release welcomed the establishment of the committee, it also explained the women's groups' objection to the name change. In the first and second paragraphs, the press release testified to the solidarity between Turkish women's organisations and the European Women's Lobby – a pan-European women's lobby organisation that had also members from Turkey, such as Defne's organisation – and compared the European Parliament's Committee on Women's Rights and Gender Equality with the proposed Turkish parliamentary committee. In the third paragraph, Defne and her colleagues situated their objection to the new name within a European social economic context by referring to how equal opportunity regulations over the years had failed to ensure real equality between men and women in Europe, which had prompted European countries to move away from them. The message here was clear: if Turkey was to be held to European standards by the committee, then the Turkish government and parliament should not be allowed to pursue an outdated measure proven to be ineffective by EU countries.

Through the press release, women's organisations tried to ensure the proper working of the new Turkish committee. They also made it public that, during their meetings with the Turkish government, the government had given assurances that, regardless of its name, the parliamentary committee would safeguard gender equality, not just equal opportunity. The last line of the press release noted the objective and context in which the committee was established in the first place, assuring European partners that, despite the problem-laden committee, the Turkish government and parliament were doing what they were asked and that accession reforms continued. In closing, the press release reiterated Turkish women's organisations' support for their country's EU accession process and the reforms necessary.

By circulating this press release through her Eurocratic networks, Defne aimed to disseminate not just information but a correct interpretation for her colleagues in Brussels. Turkish lobbyists often complained about how 'perverted information and obsessive analyses' dominated the Turkish EU field (Kaleağası 2006: 417). Defne worried that Commission officials might otherwise not notice the name change or might not understand what it amounted to in the Turkish political context, because their expertise on Turkey was circumscribed by their lack of firsthand experience with the country.

Although most EU lobbying took the form of 'information exchanges', a shared characteristic in EU lobbying across nations (Bouwen 2004), these exchanges themselves were mostly a means to political ends for Turkish lobbyists and diplomats. Defne disclosed her direct role to that end: 'The 2008 Turkey report is an edited and expanded version of the 2007 Turkey report. In 2007, I wrote an amendment and gave it to Ria [referring to the rapporteur by her first name, denoting access], which passed. There is no need for extreme bargaining on women's issues. Everyone already agrees.' To the same political end but perhaps less directly this time, the Turkish women's lobby aimed through the press release to insert their presence in and to become a legitimate party to the EU–Turkey dialogue. With the press release, they let their reservations and objections be known at the supranational level, hoping that politicians in Turkey would pay attention via the EU's brokering. To that end, the press release carried a warning that women's groups would make every effort to ensure the workings of the committee expressed their interests.

The Turkish government responded to Turkish women's lobbying at national and supranational levels by containing and minimising their concerns. For the government, the women's lobby did not need to 'obsess over words'. Nevertheless, the government recognised the women as an interest group and agreed to involve them in the process. To lose their support would look bad when the government needed to prove to the EU that it was consulting with civil society.

To keep the pressure up in Brussels, Defne organised a seminar on gender equality in Turkey with the help and participation of sympathetic Liberal MEPs, some of whom, including the vice-president of the European Parliament, held high-level political party and parliamentary posts. Held in the aftermath of the Strasbourg plenary where the draft Turkey report was voted on, the seminar brought together EU politicians and bureaucrats and Turkish civil society organisations that worked on gender equality. The timing of the seminar and choice of speakers were strategic.

Defne's political lobbying of the European Parliament paid off in one concrete way. The relevant section in the Parliament's 2008 Turkey report (adopted in 2009) reads as follows:

> [The European Parliament] Welcomes the establishment of the 'Women–Men Equal Opportunities Commission' in the Turkish parliament; welcomes the Commission's assessment that the legal framework guaranteeing women's rights and gender equality is broadly in place; urges, however, the Turkish government to ensure that it is implemented so as to have a positive effect on the situation of women in Turkey.

Getting her amendments through to the Parliament's Turkey report by lobbying the AFET rapporteur and the rapporteur of the Committee on Women's Rights and Gender Equality (both Dutch, but from different political groups), Defne's was a success story – albeit a rare one.

As a communicator, Defne found working with 'Europeans' to be 'much more comfortable and more direct, [since] what they want is clear. So, I don't get anxious about getting hold of the draft report. The more open you are [to them], the more open they are [to you]. Anyway, our mandate is open, there is nothing hidden, [but] one needs to go [to EU contacts] with content.' The most successful parliamentary lobbyists went to their contacts with a specific agenda and a clear mandate. From victims of faith-based fraud to ethnic and religious minorities, their effectiveness lay foremost in their ability to couch their interests and demands in a 'European framework'. Though not a monolith, this 'European framework' often remained suspect for Turkish diplomatic communicators, who, through a misframing of demands, often failed to convince their parliamentary colleagues.

Showing deep rivalries within the Turkish lobbying community, Defne sounded less positive about working with fellow lobbyists and representatives of Turkish interests in Brussels: 'Things are harder with the Turks. There is a hierarchy. I can manage it. I can talk to anybody anytime I want, but it's not clear who has information.... Hiding information, making money on information, misinformation, not sharing information, or not working together are obscured by a veneer of bureaucracy.' When I asked Sibel to comment on this contention, she explained it with reference to Turkey's culture of governance:

> Washington, Brussels, London – people come to work in these places after many hardships. Therefore, they do not share [information, contacts and so on]. We [Turkish representatives] struggle against each other, set our examples not by what Europeans are doing but by what our [Turkey's] Berlin embassy does. This is about our government culture. There is no risk-taking in [our] state culture. But these things will change.... There are people in Turkish institutions who question us on what we do here. They just watch. Europeans congratulate and motivate.

Rivalries within the Turkish diplomatic and lobbying communities did not stay within the group, however, but spilled over into more diverse political domains, like the European Parliament.

'Turks' of the Parliament

A small but significant group of MEPs with minority ethnic and religious back-grounds (e.g. Kurdish, Sunni Muslim, Alevi) who originated in Turkey, much like the 'Bulgarian-Turkish' MEP who authored the internal trade committee report, were instrumental to conveying Turkish interests within the Parliament. This group of MEPs constituted first contacts for anyone lobbying the Parliament about Turkey from outside, including Turkish diplomats and lobbyists. During the sixth legislature, when I was doing fieldwork, there were five such MEPs – the highest number in the Parliament's history.[5] They commonly chose their assistants and secretaries from people also of Turkish origin. Successful (and not-so-successful) Turkish lobbying in the Parliament went mostly through these MEPs.

Other than political lobbying by Hasan, Defne, Bayram or Sibel, Turkish public and private interest representatives lobbied these MEPs' offices to hold social and public events at the Parliament, for which they needed the endorsement of an MEP. These events ranged from book launching, to seminars and debates about particular issues, such as women's or minority rights, wherein MEPs, experts and others discussed matters. Other events, such as the occasional launching of (Conservative, Socialist, Liberal) 'Friends of Turkey' groups or dinners, were more like political masquerades. Over a fifteen-month period, thirteen such events took place in the Parliament. Many competed with one another over audience due to intra-group conflicts or poor organisation. Contacted by Turkish repre-sentatives with requests to organise events, Kemal, a parliamentary assistant of a Turkish-Dutch MEP, sarcastically put it: 'We do "room service" for these groups'.

Problematically, Kemal's boss and others risked being identified by their origin ('Turkish') and not by the larger European constituencies that elected them. Off the record, one parliamentary assistant of an MEP with a Turkey background confided in me that his boss had lonely moments because country colleagues con sidered this MEP 'a Turk', while Turkish officials in Brussels dismissed the MEP as 'a European'. Ayhan, the Kurdish lobbyist who put me in touch with Bayram, avoided a Kurdish-German MEP because her peers identified her mainly as 'a

Kurd', which Ayhan considered a disadvantage because other MEPs saw her agenda as too narrowly focused on one ethnic minority. Instead, he focused on non-Turkish or non-Kurdish MEPs. Political rivalries between different Kurdish lobbying groups must have been an added a factor in his choice (Berkowitz & Mügge 2014).

Some of these MEPs struggled to build a political agenda beyond the T. file, while others resorted to self-defence. Evrim, another parliamentary assistant, described her Turkish-German boss as a missionary who advocated 'for Turkey in Europe' and for a 'Turkey despite itself'. She explained the everyday dilemma her Turkish-German-European self and her MEP faced: 'I have had things to criticise. But if you are one of the four [Turkey-origin MEPs – and note here her exclusion of the Kurdish member from the group of five], you don't criticise that much. You adopt a political behaviour.' Her boss's political behaviour often amounted to relaying the Turkish 'official line', or talking points supplied by Deniz, through speeches and amendments, for which the Turkey rapporteur and his fellow MEPs frequently criticised him.

Turkish diplomats in Brussels and Ankara often tested MEPs with Turkish backgrounds by scrutinising their loyalty to the Turkish government. As a result, diplomats lobbied only those who passed the loyalty test and kept others at a distance. In turn, whether these MEPs were on good working terms with different societal and political groups from Turkey (including the government) and whether they could communicate difficult issues to counterparts affected their standing in Turkey's Europeanisation. The European Parliament's annual Turkey reports served as a litmus test for loyalty to the 'homeland' and cooperation with its agents.

Political documents and nit-picking over 'accession'

It is not news that the European Parliament's reports are essentially political documents (de Lobkowicz 2001; Muntigl et al. 2000). Their length, the contention they generate and the parties involved in their production indicate their significance. Perhaps the single most important indicator regarding the Parliament's Turkey reports has been the large number of amendments: 262 in 2008; 188 in 2009; 243 in 2010; 315 in 2011; 461 in 2012; 415 in 2013; 338 in 2014; 442 in 2015; 331 in 2016; and 397 in 2017. It is evident that the more contentious EU–Turkey relations became, the larger was the number of submitted amendments. Critical discourse analyst Ruth Wodak (2009) called attention to the ways in which the wording on paper reflected and framed EU policy options. Wodak suggested that documents produced within the EU's institutional confines 'manifest certain rules and expectations according to social conventions, and have specific functions in a discourse community and its related community of practice. The proposal itself follows certain textual devices; the contents follow an ideology or program put forward by a specific political group' (Wodak 2009: 40). Following Wodak, below I analyse the Turkey reports and the political, bureaucratic processes through which they were drafted. The documents themselves and the amendment process aptly manifest political conventions peculiar to the anti-case of Turkey's bid for EU membership and what the Parliament did about it.

Each year, MEPs proposed amendments that varied according to any concerns they had and the interests of those who lobbied them. Through parliamentary amendments, some groups struggled to mould Turkey's EU accession into an 'open-ended' process whose results no one could guarantee beforehand. Others mobilised to secure the final result of negotiations with 'accession' (full membership), however that might occur. Year after year, members proposed amendments regarding the use of the word 'accession'. This suggests that, over a decade into membership talks, the Turkish bid remained as contentious as ever. Consequently, it became all the more symbolically significant whether Turkey's EU membership remained 'potential' or moved towards becoming 'prospective'. The presence or absence of the term 'accession' was therefore critical. As I discuss later, the struggle between those who pushed 'accession' into parliamentary reports and those who pulled it out contributed to the bureaucratic politics among actors on both sides.

During negotiations of the 2008 draft report, a group of MEPs questioned the rapporteur's alleged attempt to deprive EU–Turkey relations of integrity by failing to use the word 'accession'. Noting her omission of it, they proposed amendments to reinstate the term. This was, indeed, the first time this omission had occurred in the EP's textual repository regarding Turkish membership. Seven members (five Socialists and two Liberals) jointly submitted the first amendment, which read as follows:[6]

> *Draft motion for a resolution*
> – having regard to the Negotiating Framework for Turkey of 3 October 2005,
> *Amendment*
> – having regard to the Negotiating Framework for **Turkey's EU accession** of 3 October 2005.

AFET members rejected this amendment during their subsequent meeting. Their rejection raised concerns among Turkish diplomats. Murmuring about the Parliament's strong support in 1999 and in 2004, Turkish diplomats now doubted their parliamentary counterparts' commitment to Turkey's EU bid. To their disadvantage, this was not the same Parliament that agreed to those terms.

In anticipation of rejection, however, the same MEPs raised this issue seven more times, with further amendments to the ensuing articles of the draft report, including the following:

> *Draft motion for a resolution*
> A. whereas negotiations with Turkey were opened on 3 October 2005 after approval by the Council of the Negotiating Framework, and whereas the **opening of those** negotiations is **the starting-point for a long-lasting and** open-ended process,
> *Amendment*
> A. whereas negotiations with Turkey were opened on 3 October 2005 after approval by the Council of the Negotiating Framework, and whereas the **shared objective of the** negotiations is **accession; whereas negotiations are an** open-ended process **the outcome of which cannot be guaranteed in advance,**

In response, the Christian Democrats proposed in an amendment that the process with Turkey be considered an open-ended one that should (at best) 'strengthen economic, political and human ties of the EU with Turkey'. Luisa explained what had by then become a regular practice: 'Each year the rapporteur uses "negoti-ation", to which our [Socialist] MEPs respond with numerous amendments to qualify this with "accession"'. Indeed, Socialist members together with Liberal Democrats submitted four similar amendments.

The rapporteur used 'accession' in her first Turkey report, that for 2007, but her political group, the Christian Democrats, became more vocal in their opposition to Turkey's EU accession over time in the Parliament. After many amendments to her omission of 'accession' in the 2008 draft report, the rapporteur finally agreed to the use of 'accession' in her final report. She introduced it in a compromise that read:

> A. whereas accession negotiations with Turkey were opened on 3 October 2005 after approval by the Council of the Negotiating Framework, and whereas the opening of those negotiations *was* [my emphasis] the starting-point for a long-lasting and open-ended process,

Although the rapporteur compromised, she did something else: whether many well trained eyes simply missed or ignored it, the rapporteur used her bureau-cratic entrepreneurship and switched to past tense. Although none of her fellow members had proposed an amendment for it, she had, on her own, introduced this compromise by placing accession negotiations in the past tense. According to the rapporteur, the opening of membership talks was by then *passé* and perhaps not the terms of membership but the positive perception of the Turkish bid in the Parliament had changed. This article was kept intact in the final Turkey report, with the rapporteur's use of accession as the qualifier of negotiations and her use of the past tense in which she placed them.

MEPs objected with many amendments to the rapporteur's iteration of acces-sion negotiations as a 'long-lasting and open-ended process' in her 2009 draft report. While some demanded that this be deleted in its entirety, opponents requested a clear reference to the EU conditionality. EU conditionality refers to the EU's capacity to take in new members. Opponents of Turkish membership used it as a benchmark to drag out the accession process because the EU may never be ready for Turkey. The Socialists and Liberals once more took up the fight with their MEPs from central and eastern European countries, submitting most amendments to benchmarking Turkey's accession with EU conditionality.

Concerned that their amendments might otherwise not carry, they agreed, ahead of the vote, to a reference on some conditionality. Some MEPs proposed to substitute 'whereas the opening of those negotiations was the starting-point for' with '**negotiation process with the objective of Turkey's EU membership once the membership criteria are fulfilled**', or 'a long-lasting and open-ended process with the purpose of EU membership, provided that Turkey meets the criteria,' with 'a long-lasting and open-ended process, **with the common goal of full EU member-ship as soon as the membership criteria are fulfilled**'. None of the amendments were accepted. The article was adopted intact. Even so, many Socialist and Liberal MEPs proposed new amendments with similar content in other sections of the draft report.

More direct and effective lobbying came from within the Parliament itself. Luisa shared a one-page political assessment table with me. It categorised the political and media relevance and internal and external conflict levels of the issue as 'average'. Shadow rapporteurs successfully lobbied the rapporteur behind the scenes during the amendment of the 2008 report (drafted in 2009). After negotiations with the Socialist group, the assessment stated 'the rapporteur agreed to include in her text a call to the Council to consider making progress on opening of negotiations on chapters in which Turkey, according to the Commission's assessment, fulfilled the conditions for opening'. It would be naive to think that the Socialist group initiated this textual addition without consulting the Commission. In fact, the initiative came from the Commission. This amendment carried through to the final report. Considering who asked whom to do what, this was an effective example of intra-EU lobbying.

In her subsequent draft reports, the rapporteur went back to her use of the present tense. Her efforts might have also been an attempt to zero in on Turkey's reforms to date. In 2011, the Commission had reinvigorated the accession talks with Turkey. The rapporteur's return to the present tense in her 2010 draft report was evidently because the Commission had lobbied her office on this matter. In fact, as the Christian Democrat's Turkey adviser, another Dutch national, pointed out to me, the Commission often influenced these reports to 'make Turkey better comply with accession requirements' (see also Marshall 2010). The Commission's lobbying of the rapporteur on specific legislative changes aimed to minimise any discrepancy between legislation and practice, even though we now know that this 'discrepancy' primarily came from domestic lobbying of the government and state institutions inside Turkey.

In her 2011 report, the rapporteur continued to reframe accession negotiations as 'a starting-point for a long-lasting and open-ended process', but this time accession negotiations were to be 'based on fair and rigorous conditionality and the commitment to reform'. In her 2012 report and her last report, that of 2013, accession negotiations based on the same conditionality and commitment became a framing construction. Elections held the year after changed the composition of the Parliament. Under the new Socialist rapporteur (a Hungarian-born Dutch national), MEPs continued to negotiate Turkey's Europeanisation according to the previous Turkey rapporteur's bureaucratic entrepreneurship, attesting to her legacy on EU–Turkey relations.

A structured monologue

Once the Parliament adopted a new report, Hasan and his colleagues began lobbying the Parliament over the next one. The Parliament has been the main target of Turkish lobbying – even though it is the Commission that decides the main reform criteria to be met by Ankara. Their EU counterparts perceived the Turkish arguments to be too numerous and the methods of persuasion to be too direct, and thus counterproductive, even though diplomacy is known to be a communicative practice of exercising power and authority through *indirection* (Carrier 2001). Some even felt 'bullied'.

Various parliamentary offices approached Turkish official discourses and their carriers with much caution, perhaps because the Turkish government disseminated its messages primarily through official platforms, such as the EU–Turkey Joint Parliamentary Committee (JPC), guaranteed by the Ankara Agreement. Composed of twenty-five-member delegations from European and Turkish parliaments, the JPC met twice a year, once in Turkey and once in Brussels or Strasbourg. During JPC meetings, members discussed issues that did not fit in screening reports or the Parliament's yearly reports on Turkey. Representatives of the Commission and the Council Presidency, as well as the Turkish delegation in Brussels, accompanied parliamentarians in these meetings. Representatives of various social and economic interests, high-level officials, journalists and interpreters also joined them in their meetings. Sightseeing and VIP dinners organised by host parliamentarians occasionally interrupted the two and a half days of JPC meetings.

Alfred, one parliamentary administrator whose job was to organise these meetings, characterised them as 'structured monologue'. During one JPC meeting, a Greek MEP from the Christian Democrats, Margaritis Schinas,[7] expressed his frustration with the meeting:

> I am extremely disappointed by the way this committee has evolved into a village square, where people go and shout at each other hoping someone will get attention. People try to insert a sentence here or there according to individual-national interest. JPC meetings are becoming unnecessary. That many members are absent is an indication to [*sic*] it. Substance is killed by [trivial] matters. We failed our objective of communicating.

Like MEP Schinas (later the Commission's chief spokesperson), other JPC members from both sides were far from satisfied with this platform's institutional performance. Despite many problems with it, however, the JPC remained the only official platform for EU and Turkish parliamentarians to communicate.

Parliamentarians usually limited their focus at JPC meetings to EU–Turkey relations, leaving out present and future issues on the EU's agenda, which might have had relevancy to their relations in the medium or long term. Members from both sides attended the meetings with a prefigured agenda. Most were men. Each speaker spoke his mind. Disorder seemed to be the rule, so much so that statements did not follow a logical sequence as they would in a normal conversation. In three JPC meetings I observed, politicians talked across each other about issues pertaining to their agenda that did not relate to what others had just said.

Members competed to make statements that would appear in the minutes and records of the JPC. Turkish members were more concerned in arguing with each other over the proper placement of their country in the European order and about various domestic disputes rather than about Turkey's relations with the EU.

During the JPC meeting where Schinas expressed his frustration, for example, Turkish opposition parliamentarians objected when Turkey's EU minister Bağış, in the context of Turkey's co-chairing of the UN initiative 'Alliance of Civilisations' with Spain, described Spain as representing Western civilisation. If Spain represented the West, what did Turkey represent, opposition MPs asked. Responding to his critics, Bağış suggested that Turkey was 'the most eastern of the west, and the most western of the east'. As an alternative to full EU membership, he also suggested that Turkey might adopt the 'Norwegian model' of full economic integration without political participation in the EU (Euractiv 2010).

Unlike with Turkish politicians, bureaucrats and diplomats, the European Parliament has been more open to non-official lines of communication with interest groups, perhaps because informal actors engaged with different groups in the Parliament or engaged with them with more care. In an earlier interview, Deniz stressed how his office approached EU counterparts differently. Unlike the more bull(y)ish methods of persuasion Turkish diplomats often used in communicating with their EU colleagues in Brussels, Deniz admitted: 'We don't threaten them, of course. But we say: "If you do not do such and such Turkey will become a different country, and you will have to deal with different classes of people"'.

Governmental or not, Turkish agents always lobbied specific individuals, measuring effective lobbying by personal success, both theirs and those they lobbied. Having worked with Turkish diplomats on hosting Turkish parliamentarians in Brussels for several years when we met, Ernst, Alfred's boss, suggested: 'Your [Turkish] diplomatic representation does quite well here in Brussels, but it always depends on the person. Political culture is key here. The fundamental difference between Turkey and other countries' representatives is not in structures, but in people's behaviour.' Ernst further characterised Turkish diplomats as a 'political class ... prone to submit to higher political authority.' I would add that Turkish diplomats and lobbyists were a class unto themselves. For both groups, lobbying the Parliament was all too personal!

Bureaucratic entrepreneurs and positive pedagogy

Turkish diplomats in Brussels and their colleagues in Ankara responded to the Parliament's Turkey reports by disseminating their views in official (JPC) and informal (e.g. 'Friends of Turkey' groups) parliamentary platforms. The Turkish Ministry of Foreign Affairs prepared texts – with no official signature, letterhead or logo, known as 'non-paper' in IR-speak – which communicated Turkey's views through the corridors of power in Brussels. As far as I am aware, no other country agents produced this kind of documentary response to parliamentary reports.

Every year, high-level bureaucrats drafted a new non-paper and sent it to AFET's Turkey rapporteur, shadow rapporteurs from political groups, the secretariats of parliamentary committees, AFET members, MEPs who were known to be sympathetic to the Turkish cause, and to the Commission. I had access to two such non-papers, first through my parliamentary interlocutors and later when I worked at Leyla's think-tank.[8]

The style of writing suggested that these documents carried Turkey's amendments to the Parliament's draft Turkey reports. Because of the otherwise disguised institutional identity of their author(s), the non-papers were products of bureaucratic entrepreneurship: they embodied a technopolitical quality wherein members of bureaucratic organisations used tactical knowledge and expertise to circumvent hierarchies embedded in their institutions (Page 1997: 154). Bureaucratic entrepreneurship might be risky, yet many in the Turkish bureaucracy practised it. It became especially vital in EU–Turkey relations, which were always short of specialisation and expertise. There was a circular logic to it: it rewarded individuals with higher administrative status, more responsibility and ultimately more power; bureaucratic entrepreneurs then used this power to bolster their authority and standing in the organisation.

When I asked around about the author's identity, everyone gave me Hasan's name. Having studied EU–Turkey relations and having worked in a diplomatic capacity since the late 1980s, Hasan had both a personal and a political stake as a career diplomat in Turkey's EU integration. Since our first meeting in front of the delegation offices, I had many occasions to observe him in action. He spent much time and energy influencing the Parliament's Turkey reports, drinking litres of coffee with MEPs, their assistants and staff, as well as with those from political groups and committee secretariats, socialising with them outside the Parliament over meals and drinks, and perhaps at times intimidating them over these reports. Each time I laid eyes on him, he was either handing notes to the Turkey rapporteur during AFET meetings or talking to MEPs and others he cornered outside the meeting room. This single man took onto himself the arduous task of representing Turkish public interests in the Parliament. He was proud of this initiative. Even though Turkish non-papers did not come out of his own initiative, he standardised them – not the least by training others in crafting them. His entrepreneurship endured even after he left Brussels for Ankara, from where he continued to oversee their production, always leaving a personal trace in them.

Contrary to his and his colleagues' expectations, however, lengthy documents, such as the 2008 thirty-two-page non-paper that contained amendment proposals blended with argument, opinions and recommendations, received little attention in the parliamentary offices. A year later, in 2009, Turkey's non-paper came closer to the Parliament's amendment style. It shrank to eight pages. Its author abandoned lengthy explanations of a proposed amendment or of a conflict's background. The author's voice also became less didactic and less authoritative, with the use of smaller fonts and fewer words presented in bold.

Both non-papers I had access to firmly demanded that the rapporteur adopt a rewarding tone regarding Turkey's reform performance and its active participation in the programme. Initially, the pedagogical tone of the Turkey reports had drawn no objection from Turkish officials, at least not within their informal submissions for the Parliament's Turkey reports. They demanded instead that the reports register more of Turkey's good deeds than criticisms of bad government behaviour. On its very first page, under the subheading 'Negative and Discouraging Tone', the 2008 non-paper, which misdated the draft report, read:

The draft 2009 [2008] Turkey report employs the term 'regrets' 14 times and 'is concerned' 12 times in comparison to 3 and 6 in the 2008 [2007] Final Report. Surely, this negative manner will discourage the reform process and further efforts, which have already been badly affected by external factors. Therefore, this tone which maybe [sic] critical, has to be tuned to an encouraging language by replacing most of these negative verbs by rather descriptive and neutral words, since the intention of the Report is to support the reform and accession process.

The author(s) redefined these reports as a means to enhance Turkey's Europeanisation. The non-paper further applied a normative framework to the report's discourse in addressing Turkey, followed by warnings of negative consequences if those norms were not met.

It recommended that the rapporteur place EU–Turkey relations in context by referring to them as 'accession negotiations' with 'the shared objective of accession'. Relaying common sentiments to the Turkey rapporteur, Johan, a Dutch diplomat from the Netherlands' EU representation in Brussels, suggested that Turkey's questioning the use of 'accession' in each EU official text diverted significant energy from substantive issues. For his Turkish counterparts, however, echoing Scott (1998: 93): 'There are virtually no other facts for the state than those that are contained in documents'. Thus, a word once uttered mattered most in terms of political symbolism – which was why archives mattered so much to these diplomats – such that they considered the non-use of the term 'accession' a politically motivated omission by the rapporteur. The rapporteur must have agreed with this Turkish impression; why else would she insist on *not* using the word in her reports, or switch between the present and past tense in her compromises?

The author(s) of the non-papers tried to mould the ongoing negotiation process by amending the rapporteur's 2008 words: 'Whereas Turkey has committed itself to reforms, good neighbourly relations and progressive alignment with the EU, and whereas these efforts should be viewed as an opportunity for Turkey itself to modernize'. To this passage was added: 'these efforts are both for alignment with European standards or modernisation as well as for joining the EU' (p. 2). The author(s) shifted the blame for Turkey's poor reform performance away from the government and demanded that the EU 'honour its existing commitments towards the countries already in the enlargement process, this being a strong incentive for the countries to continue their reforms' (p. 1). Progress 'has been stalled for reasons of [a] non-technical nature' (p. 3). The author(s) did not explicitly describe these reasons as political but referred to the blockage of accession negotiations by some EU member states (p. 4) and underlined the 'continuous slowdown of the reform process' and 'calls on the Turkish government to prove its political will to continue the reform process to which it committed itself in 2005' (p. 5). This 'goes beyond being critical and questions the very will of the Government to continue the reform and accession process' The Parliament was assured that 'the Government's political will remains as solid as it used to be' (p. 5). The author(s) repeatedly demanded that the European Parliament give due recognition and credit to the Turkish government for its reform efforts – efforts that might or might not have existed but that were open for interpretation and accounting, they argued, only by the Turkish people themselves.

The issues I interpret as elements of positive pedagogy were repeatedly made in both non-papers. Such continuous emphasis suggested an emerging pattern of bureaucratic entrepreneurship with its own qualities. The author(s) of both non-papers openly demanded that the rapporteur use 'a balanced tone'. As expected, Turkish colleagues found them balanced when the reports referred equally to good and bad deeds of the government in its accession performance and used a 'moderate voice' (Strauss 2010).

Prepared between Brussels and Ankara by one or more high-level Turkish bureaucrats, these non-papers had two concrete effects. First, many proposed amendments found their way into the offices of MEPs; a few even found their way into AFET debates verbatim as amendments, such as those regarding the use of the term 'accession'. Bureaucrats gently called on Turkish private interest representatives and lobbyists through informal communication platforms, such as the 'civil society consultation meetings' (*sivil toplumla istişare toplantısı*, STID) to help disseminate through their parliamentary contacts views and amendment proposals presented in the non-papers.

An early initiative of Turkey's then EU ambassador and Hasan's boss in Brussels, STID meetings were a showcase of government consultation with about ten or so Turkish private interest representatives. Since the Turkish delegation at times worked like an official AKP representation office, with most diplomats arguing for the party instead of the public they represented, representatives of rival political parties and the media were not invited to these meetings. Later I was bluntly told that the ambassador did not want to invite Bayram to STID meetings because he represented a party with which the AKP was in competition for Kurdish votes. To avoid the appearance of discriminating against Bayram, the ambassador made it a rule that no political party representative was to attend STID meetings; hence Sibel was also excluded. In this way, two opposition parties were eliminated from an informal communication channel used freely by others. After his term ended, the ambassador first became secretary general to the EUSG, which was now under the Office of the Prime Minister and which later became Turkey's EU Ministry. Later, he was elected to the Turkish parliament on the AKP ticket, where he served twice as EU minister and chief negotiator.

During and after STID meetings, Turkish diplomats reminded a handful of Turkish lobbyists that their individual efforts in Brussels served as a test for effective cooperation between Turkish public and private interest representatives – as they did also with the Turkish MEPs. Some lobbyists took this call as an opportunity to strengthen their relationship with Turkish authorities. Others used it to look good to their bosses in Turkey. During one AFET meeting, I sat behind Orhan and his boss, who was visiting from Istanbul. Orhan pointed at an amendment on the European Parliament's draft Turkey report and told his boss, '*We* put this in here'.

Orhan's behaviour was justifiable to the extent that the work of Turkish lobbyists (and diplomats) often went unrecognised, or at best underappreciated, by their higher-ups. Having to endlessly prove their professional worth to reluctant

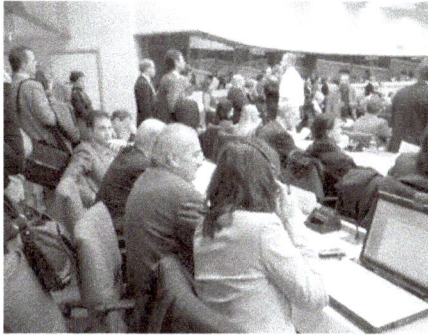

Figure 6.3 Turkish lobbyists at work

clients, like their diplomatic colleagues, Turkish lobbyists used every opportunity to display their professional skills to their employers.

Still, only a few amendments generated enough support to appear in the final report. Turkey-friendly MEPs claimed that their amendments were directly instrumental in toning down the sharp voices that appeared in the draft reports. Their Turkish colleagues welcomed this move in their post-report comments.

Turkish diplomats and lobbyists did not necessarily follow up on the results of the Parliament's Turkey debates in Brussels. The likelihood that their proposed amendments would not be passed – most were not – did not deter them from presenting themselves to their bosses in Turkey and colleagues in Brussels as successful lobbyists and professional identity-carriers.

The second concrete effect these reports and non-papers had was at a more personal level. The Turkish non-papers enabled their author(s) – and those who relayed their positions – to gain more status and promotion and helped them reinforce their position as 'experts'. After his Brussels term, I saw Hasan during the next STID meeting. By then, he had become a special adviser to chief negotiator Bağış. As I was leaving Brussels, I heard that Hasan was leading a new communications directorate at the EU Ministry in Ankara, whose creation he had personally orchestrated. Upon my return to the United States, I met him once more in the lobby of New York City's Plaza Hotel, where he was staying for a UN conference while accompanying his immediate boss, Turkey's foreign minister, Davutoğlu. During our brief talk, he proudly showed me a draft copy of a strategy paper aimed at systematising and institutionalising communication with EU counterparts, full of Turkish-EU no(ta)bles. He had personally drafted this strategy paper and with it engineered the creation of a separate unit for himself.

Referring to the strategy paper, Hasan also told me that he had to 'lobby the minister' to make it happen. Senior level bureaucrats have always had special leeway in winning over Turkish legislators, especially regarding EU-related matters (Keskin 2001). Because expertise gained in the EU field did not transfer easily to other domains of public administration or the private sector, these bureaucrats increased their presence and power by enhancing their roles and expertise during negotiations on EU-related matters. In such cases, bureaucratic entrepreneurship came in especially handy. Successive Turkish governments, including those before the AKP came to power, skirted parliamentary deliberation by issuing executive decrees drafted by civil servants, turning bureaucrats into targets for heavy lobbying while enhancing political clientelism in Turkey (Alexander 2002; Uğur 2000).

Inspired by the US presidential system but without checks and balances, Erdoğan changed the Turkish governance regime from a parliamentary democracy to a presidential system run by a technocratic government appointed by himself with the April 2017 constitutional referendum, rendering parliamentary deliberation effectively irrelevant. To cut the 'red tape' (read: bureaucratic competition or resistance) Erdoğan also turned the EU Ministry into a subunit of the Ministry for Foreign Affairs. The 24 June 2018 elections solidified Erdoğan's technocratic powers in Turkey's post-parliamentary politics and made political clientelism the new rule of the land. In this post-parliamentary governance *alla Turca*, to channel interests, influence and information effectively, bureaucrats, lawmakers and lobbyists alike needed to engage in political clientelism.

When I began writing this book, Hasan had moved back to Brussels to take up his new position as Turkey's EU ambassador. His posting required triple authorisation by the president, prime minister and the foreign affairs minister, as customary for Turkish foreign service appointments, making his Brussels appointment political – however well deserved it was. As I was finishing this book, Hasan was called back to Ankara. Appointed by Erdoğan himself, he became deputy minister of foreign affairs and director for EU affairs. As evident from his remarkable career trajectory, Hasan found his place within the post-parliamentary networks of political patronage in Turkey, with Murat and others sitting next to him.

Conclusion

Unlike bureaucratic documents that are instruments of policy-making (Hull 2012b), the European Parliament's Turkey reports were hardly classics of 'domination through knowledge' (Weber 1978: 223). They neither informed decision-makers in their making of better policies nor compelled anybody to take further action. They did not make bureaucrats who they were (cf. Hull 2012b), even though they contributed to professional careers. Although, during a later e-mail exchange with me, Hasan reminisced about his drafting amidst in-house and extra-parliamentary power struggles and insisted that it was important for the Parliament's records to demonstrate support, through precedence, for Turkish membership, no one essentially cared about past reports. Once adopted, they became mundane and inactive, an iteration within the Parliament's textual repository. Why then did EU and Turkish actors spend so much energy on preparing them?

'Writing [serves] to communicate at a distance, to store information, and to tend to depersonalize interaction', argued Goody (1986: 89–90) about power and modern statecraft. In the EU's complex policy-making process, where actors do not regularly meet face to face, material products gain a special communicative value. Representatives of Turkish and non-Turkish interests helped cross bureaucratic and social distances and facilitate the negotiation of politico-cultural forms, codes and norms through these political documents. In contrast to Goody's argument, I found that, in the production of the Parliament's Turkey reports and the Turkish responses they elicited, every bit of these documents was personal to those drafting them. Precisely because such political documents were produced in a negotiated manner, they were also products of enduring socio-political relations. They served as 'networking devices' (Preda 2002: 235; see also Harper 1998), connecting people during their production and dissemination.

In this great game of politics at the supranational and national levels, each actor and agent served its function. The Parliament, its committees and their members accomplished their self-initiated and routinised task of evaluating Turkey's performance of progress. Diplomats and lobbyists from the EU, its member states and Turkey tried to mould the final reports by lobbying the Parliament at all levels. Turkish representatives impressed on their bosses that everything was under control. In this way, they earned recognition, appreciation and promotion – regardless of actual reform performance. Meanwhile, amidst stalling negotiations, EU and Turkish government circles co-constituted one another as collocutors through these reports. Finally, politicians, bureaucrats and lobbyists from all levels and sides showed that, despite the non-movement of accession negotiations and the reform process, politics as usual was continuing in EU–Turkey affairs. Concomitantly, they proved the ongoing need for their expertise as true politicians, diplomats and lobbyists in maintaining (good) relations between otherwise reluctant parties to the Turkish bid. This further helped them consolidate their monopoly over representation of interests with which they were initially entrusted, that is, the right to speak for their respective publics or clientele. Actors from both sides thus carved further space for themselves in future bureaucratic politics surrounding Turkey's EU membership bid.

Notes

1 One time, a close friend whom I met back in 2005 in Brussels and whom I watched build a career in political communication, told me about a meeting he had with an MEP. The MEP travelled to Turkey with his wife for a week-long holiday vacation in exchange for sponsoring a Turkish event in the Parliament. But such exchange was rare. Most Turkish lobbyists preferred to work through non-monetary means. Money was a scarce resource, and Turkish clients did often not want to pay for those types of service.

2 Born in Germany, AKP's first Brussels representative and a former Union of European Turkish Democrats director was elected to the Turkish Parliament on AKP ticket during the 2018 national elections.

3 Real name.

1 Quotation from chairman's introduction to the vote on the draft 2008 Turkey report.

5 There were two female and three male MEPs. Three were from Germany (one Socialist, one Green, one far left), one from the Netherlands (Socialist) and one from Bulgaria (Liberal-Democrat).

6 By convention, all amendment proposals are put in bold italic until adopted or dismissed. I quote them here as they appear in original.

7 Real name.

8 The first report was titled 'Comments on the 2009 Draft Report of the European Parliament on Turkey's 2008 Progress Report' (dated 1 December 2008) and the second was 'Turkey's Comments and Views on the 2010 Draft Report of the European Parliament on Turkey's 2009 Progress Report and Proposals for Amendments' (dated 8 December 2009). I obtained a copy of the first non-paper from an administrator at the European Parliament and a copy of the second came to my mailbox while I was working for Leyla. Turkish diplomats and I shared citizenship. Even though they (sometimes reluctantly) talked to me about their work, they chose not to disclose written traces of it, perhaps because I was a student of the bizarre discipline of Europolitics or simply a 'citizen'. Either way, they did not feel publicly accountable to me.

Conclusion: lessons from an anti-case

When I began research for this book in 2005, Turkey was a reliable NATO member, had a budding market economy, was a predominantly Muslim society within a functioning secular state and had a maturing liberal democracy with aspirations to become the next EU member state. When I finished fieldwork in Brussels in 2009, we were approaching the fiftieth anniversary of Turkey's application for association to the European Economic Community. Between 2005 and 2009, Turkey's accession negotiations with the EU had turned into a death spiral. I quit smoking and left Brussels.

Even though I left, I continued to follow the lives and work of my interlocutors. After 2009, few could keep their positions in Brussels; among them, the no(ta)bles of Turkish Europeanisation showed remarkable dexterity and resilience. As new political opportunists rose through the ranks, many others left Brussels to continue their self-ascribed profession in Turkey or left the EU–Turkey vocation entirely for another field, falling out of the EU–Turkey policy networks. Leyla was one of them. Though she did not exactly fall out of EU–Turkey policy networks, the last I heard of her she had closed her think-tank in Brussels, left her consulting firm in Istanbul and moved to Switzerland, spending her time painting in the Swiss Alps. The diplomats and lobbyists who kept their positions, such as Deniz and Hasan, did so by increasing their power, status and influence in EU–Turkey affairs.

Meanwhile, a series of developments led MEPs to urge the Council and Commission to temporarily freeze accession negotiations with Turkey: the Brexit referendum (since the UK supported Turkish accession); the Syrian proxy war and refugee crisis; the 2016 putsch in Turkey, followed by the AKP's purge of hundreds of thousands of leftists, dissidents and Gülenists; and a general deterioration in the rule of law and fundamental rights in Turkey. In July 2017, MEPs voted for the formal suspension of the membership talks. At that point, the last opening of a negotiating chapter had been in June 2016, the JPC had not met for three years and relations were deteriorating rapidly. This was speaking the unspeakable: the EU–Turkey membership talks were officially in crisis. In October 2018, the Parliament and the Council cut pre-accession funds to Turkey. In March 2019, the Parliament officially called on the Commission and the European Council to formally suspend the accession negotiations. Diplomats and lobbyists responded to these developments with grave silence, as if nothing (that mattered) had happened.

Now we can safely draw some conclusions. First, I have argued throughout this book that *access* to polities and markets took priority over *accession* (membership) for the actors and agents of Turkish Europeanisation from both sides. I leave it up to the reader to decide whether this was so because individual actors gained personally, publicly or institutionally from the process, or whether their gains were fostered by negotiations for access (and not accession). I stand somewhere in between.

Membership negotiations are at the same time negotiations over how to govern Turkey. It would be factually wrong to suggest that Turkey had not made any preparations for EU membership. In fact, since 2005, the Turkish parliament has passed more than 1,000 laws and amendments to existing legislation and secondary legislation, and has engaged in institution-building and other relevant work to align with the EU *acquis*, and has pledged to do more. These legislative reforms took place, however, within a discursive framework (per Lukes' three-dimensional power) that largely shifted from a direct interest in membership to symbolic politics – merely the appearance of an interest in membership.

While EU and Turkish politicians and bureaucrats debated how to govern Turkey within a symbolic political discursive framework, they made room for lobbying as a legitimate communicative form of channelling vital interests, influence and information.

Unlike common depictions of lobbying as an outsider's activity, I found that the kind of lobbying that was most significant regarding Turkish Europeanisation was done not by professional lobbyists but instead came from both outside and inside Turkish and EU bureaucracies. Even then, ordinary lobbying practices were not primarily about facilitating Turkish accession per se. Instead, interest holders and their representatives used membership negotiations to get or to bar access to markets and polities in Turkey and the EU.

If we take membership negotiations as a process, joining the EU is both a technical and a political process, open to human intervention and agency. Diplomats' and lobbyists' competence manifested itself in framing issues as technical prerequisites or political demands. As a result of their technopolitical calibrations, negotiating parties had come to express diverging demands and expectations from the process, even though negotiating was supposed to bring them together. Actors often used accession prerequisites to pursue their political or economic interests. This indicates how malleable accession negotiations really were. Hence, differences between diplomacy and lobbying for accession and for realising key interests – be they private, corporate, personal or institutional – did not hinge upon whether membership was achieved. Again, a critical capacity of lobbying was the ability to manipulate the boundary between the 'technical' and 'political'. In the Turkish case, this boundary was handled with a bureaucratic politics of *non*-membership.

Turkey's actual joining of the EU has for some time not been in the immediate interests of various stakeholders and their representatives; rather, those interests are served by the continuation of accession negotiations, or at least the keeping open of the channels of communication. That the Council has not acted upon the

Parliament's 2017 and 2019 calls to suspend negotiations attests to this. Through the channel of communication maintained by politico-cultural practices, such as diplomacy and lobbying, goods, capital and services continue to circulate between Turkey and the EU. Meanwhile, a demand for brokers' expertise endures, even when they essentially dragged out the process until it ran out of steam.

Throughout the long decades of negotiations, this kind of politics largely served the interests of symbolic politics, a common negotiation practice between EU and Turkish actors. Even though membership talks between the EU and Turkey have de facto been halted, thanks to symbolic politics the parties to accession negotiations continue to co-constitute one another as collocutors amidst stalled negotiations. In the final analysis, this type of politics (further) bureaucratises political and policy relations, deepens the death spiral Turkey–EU relations are caught up in and eclipses any hope for and meaning of or future efforts in their democratisation.

In this book, I have privileged actors and agents over structures and systems. Even though state secrecy tends to remove the enigma of national interests from the daily encounters, actions and non-actions of diplomats and lobbyists, these sovereign agents prefigure diverse political and economic interests couched as national interest during the everyday life of interstate negotiations, often conflating and collapsing the distinctions between national interest, state interest, common EU interest, the interests of the executive branch of the government and business interests.

As such, my account of the EU–Turkey membership negotiations does not mean that actors failed to do their 'job'. Turkish diplomats and lobbyists, in particular, did not 'fail' in lobbying the EU. On the contrary, there was plenty of exchanging influence and interest between Brussels and Ankara. Counterintuitively, however, most exchanges about economic interests targeted state and government offices in Turkey and political platforms such as the European Parliament, instead of the Commission or EU member state offices in Brussels.

More broadly, the cultures of diplomacy and lobbying, with their own practices, norms (rules and taboos) and codes (symbols) – performed by elites and experts of the negotiation process – formed and informed international negotiations from the bottom (everyday, ground level) up, instead of being dictated from above. Embedded in localised yet shifting relations of power, when interests (and associated mandates) changed from accession to access, the informal discursive negotiation framework followed.

It would, thus, be ethnographically insensitive and irresponsible to suggest that – from no(ta)bles to ordinary actors of Turkish Europeanisation – those who were entrusted with facilitating Turkey's EU accession negotiations worked deliberately against their common mandate. Since 2005 I have observed that, in time, my interlocutors' deeds, accomplishments and non-actions – whether they took the form of policy advice or symbolic politics – changed the discursive framework within which their governments, clients and addressees negotiated.

Similarly, I do not assert that diplomats and lobbyists were told by their higher-ups or clients to act in this or that way to add to the stalling of negotiations.

Diplomats and lobbyists were charged with facilitating the workings of Turkey's national interests into common European interests in a process when both interests acquired shifting meaning. Even though 'interest' meant different things at different times to different actors, their mandate was still to make it work. But when diplomats and lobbyists acted in ways that contributed to Turkey's alienation from the EU, thus showing bureaucratic agency, they were not held accountable for actions that modified their mandate and the negotiating framework. Instead, some were promoted. Hence, Turkish and EU diplomats and lobbyists have succeeded in working for their 'mandate', even when that mandate changed from accession to access.

It would be equally insensitive to argue that my diplomatic and lobbyist interlocutors who contributed to Turkey's dis-integration from the EU have acted in this way for purely personal interests. In fact, I am confident that all performed out of a patriotic sense of duty. This is especially the case for my Turkish interlocutors, many of whom have long aspired to become the first generation of Turkish Eurocrats. Theirs was a conviction based on years of training, and personal and emotional investment in Turkey's Europeanisation. But, in the end, the Turkish bid failed, while they and their institutions gained something out of the process.

Finally, even though diplomats, bureaucrats and lobbyists gained personally, publicly or institutionally, some ultimately failed to appreciate that lobbying partially involves cultural work with those being lobbied, that is, getting to know them better in order to influence them more readily. Although their jobs were ultimately to bridge the politico-cultural distance between Brussels and Ankara, over the last decade that gap has widened ever more.

References

Abbink, Jon, and Tijo Salverda, eds. 2012. *The Anthropology of Elites: Power, Culture, and the Complexities of Distinction*. London: Palgrave Macmillan.

Abélès, Marc. 1992. *La vie quotidienne au Parlement Européen*. Paris: Hachette.

Abélès, Marc. 1997. 'Political Anthropology: New Challenges, New Aims'. *International Social Science Journal* 49 (153): 319–32.

Abélès, Marc. 2000. 'Virtual Europe'. In *An Anthropology of the European Union: Building, Imagining and Experiencing the New Europe*, edited by Irène Bellier and Thomas M. Wilson, 31–52. Oxford: Berg.

Abélès, Marc. 2009. 'Practitioners of Europe'. In *An Identity for Europe: The Relevance of Multiculturalism in EU Construction*, edited by Riva Kastoryano, 27–44. London: Palgrave Macmillan.

Abélès, Marc. 2011. *Des anthropologues à l'OMC: scènes de la gouvernance mondiale* [*Anthropologists at the WTO: Scenes of Global Governance*]. Paris: CRNS.

Abélès, Marc, and Irène Bellier. 1996. 'La Commission Européenne: du compromis culturel à la culture politique du compromise' ['The European Commission: From the Cultural Compromise to the Political Culture of the Compromise']. *Revue française de science politique* 46 (3): 431–56.

Abélès, Marc, Irène Bellier and Maryon McDonald. 1993. *Approche anthropologique de la Commission Européenne* [*Anthropological Approach to the European Commission*]. Brussels: European Commission.

Abélès, Marc, and Werner Rossade, eds. 1993. *Politique symbolique en Europe*. Berlin: Duncker & Humblot.

Abrams, Peter. 1988. 'Notes on the Difficulty of Studying the State'. *Journal of Historical Sociology* 1 (1): 58–88.

Adler-Nissen, Rebecca. 2016. 'Towards a Practice Turn in EU Studies: The Everyday of European Integration'. *Journal of Common Market Studies* 54 (1): 87–103.

Ağartan, Kaan. 2009. 'Privatization and Limits to Economic Liberalization in Turkey: Erdemir Case Study'. Unpublished PhD Dissertation, Binghamton University.

Ahearn, Raymond J. 2011. *Europe's Preferential Trade Agreements: Status, Content, and Implications*. RL41143. Congressional Research Service. https://fas.org/sgp/crs/row/R41143.pdf (accessed 15 April 2019).

Akdoğan, A. Argun. 2008. *Türk Kamu Yönetimi ve Avrupa Birliği* [*Turkish Public Administration and the European Union*]. Ankara: TODAIE.

Akipek, Sebnem, and Belgin Akçay, eds. 2013. *Turkey's Integration into the European Union: Legal Dimension*. Maryland: Lexington Books.

Aksöyek, Ataman. 2000. *Sociographie de la population turque et d'origine turque. Quarante* ans de présence en Belgique (1960–2000): dynamiques, problématiques, perspectives [*Sociography of the Turkish Population and People of Turkish Origin. Forty Years of Presence in Belgium (1960–2000): Dynamics, Problematics and Perspectives*]. Brussels: CRE.

Alemdar, Zeynep. 2009. 'Turkish Trade Unions and the European Boomerang'. *European Journal of Turkish Studies* 9. http://journals.openedition.org/ejts/3774 (accessed 7 May 2019).

Alexander, Catherine. 2002. *Personal States: Making Connections Between People and Bureaucracy in Turkey*. Oxford: Oxford University Press.

Alexander, Catherine. 2017. 'The Meeting as Subjunctive Form: Public/Private IT Projects in British and Turkish State Bureaucracies'. *Journal of the Royal Anthropological Institute* 23 (NS): 80–94.

Alimen, Nazlı. 2018. 'The Fashions and Politics of Facial Hair in Turkey: The Case of Islamic Men'. In *The Routledge International Handbook to Veils and Veiling*, edited by Anna-Mari Almila and David Inglis, 116–24. London: Routledge.

Andersen, Svein S., and Kjell A. Eliassen. 1996a. 'EU-Lobbying: Between Representativity and Effectiveness'. In *The European Union: How Democratic Is It?*, edited by Svein Andersen and Kjell A. Eliassen, 41–55. London: Sage.

Andersen, Svein S., and Kjell A. Eliassen. 1996b. *The European Union: How Democratic Is It?* London: Sage.

Appadurai, Arjun, ed. 1986. *The Social Life of Things: Commodities in Cultural Perspective*. Cambridge: Cambridge University Press.

Apthorpe, Raymond, and Des Gasper. 1996. *Arguing Development Policy: Frames and Discourses*. London: Frank Cass.

Aras, Damla. 2011. 'Turkey's Ambassadors vs. Erdoğan'. *Middle East Forum* 18 (1): 47–57.

Arat-Koç, Sedef. 2007. '(Some) Turkish Transnationalism(s) in an Age of Capitalist Globalization and Empire: "White Turk" Discourse, the New Geopolitics, and Implications for Feminist Transnationalism'. *Journal of Middle East Women's Studies* 3 (1): 35–57.

Ardener, Shirley, and Fiona Moore, eds. 2007. *Professional Identities: Policy and Practice in Business and Bureaucracy*. New York: Berghahn Books.

Arvanitopoulos, Constantine, ed. 2009. *Turkey's Accession to the European Union: An Unusual Candidacy*. Berlin: Springer.

Atan, Serap. 2004. 'Europeanization of Turkish Peak Business Organizations and Turkey–EU Relations'. In *Turkey and European Integration: Accession Prospects and Issues*, edited by Mehmet Ugur and Nergis Canefe, 100–21. London: Routledge.

Auyero, Javier, and Lauren Joseph. 2007. 'Introduction: Politics under the Ethnographic Microscope'. In *New Perspectives in Political Ethnography*, edited by Lauren Joseph, Matthew Mahler and Javier Auyero, 1–13. New York: Springer.

Avci, Gamze, and Ali Çarkoğlu, eds. 2013. *Turkey and the EU: Accession and Reform*. London: Routledge.

Aydın-Düzgit, Senem. 2012. *Constructions of European Identity: Debates and Discourses on Turkey and the EU*. London: Palgrave Macmillan.

Aydın-Düzgit, Senem, and Alper Kaliber. 2016. 'Encounters with Europe in an Era of Domestic and International Turmoil: Is Turkey a De-Europeanising Candidate Country?' *South European Society and Politics* 21 (1): 1–14.

Babül, Elif M. 2017. *Bureaucratic Intimacies: Translating Human Rights in Turkey*. Stanford: Stanford University Press.

Bachrach, Peter, and Morton S. Baratz. 1963. 'Decisions and Nondecisions: An Analytical Framework'. *American Political Science Review* 57 (3): 632–42.

Ballestero S., Andrea. 2012. 'Transparency Short-Circuited: Laughter and Numbers in Costa Rican Water Politics'. *Political and Legal Anthropology Review* 35 (2): 223–41.

Barry, Andrew. 2001. *Political Machines: Governing a Technological Society*. London: Athlone Press.

Bayley, Paul, ed. 2004. *Cross-Cultural Perspectives on Parliamentary Discourse*. Amsterdam: John Benjamins.

Bellier, Irène. 2000a. 'The European Union, Identity Politics and the Logic of Interest Representation'. In *An Anthropology of the European Union: Building, Imagining and Experiencing the New Europe*, edited by Irène Bellier and Thomas M. Wilson, 53–73. Oxford: Berg.

Bellier, Irène. 2000b. 'A Europeanized Elite? An Anthropology of European Commission Officials'. *Yearbook of European Studies* 14: 135–56.

Bellier, Irène. 2004. 'The European Commission Between *Acquis Communautaire* and Enlargement'. In *The Changing European Commission*, edited by Dionyssis G. Dimitrakopoulos, 138–50. Manchester: Manchester University Press.

Bellier, Irène, and Thomas M. Wilson, eds. 2000. *An Anthropology of the European Union: Building, Imagining and Experiencing the New Europe*. Oxford: Berg.

Benoit, Denise. 2007. *The Best-Kept Secret: Women Corporate Lobbyists, Policy, and Power in the United States*. New Brunswick: Rutgers University Press.

Berkowitz, Lenka, and Liza M. Mügge. 2014. 'Transnational Diaspora Lobbying: Europeanization and the Kurdish Question'. *Journal of Intercultural Studies* 35 (1): 74–90.

Bianchi, Robert. 1984. *Interest Groups and Political Development in Turkey*. Princeton: Princeton University Press.

Bilgic, Ali. 2016. *Turkey, Power and the West: Gendered International Relations and Foreign Policy*. London: I. B. Tauris.

Binderkrantz, Anne S., Helene H. Pedersen and Jan Beyers. 2017. 'What Is Access? A Discussion of the Definition and Measurement of Interest Group Access'. *European Political Science* 16 (3): 306–22.

BKP Development Research and Consulting. 2016. 'Study of the EU–Turkey Bilateral Preferential Trade Framework, Including the Customs Union, and an Assessment of Its Possible Enhancement Final Report'. http://trade.ec.europa.eu/doclib/docs/2017/january/tradoc_155240.pdf (accessed 8 May 2019)

Black, Annabel. 2001. 'Ambiguity and Verbal Disguise Within Diplomatic Culture'. In *An Anthropology of Indirect Communication*, edited by Joy Hendry and C. W. Watson, 255–70. London: Routledge.

Boissevain, Jeremy. 1974. *Friends of Friends: Networks, Manipulators and Coalitions*. Oxford: Blackwell.

Borneman, John, and Nick Fowler. 1997. 'Europeanization'. *Annual Review of Anthropology* 26: 487–514.

Böröcz, József. 2000. 'The Fox and the Raven: The European Union and Hungary Renegotiate the Margins of "Europe"'. *Comparative Studies in Society and History* 42: 847–75.

Bourdieu, Pierre. 1979. 'Symbolic Power'. *Critique of Anthropology* 4 (13–14): 77–85.

Bourdieu, Pierre. 1987. 'The Force of Law: Toward a Sociology of the Juridical Field'. *Hastings Law Journal* 38 (5): 808–53.

Bourdieu, Pierre. 1996. *The State Nobility: Elite Schools in the Field of Power*. Cambridge: Polity Press.

Bourdieu, Pierre. 1998. *On Television and Journalism*. Translated by Priscilla Parkhurst Ferguson. London: Pluto.

Bourdieu, Pierre. 1999. 'Rethinking the State: Genesis and Structure of the Bureaucratic

Field'. In *State/Culture: State-Formation After the Cultural Turn*, edited by George Stein-metz, 53–75. Ithaca: Cornell University Press.

Bourdieu, Pierre. 2009 [1991]. *Language and Symbolic Power*. Cambridge: Polity Press.

Bouwen, Pieter. 2002. 'Corporate Lobbying in the European Union: The Logic of Access'. *Journal of European Public Policy* 9 (3): 365–90.

Bouwen, Pieter. 2004. 'Exchanging Access Goods for Access: A Comparative Study of Business Lobbying in the European Union Institutions'. *European Journal of Political Research* 43 (3): 337–69.

Bozcalı, Fırat. Forthcoming. 'Probabilistic Borderwork: Oil Smuggling, Non-Illegality and Techno-legal Politics in the Kurdish Borderlands of Turkey'. *American Ethnologist*.

Brenneis, Donald. 2006. 'Reforming Promise'. In *Documents: Artifacts of Modern Knowl-edge*, edited by Annelise Riles, 41–70. Ann Arbor: University of Michigan Press.

Broscheid, Andreas, and David Coen. 2003. 'Insider and Outsider Lobbying of the Euro-pean Commission: An Informational Model of Forum Politics'. *European Union Politics* 4 (2): 165–89.

Brown, Hannah, Adam Reed and Thomas Yarrow, eds. 2017. *Meetings: Ethnographies of Organizational Process, Bureaucracy, and Assembly*. Chichester: Wiley.

Buğra, Ayşe. 1994. *State and Business in Modern Turkey: A Comparative Study*. Albany: SUNY Press.

Burke, Tom. 2012. 'Cameron's Policy Cannibalism: Economic Policy Eating Environment Policy'. Blog, 22 January. http://tomburke.co.uk/2012/01/22/policy-cannibalism-camerons-economic-policy-eating-environment-policy (accessed 15 April 2019).

Burrell, Alison, and A. J. Oskam, eds. 2005. *Turkey in the European Union: Implications for Agriculture, Food, and Structural Policy*. Wallingford: CABI.

Candea, Matei. 2011. '"Our Division of the Universe": Making a Space for the Non-Political in the Anthropology of Politics'. *Current Anthropology* 52 (3): 309–34.

Caporaso, James A. 2000. *The European Union: Dilemmas of Regional Integration*. Boulder: Westview Press.

Carey, Matthew. 2017. *Mistrust: An Ethnographic Theory*. Chicago: Hau Books.

Çarkoğlu, Ali, and Barry M. Rubin, eds. 2003. *Turkey and the European Union: Domestic Politics, Economic Integration, and International Dynamics*. London: Frank Cass.

Carrier, James G. 2001. 'Diplomacy and Indirection, Constraint and Authority'. In *An Anthropology of Indirect Communication*, edited by Joy Hendry and C. W. Watson, 290–300. London: Routledge.

Carroll, Brendan J., and Anne Rasmussen. 2017. 'Cultural Capital and the Density of Organised Interests Lobbying the European Parliament'. *West European Politics* 40 (5): 1132–52.

Cebeci, Münevver. 2016. 'De-Europeanisation or Counter-Conduct? Turkey's Democratis-ation and the EU'. *South European Society and Politics* 21 (1): 119–32.

Chalmers, Adam W. 2013. 'Trading Information for Access: Informational Lobbying Strategies and Interest Group Access to the European Union'. *Journal of European Public Policy* 20 (1): 39–58.

Christiansen, Thomas. 2001. 'The Council of Ministers: The Politics of Institutionalized Intergovernmentalism'. In *European Union: Power and Policy-Making*, edited by Jeremy Richardson, 135–54. London: Routledge.

Christiansen, Thomas, Knud E. Jørgensen and Antje Wiener. 2001. *The Social Construction of Europe*. London: Sage.

Christiansen, Thomas, and Simona Piattoni. 2004. *Informal Governance in the European Union*. Cheltenham: Edward Elgar.

Christoffersen, Poul S. 2007. 'Organization of the Process and Beginning of the Negotiations'. In *The Accession Story: The EU from Fifteen to Twenty-Five Countries*, edited by George Vassiliou, 34–50. Oxford: Oxford University Press.

Clément, Maéva, and Eric Sangar, eds. 2018. *Researching Emotions in International Relations: Methodological Perspectives on the Emotional Turn*. London: Palgrave Macmillan.

Clemons, Steven C. 2003. 'The Regulation of Lobbyists in the US and the Impact on Washington's Public Policy Think Tanks'. In *Lobbying and Foreign Policy: Paris, Washington, Brussels* (Note d'Ifri 54), edited by Olivier Debouzy, Steven C. Clemons and Alan Butt Philip, 21–40. Ifri: Paris.

Coen, David. 1998. 'The European Business Interest and the Nation State: Large-Firm Lobbying in the European Union and Member States'. *Journal of Public Policy* 18 (1): 75–100.

Coen, David. 2007. 'Empirical and Theoretical Studies in EU Lobbying'. *Journal of European Public Policy* 14 (3): 333–45.

Coen, David, and Jeremy Richardson. 2009. *Lobbying the European Union: Institutions, Actors, and Issues*. Oxford: Oxford University Press.

Cohen, Abner. 1979. 'Political Symbolism'. *Annual Review of Anthropology* 8 (1): 87–113.

Cohen, Abner. 1980. 'Dramas and Politics in the Development of a London Carnival'. *MAN* (NS) 15: 65–87.

Colebatch, Hal K. 2002. *Policy*. Buckingham: Open University Press.

Colebatch, Hal K., Robert Hoppe and Mirko Noordegraaf, eds. 2010. *Working for Policy*. Amsterdam: Amsterdam University Press.

Coles, Kimberley. 2007. *Democratic Designs: International Intervention and Electoral Practices in Postwar Bosnia-Herzegovina*. Ann Arbor: University of Michigan Press.

Comaroff, John L., and Jean Comaroff. 1992. *Ethnography and the Historical Imagination*. Boulder: Westview Press.

Conley Tyler, Melissa, and Craig Beyerinck. 2016. 'Citizen Diplomacy'. In *The Sage Handbook of Diplomacy*, edited by Costas M. Constantinou, Pauline Kerr and Paul Sharp. London: Sage.

Constantinou, Costas M., Pauline Kerr and Paul Sharp, eds. 2016. *The Sage Handbook of Diplomacy*. London: Sage.

Cook, Karen S., Margaret Levi and Russell Hardin, eds. 2009. *Whom Can We Trust? How Groups, Networks, and Institutions Make Trust Possible*. New York: Russell Sage Foundation.

Council of the European Union. 1991. 'European Council Maastricht 9–10 December 1991 Presidency Conclusions'. https://www.consilium.europa.eu/media/20519/1991_december_-_maastricht__eng_.pdf (accessed 15 April 2019).

Council of the European Union. 1993. 'European Council Copenhagen 21–22 June 1993 Presidency Conclusions'. https://www.consilium.europa.eu/uedocs/cms_data/docs/pressdata/en/ec/72921.pdf (accessed 15 April 2019).

Council of the European Union. 2000. 'Lisbon European Council 23–24 March 2000 Presidency Conclusions'. http://www.europarl.europa.eu/summits/lis1_en.htm (accessed 15 April 2019).

Crewe, Emma. 2005. *Lords of Parliament: Manners, Rituals and Politics*. Manchester: Manchester University Press.

Crewe, Emma. 2015. *The House of Commons: An Anthropology of MPs at Work*. London: Bloomsbury Academic.

Crewe, Emma. 2017. 'Ethnography of Parliament: Finding Culture and Politics Entangled in the Commons and the Lords'. *Parliamentary Affairs* 70 (1): 155–72.

Crewe, Emma, and Marion G. Müller, eds. 2006. *Rituals in Parliaments: Political, Anthropological and Historical Perspectives on Europe and the United States*. Frankfurt-am-Main: Lang.

Curtis, Jennifer, and Jonathan Spencer. 2012. 'Anthropology and the Political'. In *The Sage Handbook of Social Anthropology*, edited by Richard Fardon, Olivia Harris, Trevor Marchand, Mark Nuttall, Cris Shore, Veronica Strang and Richard Wilson, 168–82. London: Sage.

Davie-Kessler, Jesse. n.d. 'Affect, Embodiment, and Sense Perception. Cultural Anthropology Curated Collection'. *Cultural Anthropology*. https://www.culanth.org/curated_collections/16-affect-embodiment-and-sense-perception (accessed 7 May 2019).

Davutoğlu, Ahmet. 2001. *Stratejik Derinlik: Türkiye'nin Uluslararası Konumu* [*Strategic Depth: Turkey's International Status*]. Istanbul: Küre.

de Lobkowicz, Wenceslas. 2001. 'Enlargement of the European Union and the Role of the European Commission in This Process'. Unpublished presentation, American University in Bulgaria.

Demertzis, Nicolas, ed. 2013. *Emotions in Politics: The Affect Dimension in Political Tension*. London: Palgrave Macmillan.

Democratisation Policies Working Group. 2013. *The Silent Revolution: Turkey's Democratic Change and Transformation Inventory (2002–2012)*. Prime Ministry of Turkey: Undersecretariat of Public Order and Security Publications.

Deutsch, Karl, Sidney A. Burrell, Robert A. Kann, Maurice Lee, Martin Lichterman, Raymond E. Lindgren, Francis L. Loewenheim and Richard W. Van Wagenen. 1957. *Political Community and the North Atlantic Area*. Princeton: Princeton University Press.

DG Trade. 2019. Trade Statistics. https://webgate.ec.europa.eu/isdb_results/factsheets/country/details_turkey_en.pdf (accessed 7 May 2019).

Diez, Thomas, Apostolos Agnantopoulos and Alper Kaliber, eds. 2005. 'File: Turkey, Europeanization and Civil Society'. *South European Society and Politics* 10 (1): 1–15.

Dittmer, Jason. 2017. *Diplomatic Material: Affect, Assemblage, and Foreign Policy*. Durham: Duke University Press.

Douglas, Mary. 1986. *How Institutions Think*. Syracuse: Syracuse University Press.

Drutman, Lee. 2015. *The Business of America Is Lobbying: How Corporations Became Politicized and Politics Became More Corporate*. Oxford: Oxford University Press.

Duina, Francesco G. 2007. *The Social Construction of Free Trade: The European Union, NAFTA, and MERCOSUR*. Princeton: Princeton University Press.

Dür, Andreas. 2008. 'Interest Groups in the European Union: How Powerful Are They?' *West European Politics* 31 (6): 1212–30.

Dür, Andreas, and Gemma Mateo. 2010. 'Choosing a Bargaining Strategy in EU Negotiations: Power, Preferences, and Culture'. *Journal of European Public Policy* 17 (5): 680–93.

Eckhardt, Jappe. 2015. *Business Lobbying and Trade Governance: The Case of EU–China Relations*. New York: Palgrave Macmillan.

Economist. 2010. 'Is Turkey Turning Its Back on the West?' *The Economist*, 21 October. https://www.economist.com/leaders/2010/10/21/is-turkey-turning-its-back-on-the-west (accessed 15 April 2019).

Eder, Mine. 2001. 'Deeper Concessions and Rising Barriers to Entry: New Regionalism for Turkey and Mexico'. *Studies in Comparative International Development* 36 (3): 29–57.

Ekengren, Magnus. 2002. *The Time of European Governance*. Manchester: Manchester University Press.

Elgström, Ole, ed. 2003. *European Union Council Presidencies: A Comparative Perspective*. London: Routledge.

Eppink, Derk J. 2007. *Life of a European Mandarin: Inside the Commission*. Tielt: Lannoo.

Eryilmaz, Murat. 2012. 'Why Is ArcelorMittal Selling Its Erdemir Shares?' Steelorbis blog, 29 March. https://steelorbisen.wordpress.com/page/5/?pages-list (accessed 15 April 2019).

Euractiv. 2010. 'Turkey Offers Referendum Gamble to Europe', 30 September. https://www.euractiv.com/section/global-europe/news/turkey-offers-referendum-gamble-to-europe (accessed 15 April 2019).

Euractiv. 2013. 'Iceland Walks Out on EU Membership Talks', 23 August. https://www.euractiv.com/section/eu-priorities-2020/news/iceland-walks-out-on-eu-membership-talks (accessed 15 April 2019).

European Commission. 2001a. 'Involving Experts in the Process of National Policy Convergence. Report by Working Group 4a.' https://www.eumonitor.nl/9353000/d/commissierapportomc.pdf (accessed 15 April 2019).

European Commission. 2001b. '2001 Regular Report on Turkey's Progress Towards Accession'. Progress Report SEC (2001) 1756 final. Brussels: European Commission. http://aei.pitt.edu/44622/1/turkey_2001.pdf (accessed 15 April 2019).

European Commission. 2001c. *Enlargement of the European Union: An Historic Opportunity*. Brussels: European Commission. https://ec.europa.eu/neighbourhood-enlargement/sites/near/files/archives/pdf/press_corner/publications/corpus_en.pdf (accessed 15 April 2019).

European Commission. 2006a. 'Green Paper – European Transparency Initiative'. Brussels: European Commission. COM/2006/0194 final. https://eur-lex.europa.eu/legal-content/en/TXT/?uri=CELEX:52006DC0194 (accessed 15 April 2019).

European Commission. 2006b. 'Screening Report Turkey. Chapter 20 – Enterprise and Industrial Policy'. https://www.ab.gov.tr/files/tarama/tarama_files/20/screening_report_20_tr_internet_en.pdf (accessed 15 April 2019).

European Commission. 2009. 'Turkey 2009 Progress Report'. SEC(2009) 1334. Brussels: European Commission. https://ec.europa.eu/neighbourhood-enlargement/sites/near/files/pdf/key_documents/2009/tr_rapport_2009_en.pdf (accessed 7 May 2019).

European Commission. 2011. 'Turkey 2011 Progress Report'. SEC(2011) 1201 final. Brussels: European Commission. https://ec.europa.eu/neighbourhood-enlargement/sites/near/files/pdf/key_documents/2011/package/tr_rapport_2011_en.pdf (accessed 15 April 2019).

European Commission. 2016. "European Neighbourhood Policy." *European Neighbourhood Policy And Enlargement Negotiations - European Commission*. https://ec.europa.eu/neighbourhood-enlargement/neighbourhood/overview_en (accessed 7 May 2019).

European Parliament. 2008. *Report on the Fact Finding Visit to Cyprus – 25 to 28 November 2007 Concerning Petition 733/2004 – Famagusta Refugee Movement*. PE400.408v05–00. Brussels: European Parliament. http://www.europarl.europa.eu/meetdocs/2014_2019/documents/peti/dt/710/710127/710127en.pdf (accessed 15 April 2019).

European Public Affairs Directory. 2018. *The European Public Affairs Directory 2018*. London: Dod's Parliamentary Communications.

Eurostat. 2019. 'International Trade in Goods - a Statistical Picture - Statistics Explained.' https://ec.europa.eu/eurostat/statistics-explained/index.php?title=International_trade_in_goods_-_a_statistical_picture (accessed 8 May 2019).

Evered, Emine Ö., and Kyle T. Evered. 2016. 'From Rakı to Ayran: Regulating the Place and Practice of Drinking in Turkey'. *Space and Polity* 20 (1): 39–58.

Fabian, Johannes. 1983. *Time and the Other: How Anthropology Makes Its Object*. New York: Columbia University Press.

Favell, Adrian. 2008. *Eurostars and Eurocities: Free Movement and Mobility in an Integrating Europe*. Malden: Blackwell.

Featherstone, Kevin, and Claudio M. Radaelli. 2003. *The Politics of Europeanization*. Oxford: Oxford University Press.

Feldman, Gregory. 2019. *The Gray Zone: Sovereignty, Human Smuggling, and Undercover Police Investigation in Europe*. Stanford: Stanford University Press.

Ferguson, James. 1990. *The Anti-politics Machine: 'Development,' Depoliticization, and Bureaucratic Power in Lesotho*. Cambridge: Cambridge University Press.

Finkel, Isobel, and Thomas Buckley. 2015. 'Diageo's Turkish Unit Under Investigation by Competition Board'. Bloomberg, 11 August. https://www.bloomberg.com/news/articles/2015-08-11/diageo-s-turkish-unit-under-investigation-by-competition-board (accessed 15 April 2019).

Firat, Bilge. 2014. 'Crisis, Power, and Policymaking in the New Europe: Why Should Anthropologists Care?' *Anthropological Journal of European Cultures* 23 (1): 1–20.

Firat, Bilge. 2016. '"The Most Eastern of the West, the Most Western of the East": Energy-Transport Infrastructures and Regional Politics of the Periphery in Turkey'. *Economic Anthropology* 3 (1): 81–93.

Fletcher, Clementine. 2011. 'Diageo to Buy Turkish Distiller Mey Icki for $2.1 Billion'. Bloomberg, 21 February. https://www.bloomberg.com/news/articles/2011-02-20/diageo-said-to-be-close-to-buying-distillery-mey-icki-of-turkey (accessed 15 April 2019).

Foucault, Michel. 1991. *The Foucault Effect: Studies in Governmentality: With Two Lectures by and an Interview with Michel Foucault*. Chicago: University of Chicago Press.

Fouilleux, Eves, Jacques de Maillard and Andy Smith. 2005. 'Technical or Political? The Working Groups of the EU Council of Ministers'. *Journal of European Public Policy* 12 (4): 609–23.

Galgóczi, Béla, Jan Drahokoupil and Magdalena Bernaciak, eds. 2015. *Foreign Investment in Eastern and Southern Europe After 2008: Still a Lever of Growth?* Brussels: European Trade Union Institute.

Gambetta, Diego, ed. 1988. *Trust: Making and Breaking Cooperative Relations*. New York: Blackwell.

Garsten, Christina. 2013. 'All About Ties: Think Tanks and the Economy of Connections'. In *Power, Policy and Profit: Corporate Engagement in Politics and Governance*, edited by Christina Garsten and Adrienne Sörbom, 139–54. Cheltenham: Edward Elgar.

Garsten, Christina, and Kerstin Jacobsson. 2007. 'Corporate Globalization, Civil Society, and Post-Political Regulation: Whither Democracy?' *Development Dialogue* 49: 143–58.

Garsten, Christina, and Kerstin Jacobsson. 2013. 'Post-Political Regulation: Soft Power and Post-Political Visions in Global Governance'. *Critical Sociology* 39 (3): 421–37.

Garsten, Christina, and Adrienne Sörbom, eds. 2017. *Power, Policy and Profit: Corporate Engagement in Politics and Governance*. Cheltenham: Edward Elgar.

Garsten, Christina, and Adrienne Sörbom. 2018. *Discreet Power: How the World Economic Forum Shapes Market Agendas*. Stanford: Stanford University Press.

Geertz, Clifford. 1978. 'The Bazaar Economy: Information and Search in Peasant Marketing'. *American Economic Review* 68 (2): 28–32.

Georgakakis, Didier. 2015. 'Fields with Fields? Concluding Remarks on the Relationships Between the European Civil Society and the EU Bureaucratic Fields'. In *EU Civil Society: Patterns of Cooperation, Competition and Conflict*, edited by Håkan Johansson and Sara Kalm, 229–42. London: Palgrave Macmillan.

Georgakakis, Didier, and Jay Rowell. 2013. *The Field of Eurocracy: Mapping EU Actors and Professionals*. London: Palgrave Macmillan.

Geuijen, Karin, and Paul 't Hart. 2010. 'Flying Blind in Brussels: How National Officials Do European Business Without Political Steering'. In *Working for Policy*, edited by Hal K. Colebatch, Rob Hoppe and Mirko Noordegraaf, 171–90. Amsterdam: Amsterdam University Press.

Geuijen, Karin, Paul 't Hart, Sebastiaan Prince and Kutsal Yesilkagit. 2008. *The New Eurocrats: National Civil Servants in EU Policy-Making*. Amsterdam: Amsterdam University Press.

Giddens, Anthony. 1991. *Modernity and Self-Identity: Self and Society in the Late Modern Age*. Cambridge: Polity Press.

Goffman, Erving. 1959. *The Presentation of Self in Everyday Life*. New York: Doubleday.

Goffman, Erving. 1986. *Frame Analysis: An Essay on the Organisation of Experience*. Boston: Northeastern University Press.

Goody, Jack. 1986. *The Logic of Writing and the Organization of Society*. Cambridge: Cambridge University Press.

Gottfried, Peter, and Peter Györkös. 2007. 'The Accession of Hungary to the EU'. In *The Accession Story: The EU from Fifteen to Twenty-Five Countries*, edited by George Vassiliou, 188–206. Oxford: Oxford University Press.

Gould, Jeremy, and Henrik Secher Marcussen, eds. 2004. *Ethnographies of Aid: Exploring Development Texts and Encounters*. Roskilde: Roskilde University.

Grabbe, Heather. 2006. *The EU's Transformative Power: Europeanization Through Conditionality in Central and Eastern Europe*. London: Palgrave Macmillan.

Graham, Mark. 2002. 'Emotional Bureaucracies: Emotions, Civil Servants, and Immigrants in the Swedish Welfare State'. *Ethos* 30 (3): 199–226.

Greenhalgh, Susan. 2008. *Just One Child: Science and Policy in Deng's China*. Berkeley: University of California Press.

Greenhouse, Carol J., Elizabeth Mertz and Kay B. Warren. 2002. *Ethnography in Unstable Places: Everyday Lives in Contexts of Dramatic Political Change*. Durham: Duke University Press.

Grigoriadis, Ioannis N. 2009. *Trials of Europeanization: Turkish Political Culture and the European Union*. London: Palgrave Macmillan.

Grünert, Thomas. 1987. 'Decision-Making Processes in the Steel Crisis Policy of the EEC: Neocorporatist or Integrationist Tendencies?' In *The Politics of Steel: Western Europe and the Steel Industry in the Crisis Years (1974 - 1984)*, edited by Yves Mény, 222–307. Berlin: Walter de Gruyter.

Günay, Koray. 2008. 'The Competitiveness of the Turkish Iron and Steel Industry in the Process of Membership to the European Union.' PhD Dissertation, Işık University.

Gupta, Akhil. 2012. *Red Tape: Bureaucracy, Structural Violence, and Poverty in India*. Durham: Duke University Press.

Gürsel, Zeynep D. 2013. '#potsandpans: Rethinking Social Media in Istanbul During Occupy Gezi'. *Anthropology Now* 5 (3): 67–73.

Haas, Ernst B. 1964. 'Technocracy, Pluralism and the New Europe'. In *A New Europe?*, edited by Stephen R. Graubard, 62–88. Boston: Houghton Mifflin.

Hamilton, Keith, and Richard Langhorne. 2010. *The Practice of Diplomacy: Its Evolution, Theory, and Administration*. London: Routledge.

Handelman, Don. 1978. 'Introduction: A Recognition of Bureaucracy'. In *Bureaucracy and Worldview: Studies in the Logic of Official Interpretation*, edited by Don Handelman and Elliot Leyton, 1–14. Newfoundland: Memorial University of Newfoundland.

Hansen, Thomas B., and Finn Stepputat, eds. 2001. *States of Imagination: Ethnographic Explorations of the Postcolonial State*. Durham: Duke University Press.

Harmsen, Robert, and Menno Spiering, eds. 2016. *Euroscepticism: Party Politics, National Identity and European Integration*. Amsterdam: Brill Rodopi.

Harmsen, Robert, and Thomas M. Wilson. 2000. 'Introduction: Approaches to Europeanization'. *Yearbook of European Studies* 14: 13–26.

Harper, Richard. 1998. *Inside the IMF: An Ethnography of Documents, Technology, and Organisational Action*. San Diego: Academic Press.

Harper, Richard. 2000. 'The Social Organization of the IMF's Mission Work'. In *Audit Cultures: Anthropological Studies in Accountability, Ethics, and the Academy*, edited by Marilyn Strathern, 21–53. London: Routledge.

Hecht, Gabrielle. 2009 [1998]. *The Radiance of France: Nuclear Power and National Identity After World War II*. Cambridge: MIT Press.

Hein, Carola. 2000. 'Choosing a Site for the Capital of Europe'. *GeoJournal* 51 (1–2): 83–97.

Henderson, W. O. 1981. 'The German Zollverein and the European Economic Community'. *Zeitschrift Für Die Gesamte Staatswissenschaft* 137 (3): 491–507.

Heper, Metin. 1985. *The State Tradition in Turkey*. Beverley: Eothen Press.

Heper, Metin, ed. 1991. *Strong State and Economic Interest Groups: The Post-1980 Turkish Experience*. Berlin: Walter de Gruyter.

Hertz, Ellen. 1998. *The Trading Crowd: An Ethnography of the Shanghai Stock Market*. Cambridge: Cambridge University Press.

Hertz, Rosanna, and Jonathan B. Imber, eds. 1993. *Fieldwork in Elite Settings: Special Issue of Journal of Contemporary Ethnography* 22 (1).

Herzfeld, Michael. 1992. *The Social Production of Indifference: Exploring the Symbolic Roots of Western Bureaucracy*. Chicago: University of Chicago Press.

Herzfeld, Michael. 1997. *Cultural Intimacy: Social Poetics in the Nation-State*. New York: Routledge.

Hess, Julia M. 2009. *Immigrant Ambassadors: Citizenship and Belonging in the Tibetan Diaspora*. Stanford: Stanford University Press.

Hetherington, Kregg. 2011. *Guerrilla Auditors: The Politics of Transparency in Neoliberal Paraguay*. Durham: Duke University Press.

Heyman, Josiah McC. 2003. 'The Inverse of Power'. *Anthropological Theory* 3 (2): 139–56.

Heyman, Josiah McC. 2004. 'The Anthropology of Power-Wielding Bureaucracies'. *Human Organization* 63 (4): 487–500.

Hirschman, Albert O. 2013 [1977]. *The Passions and the Interests: Political Arguments for Capitalism Before Its Triumph*. Princeton: Princeton University Press.

Ho, Karen. 2009. *Liquidated: An Ethnography of Wall Street*. Durham: Duke University Press.

Hodder, Ian. 1994. 'The Interpretation of Documents and Material Culture'. In *The Sage Handbook of Qualitative Research*, edited by Norman K. Denzin and Yvonna S. Lincoln, 393–402. Thousand Oaks: Sage.

Hoedeman, Olivier. 2007. 'Corporate Power in Europe: The Brussels "Lobbycracy"'. In *Thinker, Faker, Spinner, Spy: Corporate PR and the Assault on Democracy*, edited by William Dinan and David Miller, 261–77. London: Pluto Press.

Hoggett, Paul, and Simon Thompson, eds. 2012. *Politics and the Emotions: The Affective Turn in Contemporary Political Studies*. New York: Continuum.

Holmes, Douglas R. 2000. *Integral Europe: Fast-Capitalism, Multiculturalism, Neofascism*. Princeton: Princeton University Press.

Holmes, Douglas R. 2013. *Economy of Words: Communicative Imperatives in Central Banks*. Chicago: University of Chicago Press.

Holmes, Douglas R., and George E. Marcus. 2005. 'Cultures of Expertise and the

Management of Globalization: Toward the Re-Functioning of Ethnography'. In *Global Assemblages: Technology, Politics, and Ethics as Anthropological Problems*, edited by Aihwa Ong and Stephen J. Collier, 235–52. Malden: Blackwell.

Høyer Leivestad, Hege, and Anette Nyqvist. 2017. *Ethnographies of Conferences and Trade Fairs: Shaping Industries, Creating Professionals*. London: Palgrave Macmillan.

Hudson, Ray. (2000), 'One Europe or Many? Reflections on Becoming European', *Transactions of the Institute of British Geographers* 25 (4): 409–42.

Hull, Matthew S. 2012a. *Government of Paper: The Materiality of Bureaucracy in Urban Pakistan*. Berkeley: University of California Press.

Hull, Matthew S. 2012b. 'Documents and Bureaucracy'. *Annual Review of Anthropology* 41 (1): 251–67.

Iklé, Fred Charles. 1964. *How Nations Negotiate*. New York: Harper & Row.

Izadi, Elahe. 2013. 'Do Women Make Better Lobbyists Than Men?' *The Atlantic*, 31 July.

Jacobs, Dirk, Karen Phalet and Marc Swyngedouw. 2006. 'Political Participation and Associational Life of Turkish Residents in the Capital of Europe'. *Turkish Studies* 7 (1): 145–61.

Jacoby, Wade. 1999. 'Priest and Penitent: The European Union as a Force in the Domestic Politics of Eastern Europe'. *East European Constitutional Review* 8: 62–7.

Jacoby, Wade. 2004. *The Enlargement of the European Union and NATO: Ordering from the Menu in Central Europe*. Cambridge: Cambridge University Press.

James, Deborah. 2011. 'The Return of the Broker: Consensus, Hierarchy, and Choice in South African Land Reform: The Return of the Broker'. *Journal of the Royal Anthropological Institute* 17 (2): 318–38.

Jenkins, Richard. 2007. 'The Meaning of Policy/Policy as Meaning'. In *Policy Reconsidered: Meanings, Politics and Practices*, edited by Susan M. Hodgson and Zoë Irving, 21–36. Bristol: Policy Press.

Joseph, Lauren, Matthew Mahler and Javier Auyero, eds. 2007. *New Perspectives in Political Ethnography*. New York: Springer.

Kalb, Don, and Herman Tak. 2006. 'The Dynamics of Trust and Mistrust in Poland: Floods, Emotions, Citizenship and the State'. In *Postsocialism: Politics and Emotions in Central and Eastern Europe*, edited by Maruska Svasek, 196–213. New York: Berghahn Books.

Kaleağası, Bahadır. 2006. *Avrupa Galaksisinde Türkiye Yıldızı [Turkish Star in European Galaxy]*. Istanbul: Doğan Kitap.

Kallas, Siim. 2005. 'The Need for a European Transparency Initiative', paper presented at Nottingham Business School. https://europa.eu/rapid/press-release_SPEECH-05-180_en.pdf (accessed 7 May 2019).

Kaplan, Sam. 2006. *The Pedagogical State: Education and the Politics of National Culture in Post-1980 Turkey*. Stanford: Stanford University Press.

Kassim, Hussein, Anand Menon, B. Guy Peters and Vincent Wright, eds. 2001. *The National Co-ordination of EU Policy: The European Level*. Oxford: Oxford University Press.

Kassim, Hussein, Guy Peters and Vincent Wright, eds. 2000. *The National Co-ordination of EU Policy: The Domestic Level*. Oxford: Oxford University Press.

Kaya, Ayhan, and Ferhat Kentel. 2005. *Euro-Turks: A Bridge or a Breach Between Turkey and the European Union? A Comparative Study of German-Turks and French-Turks*. Brussels: Centre for European Policy Studies.

Kaya, Ayhan, and Ferhat Kentel. 2007. *Belgian-Turks: A Bridge or a Breach Between Turkey and the European Union?* Brussels: King Baudouin Foundation.

Keating, Vincent Charles, and Jan Ruzicka. 2014. 'Trusting Relationships in International Politics: No Need to Hedge'. *Review of International Studies* 40 (4): 753–70.

Keohane, Robert O. 2002. 'Ironies of Sovereignty: The European Union and the United States'. *Journal of Common Market Studies* 40 (4): 743–65.

Kertzer, David I. 1988. *Ritual, Politics, and Power*. New Haven: Yale University Press.

Kertzer, David I. 1996. *Politics and Symbols: The Italian Communist Party and the Fall of Communism*. New Haven: Yale University Press.

Keskin, Yıldırım. 2001. *Avrupa Yollarında Türkiye [Turkey on the Road to Europe]*. Istanbul: Bilgi.

Kleine, Mareike. 2014. 'Informal Governance in the European Union'. *Journal of European Public Policy* 21 (2): 303–14.

Koster, Martijn, and Yves van Leynseele. 2018. 'Brokers as Assemblers: Studying Development Through the Lens of Brokerage'. *Ethnos* 83 (5): 803–13.

Kramer, Heinz. 1996. 'The EU–Turkey Customs Union: Economic Integration Amidst Political Turmoil'. *Mediterranean Politics* 1 (1): 60–75.

Kroet, Cynthia. 2017. 'Support for EU and Exit Referendums Up Across Europe: Survey'. Politico website, 16 June. https://www.politico.eu/article/eu-support-increases-in-europe-continent-but-also-exit-referendum-support (accessed 15 April 2019).

Kuus, Merje. 2014. *Geopolitics and Expertise: Knowledge and Authority in European Diplomacy*. Chichester: Wiley-Blackwell.

Laclau, Ernesto, and Chantal Mouffe. 1985. *Hegemony and Socialist Strategy: Towards a Radical Democratic Politics*. London: Verso.

LaGro, Esra, and Knud E. Jørgensen, eds. 2007. *Turkey and the European Union: Prospects for a Difficult Encounter*. London: Palgrave Macmillan.

Lagrou, Evert. 2000. 'Brussels: Five Capitals in Search of a Place. The Citizens, the Planners and the Functions'. *GeoJournal* 51 (1–2): 99–112.

Laszczkowski, Mateusz, and Madeleine Reeves, eds. 2017. *Affective States: Entanglements, Suspensions, Suspicions*. New York: Berghahn Books.

Latour, Bruno. 1988. 'Drawing Things Together'. In *Representation in Scientific Practice*, edited by Michael E. Lynch and Steve Woolgar, 19–68. Cambridge: MIT University Press.

Latour, Bruno. 2010. *The Making of Law: An Ethnography of the Conseil d'Etat*. Cambridge: Polity.

Lequesne, Christian. 1996. 'The French EU Decision-Making: Between Destabilization and Adaptation'. In *The European Union: How Democratic Is It?*, edited by Svein S. Andersen and Kjell A. Eliassen, 73–81. London: Sage.

Letsch, Constanze. 2013. 'Kurdish Smugglers Struggle to Feel Turkey Peace Dividend'. *The Guardian*, 3 July. https://www.theguardian.com/world/2013/jul/03/kurdish-smugglers-turkey-peace (accessed 15 April 2019).

Lévi-Strauss, Claude. 1987 [1950]. *Introduction to the Work of Marcel Mauss*. Translated by Felicity Baker. London: Routlege & Kegan Paul.

Lewis, David, and David Mosse, eds. 2006. *Development Brokers and Translators: The Ethnography of Aid and Agencies*. Bloomfield: Kumarian Press.

Li, Tania. 2007. *The Will to Improve: Governmentality, Development, and the Practice of Politics*. Durham: Duke University Press.

Liebow, Edward. 1995. 'Inside the Decision-Making Process: Ethnography and Environmental Risk Management'. *NAPA Bulletin* 16 (1): 22–35.

Lindquist, Johan. 2015. 'Anthropology of Brokers and Brokerage'. In *International Encyclopedia of Social and Behavioral Science*, edited by James D. Wright, 870–4. Amsterdam: Elsevier.

Lukes, Steven. 2004 [1974]. *Power: A Radical View*. London: Palgrave Macmillan.

Lukes, Steven. 2005. 'Power and the Battle for Hearts and Minds'. *Millennium* 33 (3): 477–93.

Lutz, Catherine. 2017. 'What Matters'. *Cultural Anthropology* 32 (2): 181–91.

MacMillan, Catherine. 2016. *Discourse, Identity and the Question of Turkish Accession to the EU: Through the Looking Glass*. London: Routledge.

Mahoney, Christine. 2008. *Brussels Versus the Beltway: Advocacy in the United States and the European Union*. American Governance and Public Policy. Washington, DC: Georgetown University Press.

Mango, Andrew. 1977. 'The State of Turkey'. *Middle Eastern Studies* 13 (2): 261–74.

March, James G., and Johan P. Olsen. 1998. 'The Institutional Dynamics of International Political Orders'. *International Organization* 52 (4): 943–69.

Marcus, George E., ed. 1983. *Elites, Ethnographic Issues*. Albuquerque: University of New Mexico Press.

Marquand, David. 1979. *Parliament for Europe*. London: Jonathan Cape.

Marsden, Magnus, Diana Ibañez-Tirado and David Henig. 2016. Special Issue, 'Everyday Diplomacy: Insights from Ethnography'. *Cambridge Journal of Anthropology* 35 (2): 1–152.

Marshall, Catherine. 1984. 'Elites, Bureaucrats, Ostriches, and Pussycats: Managing Research in Policy Settings'. *Anthropology and Education Quarterly* 15 (3): 235–51.

Marshall, David (2010). 'Who to Lobby and When: Institutional Determinants of Interest Group Strategies in European Parliament Committees', *European Union Politics* 11 (4): 553–75.

Masco, Joseph. 2014. *The Theater of Operations: National Security Affect from the Cold War to the War on Terror*. Durham: Duke University Press.

Mazey, Sonia, and Jeremy J. Richardson, eds. 1993. *Lobbying in the European Community*. Oxford: Oxford University Press.

Mazey, Sonia, and Jeremy J. Richardson. 2003. 'Interest Groups and the Brussels Bureaucracy'. In *Governing Europe*, edited by Jack Hayward and Anand Menon, 208–27. Oxford: Oxford University Press.

McConell, Fiona, Terri Moreau and Jason Dittmer. 2012. 'Mimicking State Diplomacy: The Legitimizing Strategies of Unofficial Diplomacies'. *Geoforum* 43 (4): 804–14.

McDonald, Maryon. 1996. '"Unity in Diversity". Some Tensions in the Construction of Europe'. *Social Anthropology* 4 (1): 47–60.

McDonald, Maryon. 2000. 'Accountability, Anthropology and the European Commission'. In *Audit Cultures: Anthropological Studies in Accountability, Ethics, and the Academy*, edited by Marilyn Strathern, 106–32. London: Routledge.

McDonald-Walker, Suzanne. 2000. *Bikers: Culture, Politics and Power*. Oxford: Berg.

McGrath, Conor. 2005. *Lobbying in Washington, London, and Brussels: The Persuasive Communication of Political Issues*. Lewiston: Edward Mellen Press.

McLaren, Lauren M. 2002. 'Turkey's Eventual Membership of the EU: Turkish Elite Perspectives on the Issue'. *Journal of Common Market Studies* 38 (1): 117–29.

Merry, Sally E. 2006. *Human Rights and Gender Violence: Translating International Law into Local Justice*. Chicago: University of Chicago Press.

Mills, Charles W. 1956. *The Power Elite*. Oxford: Oxford University Press.

Ministry of Science, Industry and Technology. 2018. *Demir Çelik Sektörü Raporu* [*Report on the Iron and Steel Sector*]. Ankara: MoSIT. https://sgm.sanayi.gov.tr/Handlers/DokumanGetHandler.ashx?dokumanId=85929937-a136-43c4-b7dd-da5225c4a5b9 (accessed 9 May 2019).

Misrahi, Frédéric. 2009. 'Nuancing Conventional Wisdom on State–Business Relations in

Turkey: The Case of Technical Product Regulations'. *European Journal of Turkish Studies* 9. https://journals.openedition.org/ejts/3804 (accessed 7 May 2019).

Misrahi, Frédéric. 2010. 'What Prospects for the Lifting of Technical Trade Barriers in the Mediterranean? Insights from the Turkish Case'. *Mediterranean Politics* 15 (2): 189–209.

Mitchell, Timothy. 1991. 'The Limits of the State: Beyond Statist Approaches and Their Critics'. *American Political Science Review* 85 (1): 77–96.

Mitchell, Timothy. 2002. *Rule of Experts: Egypt, Techno-Politics, Modernity*. Berkeley: University of California Press.

Moore, Sally F. 2000 [1978]. *Law as Process: An Anthropological Approach*. Hamburg: LIT.

Moore, Sally F. 2016. *Comparing Impossibilities: Selected Essays of Sally Falk Moore*. Chicago: HAU Books.

Morris, Zoë S. 2009. 'The Truth About Interviewing Elites'. *Politics* 29 (3): 209–17.

Mosse, David. 2005. *Cultivating Development: An Ethnography of Aid Policy and Practice*. London: Pluto Press.

Mosse, David. 2006. 'Anti-social Anthropology? Objectivity, Objection, and the Ethnography of Public Policy and Professional Communities'. *Journal of the Royal Anthropological Institute* 12 (4): 935–56.

Mosse, David, ed. 2011. *Adventures in Aidland: The Anthropology of Professionals in International Development*. New York: Berghahn Books.

Mosse, David, and David Lewis, eds. 2005. *The Aid Effect: Giving and Governing in International Development*. London: Pluto.

Mouffe, Chantal. 2005. *On the Political*. London: Routledge.

Müftüler-Bac, Meltem. 1997. *Turkey's Relations with a Changing Europe*. Manchester: Manchester University Press.

Müftüler-Bac, Meltem. 2016. *Divergent Pathways: Turkey and the European Union. Re-Thinking the Dynamics of Turkish–European Union Relations*. Leverkusen: Barbara Budrich.

Müftüler-Bac, Meltem, and Yannis A. Stivachtis, eds. 2008. *Turkey–European Union Relations: Dilemmas, Opportunities, and Constraints*. Lanham: Lexington Books.

Mulcahy, Suzanne. 2015. *Lobbying in Europe: Hidden Influence, Privileged Access*. Brussels: Transparency International.

Müller, Birgit. 2011. 'The Elephant in the Room: Multistakeholder Dialogue on Agricultural Biotechnology in the Food and Agricultural Organization'. In *Policy Worlds: Anthropology and the Analysis of Contemporary Power*, edited by Cris Shore, Susan Wright and Davide Però, 282–99. New York: Berghahn Books.

Muntigl, Peter, Gilbert Weiss and Ruth Wodak. 2000. *European Union Discourses on Un/Employment: An Interdisciplinary Approach to Employment, Policy-Making and Organizational Change*. Amsterdam: John Benjamins.

Nader, Laura. 1996. 'Coercive Harmony: The Political Economy of Legal Models'. *Kroeber Anthropological Society Papers* 80: 1–13.

Navaro-Yashin, Yael. 2012. *The Make-Believe Space: Affective Geography in a Postwar Polity*. Durham: Duke University Press.

Nedergaard, Peter. 2007. *European Union Administration: Legitimacy and Efficiency*. Leiden: Nijhoff.

Neumann, Iver B. 2012. *At Home with the Diplomats: Inside a European Foreign Ministry*. Ithaca: Cornell University Press.

Neumann, Iver B. 2013. *Diplomatic Sites: A Critical Enquiry*. New York: Columbia University Press.

Niezen, Ronald, and Maria Sapignoli. 2017. *Palaces of Hope: The Anthropology of Global Organizations*. Cambridge: Cambridge University Press.

Nordstrom, Carolyn. 2000. 'Shadows and Sovereigns'. *Theory, Culture and Society* 17 (4): 35–54.

Nuijten, Monique. 2003. *Power, Community and the State: The Political Anthropology of Organisation in Mexico*. London: Pluto Press.

Nye, Joseph S. 2004. *Soft Power: The Means to Success in World Politics*. New York: Public Affairs.

Official Journal of the European Union. 2014. 'Agreement Between the European Parliament and the European Commission on the Transparency Register for Organisations and Self-Employed Individuals Engaged in EU Policy-Making and Policy Implementation'. *Official Journal of the European Union* 277: 32014Q0919(01).

Ong, Aihwa. 2006. *Neoliberalism as Exception: Mutations in Citizenship and Sovereignty*. Durham: Duke University Press.

Öniş, Ziya. 1991. 'Political Economy of Turkey in the 1980s: Anatomy of Unorthodox Liberalism'. In *Strong State and Economic Interest Groups: The Post-1980 Turkish Experience*, edited by Metin Heper, 27–40. Berlin: Walter de Gruyter.

Öniş, Ziya. 2000. 'Luxembourg, Helsinki and Beyond: Towards an Interpretation of Recent Turkey–EU Relations'. *Government and Opposition* 35 (4): 463–83.

Öniş, Ziya. 2004. 'Turgut Özal and His Economic Legacy: Turkish Neo-Liberalism in Critical Perspective'. *Middle Eastern Studies* 40 (4): 113–34.

Orban, Leonard. 2006. 'Romania's Accession Negotiations with the EU: A Chief Negotiator's Perspective'. In *The EU and Romania: Accession and Beyond*, edited by David Phinnemore, 78–92. London: Federal Trust.

Ozbilgin, Ozge. 2013. 'Turkey Bans Alcohol Advertising and Curbs Sales'. Reuters, 24 May. https://www.reuters.com/article/us-turkey-alcohol/turkey-bans-alcohol-advertising-and-curbs-sales-idUSBRE94N0IA20130524 (accessed 15 April 2019).

Page, Edward C. 1997. *People Who Run Europe*. Oxford: Oxford University Press.

Page, Edward C., and Linda Wouters. 1994. 'Bureaucratic Politics and Political Leadership in Brussels'. *Public Administration* 72 (3): 445–59.

Page, Edward C., and Vincent Wright. 1999. *Bureaucratic Élites in Western European States*. Oxford: Oxford University Press.

Pamuk, Orhan. 2010. 'The Souring of Turkey's European Dream'. *Guardian*, 23 December. https://www.theguardian.com/commentisfree/2010/dec/23/turkey-european-dream-migrants-minorites (accessed 9 May 2019).

Panichi, James. 2015. 'When Lobbyists Collide'. Politico website, 25 September. https://www.politico.eu/article/european-lobbyists-collide-commission-brussels-washington (accessed 15 April 2019).

Papadakis, Yiannis. 2005. *Echoes from the Dead Zone: Across the Cyprus Divide*. London: I. B. Tauris.

Papadopoulos, Alex G. 1996. *Urban Regimes and Strategies: Building Europe's Central Executive District in Brussels*. Chicago: University of Chicago Press.

Peers, Steve. 1996. 'Living in Sin: Legal Integration Under the EC–Turkey Customs Union.' *European Journal of International Law* 7 (3): 411–30.

Peters, B. Guy, and Vincent Wright. 2001. 'The National Co-ordination of European Policy-making'. In *European Union: Power and Policy-Making*, edited by Jeremy Richardson, 155–78. London: Routledge.

Pina-Cabral, João de, and Antónia P. de Lima, eds. 2000. *Elites: Choice, Leadership and Succession*. Oxford: Berg.

Pinxten, Henrik. 2006. 'Neo-nationalism and Democracy in Belgium'. In *Neo-nationalism in Europe and Beyond: Perspectives from Social Anthropology*, edited by André Gingrich and Marcus Banks, 125–37. New York: Berghahn Books.

Piran, Leila. 2013. *Institutional Change in Turkey: The Impact of European Union Reforms on Human Rights and Policing*. London: Palgrave Macmillan.

Pleines, Heiko. 2005. 'Russian Business Interests and the Enlarged European Union'. *Post-Communist Economies* 17 (3): 269–87.

Polo, Jean-François, and Claire Visier. 2007. 'De l'intégration à l'européanisation, Les Groupes d'intérêt Turcs à Bruxelles' ['From Integration to Europeanization, Turkish Interest Groups in Brussels']. In *L'Europe Telle Qu'elle Se Fait: Européanisation et Sociétés Politiques Nationales* [*Europe As It Is: Europeanization and National Political Societies*], edited by Olivier Baisnee and Romain Pasquier, 77–98. Paris: CNRS.

Preda, Alex. 2002. 'Financial Knowledge, Documents, and the Structures of Financial Activities'. *Journal of Contemporary Ethnography* 31 (2): 207–39.

Price, Alan H., Christopher B. Weld, Laura El-Sabaawi and Adam M. Teslik. 2016. *Unsustainable: Government Intervention and Overcapacity in the Global Steel Industry*. Washington, DC: Wiley Rein LLP.

Radaelli, Claudio M. 1999. *Technocracy in the European Union*. New York: Routledge.

Rai, Shirin M., ed. 2010. Special Issue: Ceremony and Ritual in Parliament. *Journal of Legislative Studies* 16 (3).

Rasmussen, Maja Kluger. 2015. 'The Battle for Influence: The Politics of Business Lobbying in the European Parliament'. *Journal of Common Market Studies* 53 (2): 365–82.

Rhodes, R. A. W., Paul 't Hart and Mirko Noordegraaf. 2007. *Observing Government Elites Up Close and Personal*. London: Palgrave Macmillan.

Richardson, H. G. 1928. 'The Origins of Parliament'. *Transactions of the Royal Historical Society* 11: 137–83.

Richardson, Jeremy J., and Sonia Mazey, eds. 2015. *European Union: Power and Policy-Making*. London: Routledge.

Ridgeway, James, David Corn and Daniel Schulman. 2008. 'There's Something About Mary: Unmasking a Gun Lobby Mole'. Mother Jones blog, 30 July. https://www.motherjones.com/politics/2008/07/theres-something-about-mary-unmasking-gun-lobby-mole (accessed 2 July 2018).

Riles, Annelise. 2000. *The Network Inside Out*. Ann Arbor: University of Michigan Press.

Riles, Annelise. 2006. 'Introduction'. In *Documents: Artifacts of Modern Knowledge*, edited by Annelise Riles, 1–38. Ann Arbor: University of Michigan Press.

Riles, Annelise. 2018. *Financial Citizenship: Experts, Publics, and the Politics of Central Banking*. Ithaca: Cornell University.

Rosamond, Ben. 2000. *Theories of European Integration*. New York: St Martin's Press.

Ross, Carne. 2007. *Independent Diplomat: Dispatches from an Unaccountable Elite*. Ithaca: Cornell University Press.

Sahlins, Marshall D. 2002. *Waiting for Foucault, Still*. Chicago: Prickly Paradigm Press.

Sajdik, Martin, and Michael Schwarzinger. 2008. *European Union Enlargement: Background, Developments, Facts*. New Brunswick: Transaction Publishers.

Sandler, Jen, and Renita Thedvall. 2017. *Meeting Ethnography: Meetings as Key Technologies of Contemporary Governance, Development, and Resistance*. London: Routledge.

Sannerstedt, Anders. 2005. 'Negotiations in European Union Committees'. In *European Union Negotiations: Processes, Networks and Institutions*, edited by Ole Elgström and Christer Jönsson, 97–114. London: Routledge.

Sassen, Saskia. 1996. *Losing Control? Sovereignty in an Age of Globalization*. New York: Columbia University Press.

Sassen, Saskia. 2006. *Territory, Authority, Rights: From Medieval to Global Assemblages*. Princeton: Princeton University Press.

Schatz, Edward, ed. 2009. *Political Ethnography: What Immersion Contributes to the Study of Power*. Chicago: University of Chicago Press.

Schmid, Dorothée. 2004. 'The Use of Conditionality in Support of Political, Economic and Social Rights: Unveiling the Euro-Mediterranean Partnership's True Hierarchy of Objectives.' *Mediterranean Politics* 9 (3): 396–421.

Schumann, William R. 2009. *Toward an Anthropology of Government: Democratic Transformations and Nation Building in Wales*. London: Palgrave Macmillan.

Schwartzman, Helen B. 1989. *The Meeting: Gatherings in Organizations and Communities*. New York: Plenum Press.

Scott, James C. 1998. *Seeing Like a State: How Certain Schemes to Improve the Human Condition Have Failed*. New Haven: Yale University Press.

Sedelmeier, Ulrich. 2002. 'Sectoral Dynamics of EU Enlargement: Advocacy, Access and Alliances in a Composite Policy'. *Journal of European Public Policy* 9 (4): 627–49.

Seufert, Günter, and Karin Vorhoff, eds. 2000. 'Professional Chambers and Non-Voluntary Organizations in Turkey: The Intersection of Public, Civil and National'. In *Civil Society in the Grip of Nationalism: Studies on Political Culture in Contemporary Turkey*, 99–142. Istanbul: Orient-Institute, IFEA.

Shore, Cris. 2000. *Building Europe: The Cultural Politics of European Integration*. London: Routledge.

Shore, Cris. 2004. 'Whither European Citizenship? Eros and Civilization Revisited'. *European Journal of Social Theory* 7 (1): 27–44.

Shore, Cris. 2006. '"Government Without Statehood"? Anthropological Perspectives on Governance and Sovereignty in the European Union'. *European Law Journal* 12 (6): 709–24.

Shore, Cris, and Stephen Nugent, eds. 2002. *Elite Cultures: Anthropological Perspectives*. London: Routledge.

Shore, Cris, and Susan Wright. 1997. *Anthropology of Policy: Critical Perspectives on Governance and Power*. London: Routledge.

Shore, Cris, Susan Wright and Davide Però, eds. 2011. *Policy Worlds: Anthropology and the Analysis of Contemporary Power*. New York: Berghahn Books.

Sidaway, James D. 2000. 'Imagined Regional Communities: Undecidable Geographies'. In *Cultural Turns/Geographical Turns: Perspectives on Cultural Geography*, edited by Ian Cook, David Crouch, Simon Naylor and James R. Ryan, 234–58. Harlow: Prentice Hall.

Sideri, Katerina. 2005. 'The European Commission and the Law-Making Process: Compromise as a Category of Praxis'. *International Journal of Law in Context* 1 (2): 155–82.

Skoggard, Ian, and Alisse Waterston. 2015. 'Introduction: Toward an Anthropology of Affect and Evocative Ethnography'. *Anthropology of Consciousness* 26 (2): 109–20.

Snyder, Francis G. 1989. 'Thinking About "Interests": Legislative Process in the European Community'. In *History and Power in the Study of Law: New Directions in Legal Anthropology*, edited by June Starr and Jane Fishburne Collier, 167–200. Ithaca: Cornell University Press.

Snyder, Francis. 1993. 'The Effectiveness of European Community Law: Institutions, Processes, Tools and Techniques'. *Modern Law Review* 56 (1): 19–54.

Sontag, Deborah. 2003. 'The Erdogan Experiment'. *New York Times*, 11 May. https://www.nytimes.com/2003/05/11/magazine/the-erdogan-experiment.html (accessed 2 July 2018).

Spence, David. 1993. 'The Role of the National Civil Service in European Lobbying: The British Case'. In *Lobbying in the European Community*, edited by Sonia Mazey and J. J. Richardson, 47–73. Oxford: Oxford University Press.

Spence, David. 2002. 'The Evolving Role of Foreign Ministries in the Conduct of European Union Affairs'. In *Foreign Ministries in the European Union: Integrating Diplomats*, edited by Brian Hocking and David Spence, 18–36. London: Palgrave Macmillan.

Spencer, Jonathan. 2007. *Anthropology, Politics and the State: Democracy and Violence in South Asia*. Cambridge: Cambridge University Press.

Starr, Paul, and Ellen Immergut. 1987. 'Health Care and the Boundaries of Politics'. In *Changing Boundaries of the Political: Essays on the Evolving Balance Between the State and Society, Public and Private in Europe*, edited by Charles S. Maier, 221–54. Cambridge: Cambridge University Press.

SteelOrbis. 2015. 'Turkey Launches AD Duty Investigation on Certain HR Flat Steel Imports', 29 January. www.steelorbis.com/steel-news/latest-news/turkey-launches-ad-duty-investigation-on-certain-hr-flat-steel-imports-864474.htm (accessed 29 January 2015).

Stirrat, Roderick L. 2000. 'Cultures of Consultancy'. *Critique of Anthropology* 20 (1): 31–46.

Stoler, Ann L. 2007. 'Affective States'. In *A Companion to the Anthropology of Politics*, edited by David Nugent and Joan Vincent, 4–20. Oxford: Blackwell.

Strauss, Delphine. 2010. 'EU Warned over Enlargement Criteria'. https://www.ft.com/content/65f468f8-ec30-11df-9e11-00144feab49a (accessed 7 May 2019).

Stryker, Rachael, and Roberto J. González, eds. 2014. *Up, Down, and Sideways: Anthropologists Trace the Pathways of Power*. New York: Berghahn Books.

Suvarierol, Semin. 2009. 'Networking in Brussels: Nationality Over a Glass of Wine'. *Journal of Common Market Studies* 47 (2): 411–35.

Swartz, Marc J., Victor W. Turner and Arthur Tuden, eds. 2009. *Political Anthropology*. New Brunswick: Aldine Transaction.

Tallberg, Jonas. 2008. 'Bargaining Power in the European Council'. *Journal of Common Market Studies* 46 (3): 685–708.

Tate, Winifred. 2015. *Drugs, Thugs, and Diplomats: U.S. Policymaking in Colombia*. Stanford: Stanford University Press.

Teivainen, Teivo. 2009. 'The Pedagogy of Global Development: The Promotion of Electoral Democracy and the Latin Americanisation of Europe'. *Third World Quarterly* 30 (1): 163–79.

Telesca, Jennifer E. 2015. 'Consensus for Whom? Gaming the Market for Atlantic Bluefin Tuna Through the Empire of Bureaucracy'. *Cambridge Journal of Anthropology* 33 (1): 49–64.

Telicka, Pavel, and Karel Bartak. 2007. 'The Accession of the Czech Republic to the EU'. In *The Accession Story: The EU from Fifteen to Twenty-Five Countries*, edited by George Vassiliou, 144–57. Oxford: Oxford University Press.

Temelkuran, Ece. 2016. *Turkey: The Insane and the Melancholy*. Translated by Zeynep Beler. London: Zed Books.

TEPAV. 2006. 'Kamu Yönetimi Reformunda Mevcut Durum' ['Current Situation in Public Administration Reform']. Evaluation Paper EN-GS-2006–02. https://www.tepav.org.tr/upload/files/1271248708r1240.Kamu_Yonetiminde_Reform.pdf (accessed 15 April 2019).

Thedvall, Renita. 2006. *Eurocrats at Work: Negotiating Transparency in Postnational Employment Policy*. Stockholm: Almqvist & Wiksell International.

Thedvall, Renita. 2007. 'The EU's Nomads: National Eurocrats in European Policy-Making'. In *Observing Government Elites Up Close and Personal*, edited by R. A. W. Rhodes, Paul 't Hart and Mirko Noordegraaf, 160–79. London: Palgrave Macmillan.

Tilly, Charles. 1985. 'War Making and State Making as Organized Crime'. In *Bringing the State Back In*, edited by Peter B Evans, Dietrich Rueschemeyer and Theda Skocpol, 169–91. Cambridge: Cambridge University Press.

Tisdall, Simon. 2012. 'Turkey Accused of Pursuing Campaign of Intimidation Against Media'. *The Guardian*, 24 October. https://www.theguardian.com/world/2012/oct/24/turkey-campaign-intimidation-media (accessed 15 April 2019).

Tocci, Nathalie. 2011. *Turkey's European Future: Behind the Scenes of America's Influence on EU–Turkey Relations*. New York: New York University Press.

Togan, Sübidey. 2015. 'Technical Barriers to Trade: The Case of Turkey and the European Union'. *Journal of Economic Integration* 30 (1): 121–47.

Too, Yun Lee. 1998. 'Introduction'. In *Pedagogy and Power: Rhetorics of Classical Learning*, edited by Yun Lee Too and Niall Livingstone, 1–15. Cambridge: Cambridge University Press.

Trappmann, Vera. 2013. *Fallen Heroes in Global Capitalism: Workers and the Restructuring of the Polish Steel Industry*. London: Palgrave Macmillan.

Tsing, Anna. 2000. 'Inside the Economy of Appearances'. *Public Culture* 12 (1): 115–44.

Tuğal, Cihan. 2009. *Passive Revolution: Absorbing the Islamic Challenge to Capitalism*. Stanford: Stanford University Press.

Tulmets, Elsa. 2010. 'Experimentalist Governance in EU External Relations: Enlargement and the European Neighbourhood Policy'. In *Experimentalist Governance in the European Union: Towards a New Architecture*, edited by Charles F. Sabel and Jonathan Zeitlin, 297–324. Oxford: Oxford University Press.

Turam, Berna. 2007. *Between Islam and the State: The Politics of Engagement*. Stanford: Stanford University Press.

Turem, Z. Umut. 2011. 'A Clock-Setting Institute for the Market Age: The Politics of Importing "Competition" to Turkey'. *Differences* 22 (1): 111–45.

Uchiyamada, Yasushi. 2004. 'Architecture of Immanent Power: Truth and Nothingness in a Japanese Bureaucratic Machine'. *Social Anthropology* 12 (1): 3–23.

Uğur, Mehmet. 2000. 'Europeanization and Convergence via Incomplete Contracts? The Case of Turkey'. *South European Society and Politics* 5 (2): 217–42.

Uğur, Mehmet, and Nergis Canefe, eds. 2004. *Turkey and European Integration: Accession Prospects and Issues*. London: Routledge.

Ülgen, Sinan. 2005. *AB Ile Müzakerelerin El Kitabı Ne Bekliyoruz, Ne Olacak? [Handbook on Negotiations with the EU: What Do We Expect? What Will Happen?]* Istanbul: Istanbul Bilgi University Press.

Ülgen, Sinan. 2006. *Turkish Business and EU Accession*. London: Centre for European Reform.

Ülgen, Sinan. 2008. *Değişim Zamanı: Demir Çelik Sektörü Analizi – 2008 [Time for a Change: Sectoral Analysis of Iron and Steel – 2008]*. Istanbul: Deloitte-Turkey.

Ülgen, Sinan. 2016. 'Turkey Needs a Soft Exit from the EU'. Politico, 22 November. https://www.politico.eu/article/turkey-needs-a-soft-exit-from-the-eu (accessed 15 April 2019).

Ülgen, Sinan, and Yiannis Zahariadis. 2004. *The Future of Turkish–EU Trade Relations: Deepening vs. Widening*. EU–Turkey Working Papers 5. Brussels: Centre for European Policy Studies.

van Apeldoorn, Bastiaan. 2002. *Transnational Capitalism and the Struggle Over European Integration*. London: Routledge.

van Schendelen, Marinus P. C. M. 2010. *More Machiavelli in Brussels: The Art of Lobbying the EU*. Amsterdam: Amsterdam University Press.

Vassiliou, George, ed. 2007. *The Accession Story: The EU from Fifteen to Twenty-Five Countries*. Oxford: Oxford University Press.

Vincent, Joan. 1990. *Anthropology and Politics: Visions, Traditions, and Trends*. Tucson: University of Arizona Press.

Visier, Claire. 2009. 'The Turkish Interest Groups in Brussels'. In *Europeanisation: Social Actors and the Transfer of Models in EU-27*, edited by Sandrine Devaux and Imogen Sudbery, 95–114. Prague: CEFRES.

Visier, Claire, and Jean-François Polo. 2005. 'Les groupes d'intérêt Turcs auprès des institutions Européennes: une intégration Bruxelloise' ['Turkish Interest Groups at the European Institutions: A Brussels Integration']. *Pôle Sud* 23 (1): 9–24.

Voice of America Turkish. 2010. 'Bagis: AP Raporunu Cok Ciddiye Almayalim' ['Let's Not Take the EP Report So Seriously']. https://www.amerikaninsesi.com/a/a-17-2010-02-03-voa18-88190357/879853.html?withmediaplayer=1 (accessed 7 May 2019).

Voltolini, Benedetta. 2017. 'Framing Processes and Lobbying in EU Foreign Policy: Case Study and Process-Tracing Methods'. *European Political Science* 16 (3): 354–68.

Walters, William, and Jens Henrik Haahr. 2005. *Governing Europe: Discourse, Governmentality and European Integration*. London: Routledge.

Weber, Max. 1978. *Economy and Society: An Outline of Interpretive Sociology*. Edited by Guenther Roth. Berkeley: University of California Press.

Weber, Max. 1994. *Weber: Political Writings*. Translated by Peter Lassman and Ronald Speirs. Cambridge: Cambridge University Press.

Wedel, Janine R. 2009. *Shadow Elite: How the World's New Power Brokers Undermine Democracy, Government, and the Free Market*. New York: Basic Books.

Wedel, Janine R. 2014. *Unaccountable: How Elite Power Brokers Corrupt Our Finances, Freedom, and Security*. New York: Pegasus Books.

Wedel, Janine R. 2017. 'From Power Elites to Influence Elites: Resetting Elite Studies for the 21st Century'. *Theory, Culture and Society* 34 (5–6): 153–78.

White, Jenny B. 2014. *Muslim Nationalism and the New Turks*. Princeton: Princeton University Press.

Williams, Raymond. 2015 [1976]. *Keywords: A Vocabulary of Culture and Society*. New York: Oxford University Press.

Winner, Langdon. 1980. 'Do Artifacts Have Politics?' *Daedalus* 109 (1): 121–36.

Wodak, Ruth. 2009. *The Discourse of Politics in Action: Politics as Usual*. London: Palgrave Macmillan.

Wolf, Eric R. 1956. 'Aspect of Group Relations in a Complex Society: Mexico'. *American Anthropologist* 58 (6):1065–78.

Wolf, Eric R. 1990. 'Distinguished Lecture: Facing Power – Old Insights, New Questions'. *American Anthropologist* 92 (3): 586–96.

Woll, Cornelia. 2012. 'The Brash and the Soft-Spoken: Lobbying Styles in a Transatlantic Comparison'. *Interest Groups and Advocacy* 1 (2): 193–214.

World Bank. 2014. 'Evaluation of the EU–Turkey Customs Union'. 85830-TR. http://documents.worldbank.org/curated/en/298151468308967367/pdf/858300ESW0P-1440disclosed090260140TR.pdf (accessed 15 April 2019).

World Steel Association. 2018. 'Steel Statistical Yearbook 2018'. https://www.worldsteel.org/en/dam/jcr:e5a8eda5-4b46-4892-856b-00908b5ab492/SSY_2018.pdf (accessed 8 May 2019).

Yanık, Lerna K. 2016. 'Bringing the Empire Back In: The Gradual Discovery of the Ottoman Empire in Turkish Foreign Policy'. *Die Welt des Islams* 56: 466–88.

Yanow, Dvora. 1996. *How Does a Policy Mean? Interpreting Policy and Organizational Actions*. Washington, DC: Georgetown University Press.

Yavuz, M. Hakan. 2000. 'Cleansing Islam from the Public Sphere'. *Journal of International Affairs* 54 (1): 21–42.

Yavuz, M. Hakan. 2016. 'Social and Intellectual Origins of Neo-Ottomanism: Searching for a Post-National Vision'. *Die Welt des Islams* 56: 438–65.

Yılmaz, Gaye. 2007. 'Turkey: WTO Negotiations in the Shadow of the European Union'. In *Strategic Arena Switching in International Trade Negotiations*, edited by Wolfgang Blaas and Joachim Becker, 241–69. Aldershot: Ashgate.

Yılmaz, Hakan. 1999. 'Business Notions of Democracy: The Turkish Experience in the 1990s'. *Cahiers d'études sur la Méditerranée orientale et le monde turco-iranien* 27: 183–94.

Yurchak, Alexei. 2006. *Everything Was Forever, Until It Was No More: The Last Soviet Generation*. Princeton: Princeton University Press.

Yurdakul, Gökçe. 2013. 'Jews and Turks in Germany: Immigrant Integration, Political Representation, and Minority Rights'. In *Rethinking the Public Sphere Through Trans-nationalizing Processes*, edited by Armando Salvatore, Oliver Schmidtke and Hans-Jörg Trenz, 251–68. London: Palgrave Macmillan.

Yüzbaşıoğlu, Nazlı, and Dildar Baykan. 2018. 'Türkiye dış Politika Ağını Kadın Diplomatlarla Güçlendiriyor' ['Turkey Strengthens Its Foreign Policy Network with Women Diplomats']. Anatolian Agency, 3 March. https://www.aa.com.tr/tr/dunya-kadinlar-gunu/turkiye-dis-politika-agini-kadin-diplomatlarla-guclendiriyor/1083526 (accessed 9 June 2019).

Zabusky, Stacia E. 1995. *Launching Europe: An Ethnography of European Cooperation in Space Science*. Princeton: Princeton University Press.

Index

EU authorised representative for GPSR:
Easy Access System Europe, Mustamäe tee 50,
10621 Tallinn, Estonia
gpsr.requests@easproject.com